AMERICAN TRADE POLITICS AND THE TRIUMPH OF GLOBALISM

A deep and unresolved tension exists within American trade politics between the nation's promotion of an open world trading system and the operations of its democratic domestic political regime. Whereas most scholarly attention has focused on how domestic politics has interfered with the United States' global economic leadership, Orin Kirshner offers here an analysis of the ways in which U.S. leadership in the arena of global trade has affected American democracy and the domestic political regime.

By participating in multilateral trade agreements, the U.S. Congress has transferred its trade policy-making authority to the president and, through international trade negotiations, from the American state to the GATT/WTO regime. This reorganization of policy-making authority has resulted in the "triumph of globalism," and fundamentally alters the citizen–state relationship assumed in democratic theory. Kirshner illustrates this process through four case studies: the Reciprocal Trade Agreements Act of 1945, the Trade Expansion Act of 1962, the Trade Act of 1974, the Omnibus Trade and Competitiveness Act of 1988, and further examines the impact of the Uruguay Round Agreements Act of 1994 on the political and institutional structure of American trade politics up to the current period.

American Trade Politics and the Triumph of Globalism makes a significant contribution to the study of both international trade and domestic American politics. This is essential reading for students and scholars of trade policy, international political economy, American politics, and democratic theory.

Orin Kirshner teaches American politics at Florida Atlantic University. He has been a senior fellow at the Institute for Agriculture and Trade Policy (IATP); a visiting fellow at the Wuhan University WTO Studies School (People's Republic of China); and the executive director of the Global Environment & Trade Study (GETS).

Foreign Policy Analysis
Douglas A. Van Belle, Series editor

The Routledge series *Foreign Policy Analysis* examines the intersection of domestic and international politics with an emphasis on decision–making at both the individual and group levels. Research in this broadly defined and interdisciplinary field includes nearly all methodological approaches, encompasses the analysis of single nations as well as large–N comparative studies, and ranges from the psychology of leaders, to the effects of process, to the patterns created by specific dynamic or contextual influences on decision making.

AMERICAN TRADE POLITICS AND THE TRIUMPH OF GLOBALISM

By Orin Kirshner

Routledge
Taylor & Francis Group

NEW YORK AND LONDON

First published 2014
by Routledge
711 Third Avenue, New York, NY 10017

and by Routledge
2 Park Square, Milton Park, Abingdon, Oxon OX14 4RN

Routledge is an imprint of the Taylor & Francis Group, an informa business

Library of Congress Cataloging in Publication Data
    Kirshner, Orin, 1961–
    American trade politics and the triumph of globalism / by Orin Kirshner.
    pages cm.—(Foreign policy analysis)
    Includes bibliographical references and index.
    1. United States—Commercial policy—History—20th century.
    2. United States—Commercial treaties—History—20th century.
    3. United States—Foreign economic relations.
    4. Globalization—Political aspects—United States. I. Title.
    HF1455.K57 2013
    382'.30973—dc23
    2013036585

ISBN: 978–0–415–74286–3 (hbk)
ISBN: 978–0–415–74287–0 (pbk)
ISBN: 978–1–315–81431–5 (ebk)

Typeset in Bembo
by Swales & Willis Ltd, Exeter, Devon

Printed and bound in the United States of America by Publishers Graphics,
LLC on sustainably sourced paper.

For Isaiah and Stanley
May your songs always be sung

CONTENTS

TABLES AND FIGURE

Tables

Figure

SERIES EDITOR'S FOREWORD

I am often asked to comment on what books and articles should be on the "must read" list for someone who wants to bring foreign policy analysis (FPA) into their research portfolio. I have never put together a list of references, or done anything else like that, primarily because the field is so diverse that the response really needs to be tailored to fit the background of the person or persons who have asked. However, there are a few that I almost always mention in that conversation. Valerie Hudson's undergraduate textbook (Hudson, 2006) provides a nice overview. *Essence of Decision* (Allison, 1971), *The Functions of Social Conflict* (Coser, 1956), *The Insecurity Dilemma* (Job, 1992), *Origins of Containment* (Larson, 1985), and *Analogies at War* (Khong, 1992) all provide stimulating examples of high-quality research. However, the only one that I would actually call an FPA "must read" is Putnam's *Logic of Two-Level Games* (Putnam, 1988).

In many ways, for me to say that *Two-Level Games* is *the* one FPA must read is quite curious. There really isn't anything all that original about the theories or concepts introduced. Every causal dynamic discussed in *Two-Level Games* can also be found in *Essence of Decision*, and they all had been in common use in the FPA literature for at least a decade. Putnam's analysis is simplistic and, at best, suggestive rather than robust and, unlike *Analogies at War* or *Origins of Containment*, it doesn't offer a good example that scholars can use as a model for empirical analyses. So why would I offer *Two-Level Games* as a must read?

While it may not be theoretically innovative or empirically impressive, I would say that *Logic of Two-Level Games* is iconic, and I use iconic in the technical sense of the word. *Logic of Two-Level Games* is an idealized and extremely simple yet evocative representation of the essence of foreign policy analysis. We can talk about actor-specific theories of decision-making and any other defining characteristic of FPA that we like, but the simple analogy of a two-level game is the one thing that cuts through it all and immediately shows the commonality in the menagerie of studies and theories that might be found under the rubric of foreign policy analysis. Everything in FPA relates back to that simple idea that every decision or action is simultaneously playing out on both international and domestic political stages and, more often than not, the pressures from those two arenas are divergent rather than convergent.

Logic of Two-Level Games is the one FPA must read because it is the most elegant, evocative, and intellectually catalytic description of the essence of FPA that has ever been produced. In fact it may be the most elegant description possible. And that is why when I introduce this book as a perfect example of the insights that can be offered by bringing the two-level game to the discussion of economic policy-making, that should make it clear that I am talking about a research monograph that applies the heart and soul of FPA to a subject that is often estranged from the subfield. As the series editor, I think the result is a powerful statement and conceptual challenge that must be reckoned with.

—Douglas Van Belle

References

Allison, Graham. (1971). *Essence of Decision: Explaining the Cuban Missile Crisis*. Boston: Little Brown and Company.

Coser, Lewis. (1956). *The Functions of Social Conflict*. New York: Free Press.

Hudson, Valerie M. (2006). *Foreign Policy Analysis: Classic and Contemporary Theory*. New York: Rowman & Littlefield Publishers.

Job, Brian L. (1992). *The Insecurity Dilemma: National Security of Third World States*. Boulder, CO: Lynne Rienner Publishers.

Khong, Yuen Foong. (1992). *Analogies at War*. Princeton, NJ: Princeton University Press.

Larson, Deborah Welch. (1985). *Origins of Containment: A Psychological Explanation*. Princeton, NJ: Princeton University Press.

Putnam, Robert. (1988). Diplomacy and Domestic Politics: The Logic of Two-Level Games. *International Organization* 42: 427–460.

ACKNOWLEDGEMENTS

I would like to thank the following people for making this book possible. Ira Katznelson, who upon learning of my intellectual interests, suggested I look at American trade politics; Aristide R. Zolberg, who impressed upon me the importance of examining American trade politics from a global perspective; Elizabeth Sanders, Richard Bensel, and Herman Schwartz for introducing me to the study of the President, Congress, and the international political economy, respectively; William Diebold, Raymond Vernon, and Mark Ritchie for exposing me to the real world of American trade politics; and my two sons who never lost faith in me. It is to them that this book is dedicated.

Earlier versions of portions of this book were published as "Triumph of Globalism: American Trade Politics," *Political Science Quarterly*, 120 (4) (Fall 2005); "Superpower Politics: The Triumph of Free Trade in Postwar America," *Critical Review: A Journal of Politics and Society*, 19 (4) (2007); and "Going Global: The Reciprocal Trade Agreements Act of 1945," *Politics & Policy*, 31 (1) (February 2009).

ABBREVIATIONS

ACPFP	Advisory Committee on Post-War Foreign Policy
ACTN	Advisory Committee on Trade Negotiations
AFBF	American Farm Bureau Federation
AFL	American Federation of Labor
AFL-CIO	American Federation of Labor–Congress of Industrial Organizations
BAC	Business Advisory Council
CAP	Common Agricultural Policy
CED	Committee for Economic Development
CFR	Council on Foreign Relations
CIEP	Council on International Economic Policy
CIO	Congress of Industrial Organizations
CNTP	Committee for a National Trade Policy
CPFEP	Committee on Post-War Foreign Economic Policy
CXT	Common External Tariff
ECAT	Emergency Committee for American Trade
ECEFP	Executive Committee on Economic Foreign Policy
ECSC	European Coal and Steel Community
EEC	European Economic Community
EFTA	European Free Trade Association
EPC	Economic Policy Council
FDR	Franklin D. Roosevelt
GATT	General Agreement on Tariffs and Trade
ICC	International Chamber of Commerce
ITA	International Trade Authority
MNC	Multinational corporation
NAM	National Association of Manufacturers

NEP	New Economic Policy
NFU	National Farmers Union
NTB	Nontariff trade barrier
OEEC	Organization for European Economic Cooperation
OTCA	Omnibus Trade and Competitiveness Act
PTA	Preferential Trade Agreement
RTAA	Reciprocal Trade Agreements Act
STR	Special Trade Representative
TA	Trade Act
TAA	Trade Agreements Act
TEA	Trade Expansion Act
URAA	Uruguay Round Agreements Act
USITC	United States International Trade Commission
USTR	United States Trade Representative
VER	Voluntary Export Restraint
WTO	World Trade Organization

PART I

The Problem

1

TRIUMPH OF GLOBALISM

American Trade Politics

The tariff is not an economic question exclusively. It is a political problem as well.

E. E. Schattschneider (1935)

The Third Ministerial Conference of the World Trade Organization (WTO) was intended to launch a new round of global trade talks designed to deepen international trade liberalization and create a more open world economy. Hosted by the United States in Seattle, Washington, from November 30 to December 3, 1999, the Conference was heralded by President Bill Clinton and his advisors as "an historic opportunity for the United States to exercise leadership in setting the trade agenda for the next century." The political stakes were high. "Failure," said United States Trade Representative Charlene Barshefsky, "is not an option."[1]

Yet events did not turn out as planned. When WTO delegates arrived in Seattle, they were met by an unprecedented coalition of unions, family farmers, environmentalists, consumer rights activists, faith-based organizations, professional associations, and anti-poverty groups, who engaged in mass marches, teach-ins, and civil disobedience to protest the initiation of the so-called "Millennium Round." Although each of these groups championed its own special cause, they were united around a common political concern: they believed that the foreign trade policy-making process was undemocratic and that it elevated global free trade concerns over domestic issues. They were protesting the idea that non-elected bureaucrats working largely behind closed doors were responsible for setting international trade rules that affected agriculture, services, trade-related investment measures, intellectual property rights, public health and safety laws, and international trade in goods; and oversaw a binding international dispute settlement process with little (if any) input from the domestic citizens and groups who would be affected by these economic rules and political mechanisms.[2]

When it became obvious to local law enforcement authorities that some of these groups were intent on preventing WTO delegates from convening, the situation on the streets became more serious. Following a meeting with federal, state, and local law enforcement officials, Seattle's mayor declared a state of civil emergency and ordered Seattle police to move the protesters out of a twenty-five-block area of downtown. As seen worldwide on the Cable News Network, the protesters were met by more than 500 Seattle riot police dressed in full battle gear, who used clubs, tear gas, pepper spray, rubber bullets, flash grenades, armored personnel carriers, and mass arrests to disperse the crowd and create a no-protest zone in the center of the city. What began on November 30 as a largely peaceful effort to shut down the WTO Ministerial Conference ended on December 3 with more than 600 protesters in jail and the city of Seattle ruled by martial law.[3] For its part, the launch of a new global trade round was temporarily put on hold.[4]

At the core of what became known as "the battle in Seattle" was a political problem that has plagued American trade politics ever since the United States assumed the mantle of global economic leadership at the end of World War II: a deep and unresolved tension between the promotion of an open international trading system and the operations of the nation's democratic domestic political regime. The idea that a tension exists between America's postwar efforts to construct an open world trading system and the nation's democratic domestic political regime is not new. Indeed, scholars have identified this tension as the source of critical issues in American politics and international relations for more than five decades.[5] However, most of the attention has focused on how America's democratic domestic regime has interfered with the exercise of world economic leadership.[6] Little attention has been paid to how the exercise of world economic leadership has affected the organization of American democracy. This chapter takes up the analytical challenge and in so doing sets the book's explanatory puzzle. It examines the impact of world economic leadership on American democracy within the sphere of foreign trade politics since World War II.

This chapter sets out the book's main descriptive problem. It argues that America's promotion of an open world trading system since World War II has required a fundamental reorganization of state power within the nation's foreign trade policy-making process that has subordinated domestic economic and political concerns to matters of global economic management. This reorganization of power has provided the political and institutional foundations for a national policy of freer trade dedicated to the creation, maintenance, and expansion of a supranational regulatory authority designed to manage trade liberalization on a worldwide basis: the General Agreement on Tariffs and Trade (GATT), and its successor, the WTO. I refer to this globally oriented national policy as "world trade leadership." The chief institutional feature of this policy has been the centralization of state power within the trade policy-making process. This centralization of power has taken the form of a transfer of trade policy-making authority from Congress to the president and from the American state to the GATT/WTO. Stated more formally, the independent variable in this analysis is the exercise of world trade leadership; the dependent variable is the centralization of state power within the trade policy-making process—a phenomenon I call the "triumph of globalism." The argument presented in this chapter is *not* that the foreign trade policy-making process has become less democratic; rather, the democratic process itself has been *reorganized* in such a way as to elevate global issues and concerns over domestic ones.

The triumph of globalism in postwar American trade politics is not simply a matter of academic concern. It has far-reaching implications for American democracy as well, for, as trade-related global economic and political forces have had a growing impact on the United States, the political capacity of American citizens to harness national state power to deal with them at the domestic level has declined.

I begin by defining the terms *foreign trade policy*, *world trade leadership*, and *democracy*, which will serve as an overview for the chapter's main argument. Next, I turn to a historically grounded investigation of the triumph of globalism in four crucial case studies. This is followed by a consideration of the impact of the triumph of globalism on American domestic politics since the formation of the WTO in 1995. Finally, I bring these themes together to suggest that there is firm, empirical support for the chapter's main hypothesis: that America's postwar policy of world trade leadership has rested on a centralization of the foreign trade policy-making process—a phenomenon that has given pride of place to global concerns over domestic ones.

Triumph of Globalism: Defining Terms

Before proceeding to an empirical demonstration of the impact of world trade leadership on the operations of democracy within the trade policy-making process, it is necessary to define three terms: *foreign trade policy*; *world trade leadership*; and *American democracy*.

Foreign Trade Policy

Since World War II, America's exercise of world trade leadership has required the adoption of a foreign trade policy designed to promote the development of the GATT/WTO regime. A nation's foreign trade policy sets the political rules that regulate the relationship between its domestic economy and the world economy with respect to the cross-border exchange of goods, services, intellectual property rights, and trade-related investment. As is the case with taxes and the military, foreign trade policy has been a constituent feature of modern states since they emerged during the long sixteenth century in Europe.[7] This is because foreign trade policy concerns one of the enduring features of states: the regulation of the interface between the internal and external realms.[8] With respect to foreign trade, this regulation concerns state–market–citizen relationships at the intersection of the domestic and world economies. A foreign trade policy that opens a nation's economy to global market forces is traditionally referred to as liberal and is marked by the roll-back of state intervention into cross-border trade flows. A policy that closes a nation's borders is traditionally called protectionist and is characterized by increased intervention into those flows. Because it regulates the boundaries between the national and world economies, a nation's foreign trade policy also affects citizen–market relationships. It does so by increasing or decreasing the exposure of a nation's domestic economy—and hence citizens and society—to global market forces. A liberal foreign trade policy tends to increase the sway of global market forces in domestic society, while a protectionist policy tends to decrease their significance. Since World War II, American foreign trade policy has been broadly liberal—it has aimed at the withdrawal of the American state from the regulation of cross-border trade flows. It has done so, moreover, with an eye toward establishing a supranational regulatory authority for the management of trade liberalization on a worldwide basis: the GATT/WTO.

As a practical matter, America's exercise of world trade leadership has required the enactment of a series of legislative statutes that have reorganized trade policy-making power within the American state. At the core of these statutes has been congressional authorization for the president to enter into binding international trade agreements. The need for these statutes is rooted in the constitutional design of the American state. While Article II Section 2 of the Constitution gives the president the power to enter into international agreements, Article I Section 8 grants Congress the power to "regulate commerce with foreign nations."[9] Thus, in order for the United States to enter into international agreements affecting "commerce with foreign nations," Congress must delegate its Article I Section 8 powers to the president.

World Trade Leadership

Since World War II, the United States has played a distinctive role within the world economy and international state system as rallier of nations in support of global free trade—a role I refer to as "world trade leadership." America's exercise of world trade leadership has focused on the construction of an open international trading system—a system within which global market forces, rather than state power, determine international trade flows. The foremost objective of this system has been to encourage high levels of global economic growth by increasing the productivity of capital, labor, and agriculture on an international basis. The idea that free trade encourages global economic growth by enhancing productivity is taken as an article of faith by the three major schools of international political economy: liberalism, mercantilism, and Marxism. Indeed, although David Ricardo, Friedrich List, and Karl Marx disagreed profoundly on the distributive and political consequences of free trade, they were one in contending that open global markets provided the best political conditions for the operation of capital on a worldwide basis; specifically, by rationalizing the global division of labor, leading to productivity gains on an international basis.[10]

America's exercise of world trade leadership has centered on the construction of an international regime for freer trade: GATT, and its successor, the WTO. At the core of this regime is an elaborate set of rules for the management of international trade. These rules, negotiated among members of the regime, are treaty obligated; violating them is tantamount to a violation of international law. The most important of these rules stress trade barrier reduction on a multilateral basis and non-discrimination in the treatment of imports.[11] Taken together, these rules are designed to roll back state intervention in international trading relationships and limit trade-impacting domestic policies that conflict with the rules of the international regime.

Institutionally, the development of the GATT/WTO regime has occurred through a series of international trade negotiations known as "rounds." Each of these rounds was initiated by the United States in an effort to bring more and more countries into the regime and to expand the scale and scope of global trade liberalization.[12] Since World War II, these rounds have resulted in a radical reduction in international trade barriers, a dramatic rise in the number of countries participating in the regime, and an expansion in the economic sectors, policies, and practices covered by international trade rules. Table 1.1 documents the expansion of the postwar world trading system through these rounds. Although economists differ as to the precise impact of these rounds on the expansion of international trade in the post–World War II era, there is widespread agreement that they have played a major role in the trade-related integration of national economies, as well as in global economic growth.[13]

American Democracy and Foreign Trade Politics

For the purpose of this analysis, democracy can be defined as the ensemble of institutions, rules, and procedures that link citizens to the state in the trade policy-making process. The more decentralized and accessible these institutions, rules, and procedures are, the more open and accountable is the democratic policy-making process. Conversely, the more centralized and inaccessible these institutions, rules, and procedures are, the less open and accountable is the democratic policy-making process. If the institutional arrangements, rules, and procedures governing the trade policy-making process remained unchanged over time, there would be little, if any, impact on democracy. But this has not been the case. Since World War II, when the United States assumed the mantle of world trade leadership, a profound change has occurred in the balance of power between the president and Congress at the domestic level and between the American state and the GATT/WTO regime at the global level. This change has made the foreign trade policy-making process less open and accountable to the citizens whose lives and livelihoods are affected by America's world trade leadership role.

TABLE 1.1 Growth of the International Trading System—GATT Trade Rounds

Year	Round	Subjects	Countries
1947	Geneva	Tariffs on goods	23
1949	Annecy	Tariffs on goods	13
1951	Torquay	Tariffs on goods	38
1956	Geneva	Tariffs on goods	26
1960–61	Dillion	Tariffs on goods	26
1964–67	Kennedy	Tariffs on goods	62
1973–79	Tokyo	Tariffs on goods	102
		Nontariff barriers[1]	
1986–94	Uruguay	Tariffs on goods	123
		Nontariff barriers[2]	
		Agriculture	
		Investment	
		Services[3]	
		Intellectual property rights[4]	
		Binding dispute-settlement process	

Source: World Trade Organization, *Trading into the Future*, 2nd ed. (Geneva: WTO, 1999)

Notes:

1 Subsidies; Anti-Dumping Practices; Countervailing Duties; Technical Barriers to Trade; Import Licensing Procedures; Government Procurement.

2 Subsidies; Anti-Dumping Practices; Countervailing Duties; Technical Barriers to Trade; Import Licensing Procedures; Government Procurement; Sanitary and Phytosanitary Measures; Rules of Origin; Safeguards.

3 Movement of Natural Persons; Financial Services; Maritime Transport Services; Basic Telecommunications; Professional Services.

4 Copyrights; Trademarks; Geographic Information Systems; Patents; Layout Designs of Integrated Circuits; Protection of Undisclosed Information; Anti-Competitive Practices in Services Contracts.

If Congress and the president were similar institutions, or if the representation of citizen interests were the same at the domestic and global levels, this shift in trade policy-making power would have little effect on democracy. However, Congress and the president are radically different institutions, and the representation of citizen interests is profoundly different in the domestic and international realms.

The most significant differences between the president and Congress that affect citizen–state relationships are the institutions' orientation to the domestic and international realms as well as their internal political structures. Max Weber once said that "as structures of power, political organizations vary in the extent to which they are turned outward";[14] and within the American state it is the president—rather than Congress—which is externally oriented. Within the constitutional system, the president's external orientation is rooted in the chief executive's expressed powers to wage war, enter into international negotiations, make binding international agreements, appoint and receive ambassadors, and recognize foreign governments.[15] These expressed powers are reinforced by the president's claim to possess inherent constitutional powers to function as the sole representative of the United States as a sovereign and unified actor at the level of international politics—a claim given constitutional legitimacy by the Supreme Court in its 1936 *Curtiss-Wright* decision.[16]

The president's external orientation is buttressed by its centralized political structure, which facilitates foreign policy coherence and consistency, a unified national viewpoint, and the ability to act with secrecy and dispatch. Although conflicts exist within the executive branch between competing bureaucracies, agencies, and personnel, it is the president who sits at the apex of the policy-making process.[17] The centralized political structure of the executive branch is rooted in the president's institutional role as chief executive and head of state, and the fact that the president is elected on a nationwide basis.

In contrast to the president, Congress is a profoundly decentralized institution with a domestic political orientation. The decentralized organization of Congress is principally rooted in its fragmented electoral design. Whereas the president is elected nationally in what constitutes a single electoral system, members of Congress are elected from subnational political units (states and congressional districts) comprising 535 separate electoral systems: 100 in the Senate and 435 in the House of Representatives. The decentralized character of Congress is reinforced by the division between the Senate and the House, a committee system that fragments policy into functional issue areas, and a weak party system that results in strong constituency ties and weak leadership sanctions over members.[18]

The domestic political orientation of Congress flows principally from its decentralized political structure. Whereas the president is in the position to raise claims to represent the United States as a single political unit at the international level, individual members of Congress are not. Members of Congress are elected to represent local constituencies and issues, and although individual members may develop a national perspective and foreign policy expertise, they are usually expected to cater to their local constituencies as well—regardless of national or foreign policy consequences.[19] Moreover, although the Constitution grants the Senate the power to ratify treaties and vote on the president's ambassadorial appointments, the House of Representatives does not participate in this process; nor do any members of Congress possess constitutional authority to represent the nation as a single unit in foreign affairs.

The institutional organization of the president and Congress has important consequences for citizen–state relationships in the sphere of trade politics at the domestic level. On the one hand, the president's outward orientation and centralized political structure make the chief executive comparatively more attuned to the needs of American citizens with global economic and political interests and more insulated from domestic politics.[20] On the other hand, the inward orientation of Congress and its decentralized political structure make it comparatively more responsive to American citizens with domestic economic and political concerns and considerably more removed from global politics than is the president.

Indeed, the Framers of the Constitution sought to create such differences between the branches and the representation of citizen interests in domestic politics.[21]

The delegation of Congress's Article I Section 8 authority to the president makes possible a related shift of power that further alters citizen–state relationships. This shift occurs when the president negotiates and implements international trade agreements within the GATT/WTO regime. The negotiation of these agreements severs the citizen–state relationship almost completely. It does so by moving the trade policy-making process from the national level, where citizen–state relationships are constituted, to the realm of global politics, where the operative political relationships are state-to-state. The GATT/WTO regime is an agreement among sovereign states and operates entirely beyond the bounds of citizen–state relationships. Indeed, the regime contains no provisions for the direct representation of citizen interests within its deliberations. It is left up to individual states to decide for themselves how (or if) their negotiating positions will represent the interests of their citizens, or which citizen interests (if any) will be represented. Furthermore, because the GATT/WTO regime operates at the level of state-to-state relationships, the myriad international trade agreements upon which it rests are placed in a "locked box" outside the realm of domestic politics. As sovereign states, members of the GATT/WTO regime possess the power to backtrack on their international commitments; doing so, however, is a violation of international law, is likely to undermine their credibility in future negotiations, and may lead to regime-authorized economic sanctions. Moreover, in the special case of the United States, failure to adhere to its regime commitments poses an additional threat: it endangers America's self-appointed world trade leadership role.

Triumph of Globalism: Historical Evidence

It remains to be shown that the exercise of world trade leadership has resulted in the centralization of state power within American trade politics and in a shift in policy-making power from the domestic to the global levels. To demonstrate this relationship, I adopt a case-study approach that focuses on America's initiation of the four most significant postwar international trade rounds and their impact on the nation's foreign trade policy-making process.

Since World War II, eight international trade rounds, each initiated by the United States, have been concluded. Yet scholars of the postwar world trading system generally agree that four of these rounds marked watersheds in the development of the GATT/WTO regime:[22] the first Geneva Round (1947); the Kennedy Round (1964–1967); the Tokyo Round (1973–1979); and the Uruguay Round (1986–1994). America's participation in each of these watershed trade rounds required the enactment of a foreign trade statute delegating Congress's Article I Section 8 powers to "regulate commerce with foreign nations" to the president. These foreign trade acts were: the Reciprocal Trade Agreements Act

(RTAA) of 1945; the Trade Expansion Act (TEA) of 1962; the Trade Act (TA) of 1974; and the Omnibus Trade and Competitiveness Act (OTCA) of 1988. The enactment of these statutes represented critical choice points in American trade politics that involved a trade-off between the exercise of world trade leadership and the operation of democracy.[23]

Because these acts were critical choice points, they constitute what Harry Eckstein calls "crucial cases." As Eckstein explains: "The essential abstract characteristic of a crucial case can be deduced from its function as a test of theory. It is a case that *must closely fit* a theory if one is to have confidence in the theory's validity, or, conversely, *must not fit* equally well any rule contrary to that proposed."[24] Thus, the argument that the exercise of world trade leadership has required a reorganization of American democracy within the sphere of trade politics and the transfer of trade policy-making authority from the domestic to the global levels must be confirmed in these cases in order to have confidence in this hypothesis.

The selection of these crucial cases is justified on methodological grounds as well. First, selecting a small number of cases allows for more in-depth examination of changes in the institutional organization of the trade policy-making process. Furthermore, the fact that these cases are spread across the whole postwar period allows us to view these institutional changes as they developed over time, facilitating comparative analysis of these changes as America's exercise of world trade leadership moved forward.

My analysis of each of these statutes is divided into three parts: their global objectives; how they altered the Congress–president relationship; and how they affected the relationship between the American state and the GATT/WTO regime—specifically, in terms of the domestic political and economic policy consequences of the statute's implementation within the context of an expanding international trading system.

Case I: The RTAA of 1945 and the Geneva Round

Global Objective

The RTAA of 1945 marked the first major assertion of American world trade leadership in the postwar era.[25] The basic goal of the act was to allow the United States to use its enormous global economic power in the immediate aftermath of World War II to build a new international trading system to complement its creation of a new international monetary order as well as its reconstruction efforts in Western Europe and Japan.

Domestic Institutional Reorganization

It was under the authority of the RTAA of 1945 that the United States launched the GATT.[26] Although the statutory language of the RTAA of 1945 was similar to that of the first RTAA (passed in 1934), its purpose was entirely different. As Assistant Secretary of State William A. Clayton put it to the House Ways and Means Committee:

> I believe all of us would profit from an effort to look at this bill, not in terms of what we thought about reciprocal trade agreements in 1934, 1937, 1940, and 1943, but as a new instrument for use in the world of tomorrow. For it is, in fact, a new instrument—made so not by new language, but by a new world. Those who judge the trade agreements program solely in the context of its prewar operation are likely to miss the new and portentous meaning of this idea . . . . [B]efore the war the trade agreements program was an instrument for defense against an epidemic of destructive and demoralizing trade warfare. Today, with the end of the great holocaust finally within sight, this same instrument is transformed into a powerful device for shaping a better world.[27]

At the core of the RTAA of 1945 was authorization for the president to use Congress's Article I Section 8 power to "regulate commerce with foreign nations" for a period of three years.[28] During that time, the president was empowered to enter into binding international trade agreements allowing cuts in America's tariff rates by up to 50 percent of their 1945 levels. The president was further empowered to use his administrative authority as chief executive to make these agreements and their tariff rate changes part of America's domestic law through *proclamation*—that is, without further congressional authorization. Furthermore, the act gave the president the sole power to decide what manufactured products would be subject to international negotiation, under what terms the negotiations would be conducted, and the extent to which tariffs would be cut. Although the act required the president to "give reasonable public notice of the intention to negotiate" and to take the views of interested parties and the Departments of Treasury, State, Navy, and War into account, it empowered him to devise whatever administrative process he wanted for carrying out the powers in the act. What is more, the president was not bound by the views he received from the public, Congress, or executive bureaus or agencies.

State–GATT Relations

Although Congress authorized the president to reduce U.S. tariffs by up to 50 percent and to enter into international trade agreements to do so, the chief executive was *not* authorized to use this grant of power to launch the GATT. As a result, the Truman administration launched the GATT and committed the United States to its binding rules and regulations by executive agreement, using the president's constitutional powers as head of state to enter into such an agreement without congressional assent. The chief means of this end-run around Congress was a specially designed legal instrument, the Protocol of Provisional Application. Rather than setting up the GATT as a full-fledged international organization comprised of members, the global trade authority was negotiated and entered into in the form of a provisional international agreement comprised of Contracting Parties. Although the GATT was not legally binding on Congress, it *was* legally binding on the president, which, in light of the president's control of foreign trade policy, was tantamount to binding American trade policy to the new international regime.

In addition to launching the GATT, the Truman administration used the RTAA of 1945 to enter into international trade agreements with twenty-two countries, leading to an overall average cut in U.S. tariffs of about 35 percent of 1945 levels. Through the use of executive agreements, these tariff cuts were bound at the international level within the framework of the GATT, which effectively removed them from further domestic consideration.

Case II: The TEA of 1962 and the Kennedy Round

Global Objective

The second major assertion of American world trade leadership came with the TEA of 1962, which authorized the president to use Congress's Article I Section 8 power to initiate the Kennedy Round of Multilateral Trade Negotiations.[29] The TEA was the first trade act of the postwar era that moved beyond the framework of the RTAA of 1945. It marked the greatest expansion of presidential power within the trade policy-making process since the RTAA of 1945.[30] The chief global objective of the act was to respond to a major change in the structure of the world trading system: the emergence of the European Economic Community (EEC) as an international trading power. The TEA and the Kennedy Round were designed to steer the EEC toward a low-tariff, GATT-centered foreign trade policy.

Domestic Institutional Reorganization

The statutory core of the TEA was Title II, which gave the president unprecedented power to negotiate trade agreements and lower American tariffs. Section 201 of Title II declared that

> whenever the President determines that any existing duties or other import restrictions of any foreign country or the United States are unduly burdening and restricting the foreign trade of the United States . . . the President may proclaim such modifications of existing duties and other import restrictions . . . as he determines to be required or appropriate to carry out any such trade agreement.[31]

This section, and Section 202, authorized the president for five years to reduce American tariffs by up to 50 percent of their 1962 rates and to reduce to zero any rate of duty of 5 percent or less. Chapter 2 of Title I was even more sweeping in scope. It granted the president special authority to eliminate tariffs entirely in the case of any trade agreement with the EEC in which the combined EEC and U.S. share of world exports was 80 percent or more. This measure was designed, in part, to entice England into the EEC, inasmuch as it was only with the addition of England that the combined U.S.–EEC total would reach the 80 percent threshold in most industrial sectors.[32] In each case, the president was empowered to decide how much rates should be reduced and the methodology for determining the 80 percent threshold. The act also gave the president the authority to negotiate on a sector-by-sector basis (rather than item-by-item, as under prior trade acts). This sector-by-sector approach allowed the president to aggregate many small items into general categories and then negotiate tariff reductions on those sectors as a whole. This greatly increased the efficiency of international negotiations, the task of determining rates, and the administration of trade policy after rates had been cut.[33]

State–GATT Relations

The Johnson administration used the TEA and the Kennedy Round to expand the reach of the GATT trading system. Again, this was done through the use of executive agreements and was not authorized by Congress. In fact, in the course of debate on the TEA, Congress explicitly stated that passage of the act was not an endorsement of the GATT system.

The Kennedy Round resulted in international trade agreements among sixty-two countries, including the United States, and an overall reduction in America's tariff of about 35 percent. It also eliminated most duties of 5 percent or less. These tariff cuts were bound within the framework of the GATT, which effectively removed them from the sphere of domestic trade politics. Although the special EEC authority was never used (England failed to join the EEC by the end of the round), by the time the Kennedy Round tariff cuts took full effect, tariffs among industrial countries (with the exception of a few sectors) no longer posed a significant barrier to trade, and U.S. tariffs stood at their lowest level in history—about 8 percent.

Case III: The TA of 1974 and the Tokyo Round

Global Objective

The third major assertion of American world trade leadership came with the TA of 1974, which allowed the president to launch the Tokyo Round of Multilateral Trade Negotiations. At the core of the TA was a new delegation of

Congress's Article I Section 8 power to the president for a period of five years.[34] Specifically, the president was authorized to reduce America's tariffs by up to 60 percent of 1975 rates, to cut rates of 5 percent or less to zero, and to proclaim these reductions without returning to Congress. The main objective of the act was to respond to a major structural change in the world trading system: the emergence of Japan as a great economic power. The TA and the Tokyo Round were designed to deepen Japan's integration into the GATT regime, to encourage Japan to adopt an outward-looking, GATT-centered trade policy, and to continue to steer the EEC toward a liberal trade policy within the framework of the GATT.

Domestic Institutional Reorganization

The most significant aspect of the TA was its authorization for the president to negotiate on nontariff trade barriers. Section 102 urged the president to take all "appropriate and feasible" steps within his power to "harmonize, reduce, or eliminate" nontariff trade barriers or other distortions of international trade. In granting this blanket authority, Congress made clear that American nontariff trade barriers were to be placed on the international negotiating table as well. Because nontariff trade barriers are any barriers to trade, this was a remarkable grant of policy-making power. In effect, it authorized the president to independently and unilaterally survey the entire American economy and regulatory landscape to determine what was and what was not a nontariff barrier to trade, engage in negotiations with foreign countries with an eye toward making changes in American domestic law, and enter into international agreements committing the United States to make such changes. Although the act required the president to consult with appropriate congressional committees prior to signing a nontariff trade barrier agreement and to transmit these agreements to Congress for nonbinding review, the only point in the process where Congress actually had the opportunity to block presidential action came with the implementing legislation.

Nontariff trade barrier agreements did not become binding on the United States until Congress enacted legislation making the changes in U.S. domestic law required by the agreement. (If the changes applied solely to administrative rules and regulations, the president was allowed to implement agreements unilaterally.) Although Congress reserved the right to approve or reject nontariff trade barrier agreements that required changes in U.S. domestic law, the national legislature agreed to a process of implementation that radically enhanced the chances for enactment: the so-called "fast track" procedure.

The central purpose of fast track was to make it difficult for Congress to reject a nontariff trade barrier agreement negotiated by the president.[35] Under fast track, Congress bound itself to an expedited process for considering legislation implementing these agreements. Most significantly, Congress was not allowed to amend legislation implementing these agreements; it had only sixty days in which to review the legislation before voting on it; and once a motion to vote on a bill was accepted, the House and Senate were allowed only twenty hours of floor debate on the measure. The final vote on a bill was simply up or down.[36]

The fast-track procedure further enhanced presidential power by allowing the chief executive to bundle all trade agreements into a single "implementing bill." This meant that Congress was forced to consider all trade agreements and the changes they made in U.S. domestic law as a single package. Voting down a single agreement while accepting others was not an option: all of the agreements stood or fell together. This bundling process put Congress in the unenviable position of voting for or against the work of an entire international trade round—rather than on the substance of specific trade agreements. Because the vote came after the conclusion of years of detailed international negotiations, often involving complex compromises, and to which the president had given his seal of approval, Congress essentially was presented with a *fait accompli.*[37]

State–GATT Relations

The Tokyo Round resulted in international trade agreements among 102 countries. (In the TA of 1974, Congress finally included language expressing support for the GATT.) The Tokyo Round resulted in tariff reductions of about 35 percent. These reductions were bound within the framework of the GATT, which removed them from the sphere of domestic politics. The round also produced a number of agreements that established international rules for the global management of a range of nontariff trade barriers. These agreements, too, were bound at the international level and placed within the administrative purview of the GATT. They included domestic antidumping rules, subsidies and countervailing duties, government procurement practices, methods of customs valuation, technical standards, and import licensing.

Case IV: The OTCA of 1988 and the Uruguay Round

Global Objective

The fourth major assertion of American world trade leadership came with the OTCA of 1988, which authorized the president to use Congress's Article I Section 8 power to negotiate trade agreements within the framework of the Uruguay Round of Multilateral Trade Negotiations.[38] The principal goals of the OTCA were to expand GATT disciplines to cover new sectors of the global economy, institutionalize a new dispute settlement system within the GATT, strengthen the GATT's operational machinery, and further liberalize trade in traditional areas such as tariffs and quotas. The OTCA also was designed to move international trade rules deeper into the domestic regulatory regimes of GATT members. This goal reflected the success of decades of trade liberalization and global economic integration, which expanded the range of domestic policies and practices affecting international trade flows.

Domestic Institutional Reorganization

The OTCA granted the president the power to reduce U.S. tariffs by up to 50 percent of their prevailing rates and to implement tariff changes through proclamation for a period of five years. Tariffs of 5 percent or less could be eliminated entirely. The president also was granted new open-ended authority to negotiate on nontariff trade barriers, subject to congressional consideration on a fast-track basis. The OTCA granted the president fast-track authority for three years, after which he was authorized to request an additional two-year extension from Congress. Although this "reverse fast track" provision required the president to request an extension of fast-track authority, the OTCA established rules that made it difficult for Congress to deny the request. Under these rules, the vote on fast-track extension was a vote to *disapprove* the new authority; in other words, the president would be allowed to retain fast-track authority unless Congress voted to take it away. Furthermore, congressional consideration of a "disapproval resolution" was itself subject to fast-track rules, which streamlined congressional procedures, limited floor debate, prohibited amendments, and, generally, made disapproval difficult. All the president was required to do to retain his authority for a full five years was to certify to Congress that, despite progress in the negotiations, more time was needed to conclude them.[39] Although the president's tariff and nontariff trade barrier negotiating authority was subject to a number of consultation procedures with Congress, none of them was binding. As in the past, the president was given full authority to formulate U.S. foreign trade policy and to negotiate on tariff and nontariff trade barriers as he saw fit. While the president was required to receive advice from executive branch bureaus and agencies, interested congressional committees, and the private sector, this advice was on a take-it-or-leave-it basis.

State–GATT Relations

The Uruguay Round resulted in binding international trade agreements among 123 countries and led to the most significant reform of the world trading system since World War II. Economically, the Uruguay Round moved well beyond the GATT's principal focus on trade in industrial goods and tariffs, producing new and unprecedented agreements covering agricultural policies, consumer health and safety laws, trade in services, trade-related investment measures, and intellectual property rights. The round also resulted in a wide range of agreements covering specific national trade policy practices and included a "built-in" agenda for further negotiations on basic telecommunication services, maritime transport services, movement of natural persons, financial services, subsidies, government procurement, safeguard measures, and professional services.[40] Furthermore, these agreements were retroactive: they applied to all preexisting national legislation.[41]

Politically, the round established a powerful new international organization to oversee world trade and enforce international trade rules, the WTO. The WTO replaced the GATT and, since 1995, has provided the institutional framework for the multilateral trading system. Under the GATT regime, the organization's governing body was weak and its system for settling disputes among the Contracting Parties lacked an adequate enforcement mechanism. The WTO was designed to remedy these problems and led to a "profound change in the legal structure of the institutions for world trade."[42] Perhaps the most significant institutional innovation of the WTO is its dispute settlement procedures, which provide an institutionalized process for the settlement of disputes among WTO members. If one or more WTO members believe that another member is violating its commitments under the Uruguay Round trade agreements, they can file suit in the WTO with a dispute settlement body (DSB). The DSB establishes ad hoc dispute settlement panels for each case. These panels are composed of individuals, chosen from a predetermined roster, who have demonstrated, through prior associations or actions, a commitment to trade liberalization and to the rules of the WTO.[43] The panel process itself is highly secretive. Panel hearings are held behind closed doors, only disputants (that is, governments) are allowed to attend, and the public is not represented. Panel deliberations and decisions are made in closed sessions, and the opinions expressed in panel reports are anonymous.[44] Furthermore, the decision of a dispute settlement panel is binding. It is automatically adopted sixty days after completion, unless there is a consensus among all WTO members (including the country that has won the panel decision) to reject the ruling, or the losing country files an appeal with a standing Appellate Body. In the case of an appeal, the Appellate Body has ninety days in which to uphold, modify, or reverse the legal findings and conclusions of the dispute settlement panel. If the Appellate Body rules that a member's action violates its commitments under the Uruguay Round Agreements, the defendant is ordered to change its action to bring it into conformity with its international obligations. If the member refuses, it faces economic sanctions.

Triumph of Globalism: The WTO in American Domestic Politics

To date, the triumph of globalism in American trade politics has reached its zenith with the enactment of the URAA of 1994.[45] The URAA made America's Uruguay Round commitments binding on the United States and was passed using the fast-track authority granted in the OTCA of 1988. The URAA elaborates a complex set of institutional rules and procedures that delineate the relationship between the president and Congress; the distribution of economic decision-making power between national, state, and local governments; and the institutional relationship between this domestic policy-making system and the operations of the WTO. It forms the basis of all WTO-centered U.S. trade policy today.

At the federal level, the URAA commits the United States to the WTO and its substantive trade agreements as a matter of domestic law. It also establishes the process through which the United States adheres to the dispute settlement procedures of the WTO. Here, the URAA binds the United States to decisions made by WTO dispute settlement panels regarding changes in regulatory rules and procedures at the national, state, and local levels. Although the act states that the Senate Finance Committee and the House Ways and Means Committee may vote to indicate their agreement or disagreement with a panel's ruling and the proposed contents of the final rule or other modification, it goes on to say that "*any such vote shall not be binding on the department or agency which is implementing the rule or other modification*" (emphasis added).[46] This clause officially denies these committees any power to actually alter the president's action.

With respect to state law, the URAA declares that one of its overriding objectives is to promote the conformity of state laws to WTO agreements and dispute settlement panel decisions. To this end, the act establishes statutory procedures that empower the president to play the role of national trade policy investigator and prosecuting attorney, identifying illegal breaches of the WTO at the state and local levels and then—if necessary—suing for compliance in federal court. Although the URAA establishes an elaborate federal–state consultation process that gives states an opportunity to participate in the formulation of policies that affect them, it denies them power to block executive branch action. This president-centered administrative system applies as well to the WTO dispute settlement process, which allows foreign nations to challenge the WTO legality of state and local laws and practices. In the event a state or local law or practice is found by the WTO dispute settlement process to violate WTO rules, it is the president, not the state, who controls the domestic political response. While Title I requires the president to consult with Congress whenever state laws become the object of a foreign trade dispute or negotiation, it gives Congress no power to block presidential action.

For all practical purposes, the only checks on the exercise of executive power under the URAA of 1994 are various nonbinding consultation provisions. Although the act does provide a mechanism through which Congress can withdraw the United States from participation in the WTO, this provision establishes extremely high legislative hurdles for withdrawal action to be taken.[47]

Since 1995, the impact of the WTO-URAA regime on American trade policy-making and domestic regulatory matters has been considerable. From 1995 to 2010, the United States was a defendant in 111 dispute settlement cases.[48] At the time of this writing, seventy-five of these cases had been resolved, and thirty-six were still in the process of consultation, adjudication, or appeal. Of the seventy-five cases that had been resolved, the United States lost sixty-eight cases—*a loss rate of 91 percent*. Of the cases lost, the United States has implemented changes in its domestic laws and regulations in fifty-nine cases—*a compliance rate of 87 percent*.

The majority of these cases involved changes in the administrative rules or practices used by various executive branch bureaus and agencies to implement laws
democratically enacted by Congress. Because these cases involved administrative
rule changes, many of which were complex and technical in nature, they received
scant public attention. Indeed, these changes were made under the guidelines of
the Administrative Procedures Act, which merely requires notice of such changes
in the Federal Register. Although notice in the Federal Register formally makes
the actions of executive branch bureaus and agencies transparent, the fact is that
few Americans read (or even know about) it. Furthermore, although the Administrative Procedures Act often requires public hearings on proposed rule changes,
administrative agencies seeking such changes are not legally bound to follow the
views they receive. For all practical purposes, then, these changes occurred well
out of public view.[49] Although the vast majority of these cases have received scant
public attention, ten have been front-page news and have led (or are leading) to
the alteration of important U.S. laws or presidential actions designed to specifically address domestic concerns. These actions are listed in Table 1.2.

TABLE 1.2 U.S. Actions Pursuant to WTO Dispute Settlement Procedures, Major Cases

1997	The president's decision to weaken sections of the Clean Air Act of 1990 restrict-ing imports of high-pollution-content reformulated gasoline.
1998	The president's decision to weaken sections of the Endangered Species Act of 1989, designed to protect endangered sea turtles caught during shrimp trawling.
2003	The president's decision to lift tariffs on a wide range of steel imports, designed to protect the domestic industry from rising foreign competition.
2004	Congressional enactment of legislation changing the U.S. tax code to eliminate export subsidies to foreign sales corporations.
2004	Presidential action to work with Congress to eliminate the so-called Byrd Amendment in U.S. trade law, which provides kickbacks to U.S. companies harmed by foreign subsidies.
2005	Presidential action to work with Congress to change U.S. laws governing elec-tronic gaming rules, especially the Interstate Horseracing Act of 1978.
2005	Presidential action to work with Congress to eliminate subsidies to U.S. cotton farmers.
2007	Presidential agreement to negotiate on reducing or eliminating subsidies and other forms of domestic support for corn products.
2007	Presidential agreement to negotiate on reducing or eliminating subsidies and other forms of domestic support for wheat, corn, grain sorghum, barley, oats, upland cotton, and rice; feed program payments for beef and veal, dairy, hogs and pigs, sheep and lamb, and all other livestock; assistance program payments for apples, apricots, peaches, pears, and all other trees, bushes and vines; programs exempting agricultural producers from payment of gasoline and diesel fuel taxes, and taxes based on overall farm income; and programs related to the operation and maintenance of irrigation works by the U.S. Department of the Interior.
2008	Presidential agreement to negotiate on the Dolphin Protection Consumer Infor-mation Act of 1990, allowing the labeling of tuna imports as "dolphin-safe."

In addition to the cases already brought against the United States, WTO members have raised concerns regarding a wide range of democratically enacted and implemented U.S. state and regulatory matters designed to respond to domestic economic, social, and political demands. The raising of these concerns by foreign governments suggests that these issues are ripe for international challenge. In light of the fact that the United States has lost 91 percent of the cases brought against it, and has a compliance rate of 87 percent, these emerging issues must be taken seriously. Indeed, as the U.S. International Trade Commission stated in a July 2003 letter to the General Accounting Office: "In light of continued adverse findings by the Appellate Body, it appears likely that the United States will be subject to additional adverse WTO rulings, with all the attendant consequences."[50] These federal and state regulatory issues include: dumping, subsidy offsets, and domestic safeguard measures; the extra-territorial application of U.S. environmental, banking, tax, and export laws; the use of trade restrictions to enforce domestic environmental laws; government procurement regulations at the national and state levels, including programs to help small businesses and minorities compete for contracts; federal programs designed to provide benefits to small businesses located in historically under-utilized business zones; subsidized export guarantees to farmers and ranchers; subsidized crop insurance programs; tax incentives for the fishery, lumber, aeronautics, and shipbuilding industries; the Jones Act, restricting foreign participation in domestic waterborne shipping; user fees at port facilities; "Buy American" and "Buy-in-State" programs; state and municipal laws requiring safety certifications for products sold or installed within their jurisdictions, including environmental and consumer health and safety standards; state-based tax on foreign-owned corporations based on total worldwide profits (the unitary tax); and state-based governance of professional standards.[51] In addition, more than thirty specific U.S. federal statutes, enacted by Congress through domestic democratic political processes involving, among other things, public hearings, open floor debates, and roll-call voting, have been singled out by trading partners for possible litigation. These federal statutes and the violations they are said to constitute are listed in Table 1.3.

Concerns about the impact of the WTO on American democracy go well beyond the views articulated by the Seattle protesters in 1999. According to the International Affairs and Trade Director of the Department of Commerce: "The fact that these [WTO] decisions have not yet [sic] impacted a substantial number of cases is far less significant than the fact that they have the potential to do so."[52] The Congressional Budget Office put it this way:

> Foreign trade can no longer be dealt with apart from other domestic economic policies and concerns. Governments often employ trade policies less for commercial ends than to achieve other goals—economic, political, and social. Significant trade liberalization thus means changing these national programs, and for this reason domestic policies will increasingly be the focus of trade negotiations.[53]

TABLE 1.3 Federal Statutes under International Scrutiny

The Helms-Burton Act of 1996 (extra-territorial application of U.S. law)
Iran and Libya Sanctions Act of 1996 (extra-territorial application of U.S. law)
Iran Non-Proliferation Act of 2000 (extra-territorial application of U.S. law)
Export Administration Act of 1979 (extra-territorial application of U.S. law)
The Jones Act (discriminatory)
Trade Expansion Act—Section 231 (protectionist)
The U.S. Outer Continental Shelf Lands Act (protectionist)
Omnibus Trade and Competitiveness Act—Section 301 (unilateral actions)
The Customs and Trade Act of 1990 (port fees—discriminatory)
The Omnibus Budget Reconciliation Act of 1990 (port fees—discriminatory)
Buy American Act (BAA) of 1933 (government procurement—discriminatory)
The Highway Administration Act (government procurement—discriminatory)
The Urban Mass Transit Act (government procurement—discriminatory)
The Airports Improvement Act (government procurement—discriminatory)
The Merchant Marine Act of 1936 (government procurement—discriminatory)
The Hazardous Materials Transportation Act of 1994 (government
    procurement—discriminatory)
The Amtrak Authorization Act (government procurement—discriminatory)
National Science Foundation Act of 1988 (government procurement—discriminatory)
Commercial Space Act of 1998 (government procurement—discriminatory)
Small Business Act of 1953, as amended (government procurement—discriminatory)
American Fisheries Act of 1988 (limits on foreign ownership)
Submarine Cable Landing License Act of 1921 (limits on foreign ownership)
Federal Power Act (limits on foreign ownership)
Geothermal Steam Act (limits on foreign ownership)
Nuclear Energy Act (limits on foreign ownership)
The Nutrition Labeling and Education Act of 1990 (discriminatory)
U.S. Clean Air Act of 1990 (discriminatory)
Marine Mammal Protection Act of 1988 (dolphin-safe tuna—discriminatory)
U.S. Endangered Species Act of 1989 (sea turtles—transparency/discriminatory)
The Farm Security and Rural Investment Act of 2002 (violation of Agreement on
    Agriculture)
Federal Agriculture and Reform Act of 2002 (violation of Agreement on Agriculture)
The Agricultural Risk Protection Act of 2000 (violation of Agreement on Agriculture)
The Agricultural Trade Act of 1978 (violation of Agreement on Agriculture)

Source: WTO, Trade Policy Review Body, "Trade Policy Review: United States," Document Number WT/TPR/S/88, August 15, 2001; European Commission, *Market Access Sectoral and Trade Barriers Database*, "United States: General Features of Trade Policy, 2003"; and WTO Dispute Settlement Data Base, http://www.wto.org/english/tratop_e/dispu_e/dispu_status_e.htm (accessed August 3, 2013).

The domestic laws, rules, and regulations already (or potentially) subject to WTO scrutiny are less important in and of themselves than what they collectively suggest about the impact of the international trading system on the United States going forward: as foreign trade and international trade rules push deeper and deeper into the American economy (in large measure the result of U.S. world trade leadership),[54] more and more economic, social, and political issues tradition-ally considered domestic are likely to become the objects of international negotia-tion and arbitration within the framework of the WTO. Indeed, as then-WTO Director General, Renato Ruggiero, declared in 1996:

> One by one, trade and investment barriers will continue to be swept away by globalization, like leaves on an autumn day. . . . The new challenge will be less to regulate relations among national economies, than to establish the rules and structures of a transnational economy.[55]

Conclusion

The findings of this chapter lend some credence to the claims of the Seattle protesters. Although America's trade policy-making process is not necessarily undemocratic, the exercise of world trade leadership *has* involved the centrali-zation of the nation's domestic democratic political system and the prioritiza-tion of global over domestic concerns. Specifically, the exercise of world trade leadership has rested on a shift of trade policy-making power at the domestic level from Congress to the president, and at the global level from the American state to the GATT/WTO—a shift of power I have termed the "triumph of globalism." The principal vehicle for this power shift has been a series of foreign trade statutes that have permitted Congress to delegate its Article I Section 8 power to "regulate commerce with foreign nations" to the president, and the subsequent use to which the president has put this power: the creation of a supranational regulatory authority for the management of trade liberalization on a global basis. If Congress and the president were similar institutions, or if citizen–state relationships were the same in domestic and global politics, then this shift would be merely technical in character. But Congress and the presi-dent are not similar institutions, and the representation of citizen interests is different at the domestic and international levels. As a result, the triumph of globalism fundamentally alters the nature of citizen–state relationships in the foreign trade policy-making process.

Yet the triumph of globalism is not simply a matter of academic concern. It poses real and growing problems for domestic democratic accountability as well. At the end of World War II, when America's superpower status served to protect the domestic economy from foreign competition, and when the rules of the international trading regime dealt solely with tariffs on goods, the triumph of globalism in American trade politics raised few issues of domestic democratic concern. External economic and political forces attached to foreign trade simply did not affect the vast majority of American citizens. However, as foreign trade and international trade rules have pushed deeper and deeper into the American economy, the triumph of globalism has brought issues of democratic representa-tion to the fore. Specifically, as the domestic consequences of America's world trade leadership role have emerged as the source of growing public concern, the triumph of globalism has made it increasingly difficult for American citizens to harness national state power to deal with them.

It should go without saying that identifying the triumph of globalism as a constituent feature of postwar American trade politics is not the same thing as explaining its origins. What, then, accounts for this phenomenon? The remainder of this book is dedicated to answering this question. Chapter 2 examines how political scientists have approached the study of American trade politics in the past. It argues that political science trade theory is deeply divided among three explanatory approaches. One traces the policy to society-based factors; another traces it to state-level factors; and a third traces it to international factors. For more than three decades students of American trade politics have argued that the next major theoretical move for this research domain is to integrate these approaches into a single analytical framework. To date, however, such a move has not been made. Chapter 2 clears the conceptual terrain for the construction (in Chapter 3) of a theory of postwar American trade politics that integrates society, state, and systemic variables into a single explanatory framework. Chapter 3 develops this framework. It elaborates a theory of postwar American trade politics that traces the nation's policy of world trade leadership to a pattern of society–state relationships at the domestic level anchored in the nation's superpower position in world trade. I call this pattern "superpower trade politics." In Chapters 4–7, I deploy this framework to explain the formulation and enactment of the four crucial trade statutes at the legislative core of the triumph of globalism: the RTAA of 1945, the TEA of 1962, the TA of 1974, and the OTCA of 1988.

The book's conclusion (Chapter 8) revisits its main themes. It argues that America's postwar policy of world trade leadership has led to a reorganization of state power in the trade policy-making process which has resulted in a fundamental alteration in citizen–state relationships as well as the elevation of matters of global economic management over issues of domestic concern. Furthermore, it argues that this triumph of globalism in postwar American trade politics has been the product of a globally oriented pattern of domestic politics anchored in the nation's superpower position in world trade. Finally, Chapter 8 ends on an analytical and normative note. Analytically, it argues that the book's explanatory focus should alert scholars to the value of conducting studies of American politics and policy that problematize the external–internal relationship. This is particularly apposite, given the trade-related globalization of the American economy and the growing reach of the WTO into an expanding array of domestic policies traditionally considered domestic (such as agricultural policy, environmental policy, and consumer health and safety policy). Normatively, the chapter concludes with a brief exploration of the practical feasibility of altering trade politics in such a way as to reconcile the exercise of world trade leadership with American democracy.

Notes

1 Robert G. Kaiser and John Burgess, "A Seattle Primer: How Not to Hold WTO Talks," *Washington Post*, December 12, 1999.
2 It is interesting to note that the views of the Seattle protesters were shared by a substantial number of Americans. According to a study by the Program on International Policy Attitudes (PIPA) regarding Americans' attitudes about freer trade and the WTO: "Americans' views of international trade are complex and cannot be explained as a simple preference for free trade or protectionism. . . . Americans show strong concern that, though trade has benefitted business and the wealthy, it has not benefitted American workers and has widened the gap between rich and poor. Americans also show concern that trade has been harmful to the environment, to international labor standards, and to poor countries." Accessed on the website of PIPA at www.americans-wolrd.org/digest/global_issues/intertrade/summary.cfm. January 30, 2004.
3 National Lawyers Guild, Seattle Chapter, *Bringing in an Undemocratic Institution Brings an Undemocratic Response* (Seattle: National Lawyers Guild, 2000).
4 A new global trade round was successfully launched in 2001 in Doha, Qatar, which, due to its out-of-the-way location and restrictive visa processes saw little civil society presence. At the time of this writing the Doha Round remains ongoing.
5 Stanley Hoffman, ed., *Gulliver's Troubles; or, the Setting of American Foreign Policy* (New York: McGraw Hill, 1968), 87–213; William Y. Elliot, *The Political Economy of American Foreign Policy* (New York: Henry Holt and Co., 1955), 362–382; Norman S. Buchanan and Friedrich A. Lutz, *Rebuilding the World Economy* (New York: Twentieth Century Fund, 1947), 293–315.
6 See, for example, Michael Mastanduno, "The United States Political System and International Leadership: A 'Decidedly Inferior' Form of Government," in G. John Ikenberry, ed., *American Foreign Policy: Theoretical Essays*, 2nd ed. (New York: Harper Collins, 1996); Robert L. Paarlberg, *Leadership Abroad Begins at Home: U.S. Foreign Economic Policy After the Cold War* (Washington, D.C.: The Brookings Institution, 1995); Patrick Low, *Trading Free: The GATT and U.S. Trade Policy* (Washington, D.C.: Twentieth Century Fund, 1993); I. M. Destler, *American Trade Politics*, 2nd ed. (Washington, D.C.: Institute for International Economics, 1992); Stephen D. Krasner, "United States Commercial and Monetary Policy: Unraveling the Paradox of External Strength and Internal Weakness," in Peter J. Katzenstein, ed., *Between Power and Plenty: Foreign Economic Policies of Advanced Industrial States* (Madison: University of Wisconsin Press, 1978).
7 See Charles Tilly, *Coercion, Capital, and European States, AD 990–1992* (Cambridge, MA: Blackwell, 1994); and Immanuel Wallerstein, *The Modern World System I: Capitalist Agriculture and the Origins of the European World Economy in the Sixteenth Century* (New York: Academic Press, 1974).
8 J. P. Nettl, "The State as a Conceptual Variable," *World Politics* 20 (4) 1968: 559–592.
9 U.S. Const. art. I, sec. 8.
10 See David Ricardo, *The Principles of Political Economy and Taxation* (Amherst, NY: Prometheus Books, 1996), 89–104; Friedrich List, *The National System of Political Economy, Volume II, the Theory* (New York: Augustus M. Kelley, 1966), 6–21; and Karl Marx, "On the Question of Free Trade," speech delivered to the Democratic Association of Brussels on January 9, 1848 in Karl Marx and Friedrich Engels, *Collected Works*, vol. 6 (New York: International Publishers, 1976).
11 Jock A. Finlayson and Mark W. Zacher, "The GATT and the Regulation of Trade Barriers: Regime Dynamics and Functions," in Stephen D. Krasner, ed., *International Regimes* (Ithaca, NY: Cornell University Press, 1983).
12 Low, *Trading Free: The GATT and U.S. Trade Politics*.

13 Jagdish Bhagwati, *Protectionism* (Boston, MA: MIT Press, 1988), 1–15.

14 Max Weber, *Economy and Society*, vol. 2 (Berkeley: University of California Press, 1968), 910.

15 See Edward S. Corwin, *The President: Office and Powers*, 5th rev. ed. (New York: New York University Press, 1984); Richard M. Pious, *The American Presidency* (New York: Basic Books, 1979); and Louis W. Koenig, *The Chief Executive* (New York: Harcourt Brace Javanovich, Inc., 1975).

16 Joan Biskupic and Elder Witt, *The Supreme Court and the Powers of the American Government* (Washington, D.C.: Congressional Quarterly, Inc., 1997), 189.

17 Thomas E. Cronin, *The State of the Presidency* (Boston: Little, Brown, and Co., 1980); and Clinton Rossiter, *The American Presidency* (Baltimore: The Johns Hopkins University Press, 1960).

18 Roger H. Davidson and Walter J. Olezek, *Congress and Its Members* 3rd ed. (Washington, D.C.: Congressional Quarterly, Inc., 1990); Randall Ripley, *Congress: Process and Policy*, 3rd ed. (New York: W. W. Norton and Company, 1983); and David R. Mayhew, *Congress: The Electoral Connection* (New Haven: Yale University Press, 1974).

19 Walter J. Olezek, *Congressional Procedures and the Policy Process* (Washington, D.C.: Congressional Quarterly, Inc., 1989); Richard E. Fenno, *Home Style: House Members in Their Districts* (Boston: Little, Brown, and Co., 1978); and Lewis A. Froman, *Congressmen and Their Constituencies* (Chicago: Rand McNally and Co., 1963).

20 It may be argued that if the president is responsive to the demands of public opinion, the institutional shift of power between Congress and the chief executive may not affect the character of American democracy. However, a large body of literature exists that belies this interpretation. First, the relationship between public opinion and how elected officials form their policy preferences is complex; indeed, often a relationship is difficult, if not impossible, to find. Second, elected officials, and the president in particular, are in the position to shape public opinion—and they often do. Third, the capacity of the president to operate independently from public opinion, and to shape the public's perception of presidential actions, is most pronounced in the field of foreign policy, including foreign trade policy. Finally, presidential independence from and manipulation of public opinion has been well documented in the field of trade policy itself. See, for example, Raymond A. Bauer, Ithiel de Sola Pool, and Lewis A. Dexter, *American Business & Public Policy: The Politics of Foreign Trade*, 2nd ed. (Chicago: Aldine, Atherton, Inc., 1972); and John R. MacArthur, *The Selling of "Free Trade"* (New York: Hill and Wang, 2000).

21 Clinton Rossiter, ed., *The Federalist Papers, Nos. 46, 50, and 74* (New York: Mentor, 1961).

22 John Croome, *Reshaping the World Trading System: A History of the Uruguay Round* (Geneva: World Trade Organization, 1995); Ernest H. Preeg, *Traders in a Brave New World: The Uruguay Round and the Future of the International Trading System* (Chicago: University of Chicago Press, 1995); Low, *Trading Free*; Miriam Camps and William Diebold, Jr., *The New Multilateralism: Can the World Trading System Be Saved?* (New York: Council on Foreign Relations, 1986); Gilbert R. Whinham, *International Trade and the Tokyo Round Negotiation* (Princeton: Princeton University Press, 1986); and Ernest Preeg, *Traders and Diplomats: An Analysis of the Kennedy Round of Negotiations under the General Agreement on Tariffs and Trade* (Washington, D.C.: The Brookings Institution, 1970).

23 It is important to point out that in all these instances, a majority of members of Congress supported granting the president increased policy-making powers. The question as to why Congress would go along with this institutional reorganization is the subject of heated debate among students of postwar American trade politics. For an excellent overview of this debate, see Sharyn O'Halloran, *Politics, Process, and American Trade Policy* (Ann Arbor: University of Michigan Press, 1994). Furthermore, it might be

asked, as a counterfactual, what Congress might have done had it not been constrained by the exercise of world trade leadership. The specialist literature on postwar American trade politics suggests that, absent one or a combination of factors at the international and/or domestic (state and society) levels, the domestic political orientation of Congress and its fragmented internal organization would have led to some form of economic nationalism, with protectionism and managed trade at its center. The classic study of Congress acting on its own in the foreign trade policy-making process is E. E. Schattschneider, *Politics, Pressures and the Tariff: A Study of Free Private Enterprise in Pressure Politics, as Shown in the 1929–1930 Revision of the Tariff* (New York: Prentice-Hall, 1935).

24 Harry Eckstein, "Case Study and Theory in Political Science," in Fred L. Greenstein and Nelson Polsby, eds., *Handbook of Political Science*, vol. 7 (Reading, MA: Addison-Wesley Publishing Company, 1975), 118.

25 At this point it might be asked: why not begin this analysis of the triumph of globalism with the original RTAA of 1934? The reason is simple: while similar in language, the RTAA of 1945 was a fundamentally different instrument than was the RTAA of 1934. The main difference between these statutes is found in their objectives and methods. With respect to objectives, the RTAA of 1945 was a global policy designed to launch an international trade regime; while the RTAA of 1934 was a domestic policy designed to expand U.S. exports at a time of severe economic crisis and high unemployment. In terms of methods, the RTAA of 1945 was a multilateral policy; while the RTAA of 1934 was a bilateral policy. As David A. Lake explains: "The RTAA [of 1934] simply reflected a recognition in the United States that lower tariffs abroad and an ability to bargain bilaterally for such reductions were necessary for the restoration of its export markets. It was a tactical and pragmatic response to the international closure precipitated in part by its own earlier actions. The RTAA [of 1934] demonstrated only the willingness of the United States to trade limited reductions in its own tariff wall in return for substantial reductions by others." See David A. Lake, *Power, Protection and Free Trade: International Sources of U.S. Commercial Strategy, 1887–1939* (Ithaca, NY: Cornell University Press, 1988), 204. He continues, "The RTAA [of 1934] was not intended to overturn the American system of protection . . . . Nor did [it] emphasize the long-term health of the international economy or the necessity of lowering protection at home regardless of the actions of other countries" (206–207). For his part, William Diebold argues that, while similar in terms of shifting trade policy-making power from Congress to the president, it was "the turn from bilateral to multilateral methods" that marked the departure of the RTAA of 1945 from the RTAA of 1934. See William Diebold, Jr. "A Watershed with Some Dry Sides: The Trade Expansion Act of 1962" (revised text supplied to the author), 23. Due to the differences between the RTAA of 1934 and the RTAA of 1945 in their objectives (domestic vs. global) and methods (bilateral vs. multilateral), the triumph of globalism cannot be said to have been operational in the enactment of the RTAA of 1934.

26 John H. Jackson, "The General Agreement on Tariffs and Trade in United States Domestic Law," *Michigan Law Review* 66 (1967): 249–322.

27 Testimony of William A. Clayton. U.S. Congress, House Committee on Ways and Means, *1945 Extension of Reciprocal Trade Agreements Act: Hearings before the Committee on Ways and Means*, HR 2652, 79th Cong., 1st sess. April 1945, 14–15

28 *The Reciprocal Trade Agreements Act, 1945*, Public Law 79–130, 59 Stat. 410.

29 *The Trade Expansion Act, 1962*, Public Law 87–794, 76 Stat. 1962.

30 Jackson, "The General Agreement on Tariffs and Trade," 249–322; and Harry C. Hawkins and Janet L. Norwood, "The Legislative Basis of U.S. Commercial Policy," in William B. Kelley, Jr., ed., *Studies in United States Commercial Policy* (Chapel Hill: University of North Carolina Press, 1963).

31 Public Law 87–794, Section 201.

32 Congressional Quarterly, *Special Report: The Trade Expansion Act of 1962* (Washington, D.C.: Congressional Quarterly Press, 1962).

33 Ibid.

34 *Trade Act, 1975*, Public Law 93–618, 88 Stat. 1978.

35 Harold H. Koh, "The Fast Track and United States Trade Policy," *Brooklyn Journal of International Law*, XVIII (1992): 143–180. The fast-track procedure also was designed to circumvent the constitutionally stipulated process for implementing international treaties. According to the Constitution, international treaties only become binding on the United States if they secure a two-thirds super-majority in the Senate. Although international trade agreements have the status of treaties at the level of international law, since World War II, Congress, the president, and the Supreme Court have consistently held that simple majority votes in both houses of Congress are sufficient to implement international trade agreements.

36 Public Law 93–618, Chapter 5, Section 151.

37 The Trade Act's fast-track authority was used to implement the Tokyo Round of Multilateral Trade Agreements, which were submitted to Congress by the president in the Trade Agreements Act (TAA) of 1979. Although substantial political controversy surrounded the enactment of the TAA, the fast track procedure worked well, contributing to overwhelming bipartisan support for the implementing legislation, which passed the Senate 90–4 and the House 395–7. See I. M. Destler, *American Trade Politics*, 2nd ed., 74–75.

38 *The Omnibus Trade and Competitiveness Act, 1988*, Public Law 100–418, 102 Stat. 1107.

39 Public Law 100–418, Title I, Section 1103. The fast-track authority in the OTCA was used to implement the Uruguay Round of Multilateral Trade Agreements, which were submitted to Congress by the president in the Uruguay Round Agreements Act (URAA) of 1994. The enactment of the URAA generated even more intense political battles than did the implementation of the Trade Agreements Act of 1979. Despite these battles, however, the fast-track process worked well, contributing to overwhelming bipartisan support for the measure in both houses of Congress.

40 Preeg, *Traders and Diplomats in a Brave New World*.

41 Under the GATT, trade agreements did not apply to inconsistent legislation existing prior to the agreement; after the Uruguay Round, they did so apply. See John H. Jackson, William J. Davey, and Alan O. Sykes, *Legal Problems of International Economic Relations*, 3rd ed. (Minneapolis: West Publishing Company, 1995), 300–301.

42 Ibid., 289.

43 Because the WTO is designed to promote free trade, and manages international agreements designed to facilitate trade liberalization, this requirement should come as no surprise. One result, however, has been an overwhelming free trade bias in panel decisions. Indeed, according to one authority, approximately 90 percent of all panel decisions result in "full or partial victory" for the plaintiffs (i.e., those who allege breaches of WTO free trade agreements). Ibid., 339.

44 *Final Act of the Uruguay Round of Multilateral Trade Negotiations, Annex 2*, 353–377, accessed at www.wto.org/english/docs_e/legal_e.htm, June 7, 2005. More recently, WTO dispute settlement panels have begun to allow non-governmental organizations (NGOs) to provide testimony in some cases (principally relating to the environment), going so far as to accept *amicus curiae* briefs. However, in the handful of cases in which NGOs are allowed to testify or submit briefs, it is only on an advisory basis. Their input is nonbinding.

45 *Uruguay Rounds Agreements Act of 1994*, Public Law 103–465. At the time of this writing the ninth international trade round, the Doha Round of Multilateral Trade Negotiations, remains ongoing. As a result, the round has not led to changes in U.S. domestic law. Thus, the Uruguay Round agreements remain the international framework for world trade.

46 Public Law 103–465, Title I, Subtitle C, Section 123, Paragraph [g]. Although members of Congress have voiced concern about specific rules and regulations altered by executive branch bureaus and agencies under the URAA, this title and section have never been used to block executive branch action. Furthermore, even if it were so used, the URAA specifies that any such action is not binding on the president or other executive branch bureaus and agencies.

47 Public Law 103–465, Section 125 of Subtitle C allows Congress to withdraw the United States from the WTO through the passage of a joint resolution in both Houses. However, this section establishes extremely high legislative hurdles for a joint resolution to become binding: the ability to muster a two-thirds vote in each House of Congress—enough to override an inevitable presidential veto.

48 See WTO, "Dispute Settlement—Index of Dispute Issues," accessed on the website of the World Trade Organization at http://www.wto.org/english/tratop_e/dispu_e/dispu_subjects_index-e.htm, September 2011.

49 A list of these dispute settlement cases, the country or countries that brought action against the United States, and the action(s) taken by the United States to implement WTO rulings or negotiated settlements can be found at the website of the World Trade Organization, www.wto.org/english/tratop_e/dispu_e.htm, accessed January 30, 2011.

50 U.S. General Accounting Office, *World Trade Organization: Standard of Review and Impact of Trade Remedy Rulings*, GAO-03-824 (Washington, D.C.: 2003), Appendix V, "Comments from the United States International Trade Commission," 116.

51 WTO, Trade Policy Review Body, "Trade Policy Review: United States," Document Number WT/TPR/S/88, August 15, 2001; European Commission, *Market Access Sectoral and Trade Barriers Database*, "United States: General Features of Trade Policy, 2003."

52 Government Accounting Office, *World Trade Organization: Standard of Review and Impact of Trade Remedy Rulings*, Report to the Ranking Minority Member, Committee on Finance, U.S. Senate, GAO-03-824, July 2003, 111.

53 Congress of the United States, Congressional Budget Office, *The GATT Negotiations and U.S. Trade Policy* (Washington, DC: Congressional Budget Office, 1987), xii.

54 In addition to the political effects of America's world trade leadership role, the expansion of foreign trade in the postwar period has been promoted by two major economic developments: growing efficiencies in transportation and communications technologies, and the rise of export-led growth in developed and developing countries.

55 Renato Ruggiero, "Beyond Borders: Managing a World of Free trade and Deep Interdependence," speech delivered before the Argentina Council on Foreign Relations, September 10, 1996, World Trade Organization PRESS/55, September 10, 1996.

PART II
Theory

2

POLITICAL SCIENCE TRADE THEORY

> Whether as a prejudice of common sense, a postulate of logicians, or a habit of prosecuting attorneys, the monism of cause can be, for history, only an impediment. History seeks for causal wave-trains and is not afraid, since life shows them to be so, to find them multiple.
>
> *Marc Bloch (1953)*

The argument presented in Chapter 1 begs a fundamental question: what accounts for America's postwar policy of world trade leadership? Answering this question is crucial for an understanding of the causal origins of the triumph of globalism, for, as I argued in Chapter 1, the triumph of globalism has been the result of America's exercise of world trade leadership. Where, then, are we to turn for fruitful modes of analysis capable of explaining the mainsprings of this global policy?

In my view, existing theories of trade politics are not up to the task. The problem, however, is not the lack of adequate theories, but of too many theories to be adequate. Indeed, students of trade have traced the causal origins of the policy to a wide variety of explanatory factors. These include: the pattern of group or class mobilization into politics; the business cycle; the impact of global, national, and regional markets on the policy preferences of business, labor, and agriculture; the structure and dynamics of capitalism; the institutional organization of the American national state, particularly the relationship between the president and Congress; the coalition-building efforts of public officials; the impact of ideas on public officials and the institutions, processes and rules they create; the role of epistemic communities in policy formation; political parties and their relationship to voters; party competition; the strategic interaction of states; war and global economic conditions; international security structures; and the distribution of power among states within the international system. This is a sticky wicket. And if the reader is left dazed and confused, the student of trade is left on their knees.

There are two ways of dealing with this problem. One is to pick one of these theoretical perspectives in an effort to squeeze more juice out of the lemon. The drawback of such an approach is that it recapitulates extant perspectives, although it certainly may advance them within their limited domain. Another is to attempt to see the forest from the trees in an effort to bridge analytical divides. The advantage of such an approach is its promise of being able to advance novel theories through the construction of meta-theories. And this is the approach I shall take.

More specifically, my theoretical approach is to integrate three broad analytical perspectives within the political science literature on trade. One perspective operates at the international level and focuses on the structures and processes of the international political economy, as well as the relative power of nation-states in the system. Another focuses on the interests of domestic economic groups and their pattern of mobilization into trade politics and policy-making. The third examines the policy preferences of public officials operating within differentially empowered and organized state institutions. For the purpose of ease of use, I will refer to these perspectives as system, society, and state.

The idea of rolling system, society, and state into a single meta-theory is not new. Indeed, for more than three decades political scientists who study trade have argued that such integration is the next logical theoretical move for this research domain.[1] To date, however, such a move has not been made. Nowhere is this clearer than in the attempts by political scientists to explain why the United States maintained a liberal trade policy in the last two decades of the twentieth century despite its (supposed) decline vis-à-vis other nations, and the concomitant expansion of imports into the American market—both of which might have been expected to lead the nation to adopt a protectionist or neo-mercantilist trade policy. David A. Lake explained this apparent anomaly with reference to a new distribution of national economic power within the international state system—what he called "a structure of multilateral opportunism."[2] On the other hand, Helen V. Milner explained it with reference to the emergence in the postwar period of "global industries," which were able to counteract rising protectionist pressures in Congress through lobbying efforts of their own.[3] Finally, I. M. Destler traced the maintenance of a liberal trade policy to a "pressure-diverting policy management system" at the level of the American state—a system that built a free trade bias into the trade policy-making process, while at the same time insulating national policy-makers from rising protectionist pressures, particularly in Congress.[4] Each of these studies contained some truth. However, because the authors focused on different causal forces, they reached radically different conclusions. They each had something to say, but they talked past each other.

That trade should provide the case material for such divergent perspectives should come as no surprise; for the morphology of the policy invites them. It does so because trade policy sets the political rules that regulate the insertion of a nation's economy into the world economy with respect to the cross-border exchange of goods, services, trade-related investment, and trade-related intellectual property rights. Thus trade is situated at the intersection of domestic politics and the international system; and it engages the economic interests of society-based groups as well as the political interests of public officials. Given trade's morphology, it is a wonder that political science trade theory is not replete with studies that place a consideration of society–state relationships within the context of the economic and political structures and processes of the international system. That it has not provides an opportunity for theory construction. Indeed, it may be argued that political science trade theory possesses a built-in agenda for theory construction. It suggests an approach for explaining the origins of America's postwar policy of world trade leadership (and hence the triumph of globalism) that focuses on the impact of the international political economy on society–state relationships at the level of domestic politics.[5]

Clearly the first step in the construction of such an approach is to examine what political scientists have to say about the operation of system, society, and state forces in trade politics; in particular American trade politics. And here three studies stand out for detailed treatment: Stephen D. Krasner's *World Politics* article, "State Power and the Structure of International Trade" (1976); E. E. Schattschneider's, *Politics, Pressures and the Tariff* (1935); and Raymond A. Bauer, Ithiel de Sola Pool, and Lewis Anthony Dexter's, *American Business & Public Policy: The Politics of Foreign Trade* (1963).[6] Three aspects of these studies make them particularly worthy of attention. First, and most important, each was the first to highlight the causal role of system, society, and state forces (respectively) in trade politics. Therefore, focusing on these works clears the conceptual terrain by taking us back to first analytical principles. Second, so original and provocative were the arguments and findings of these studies that they became instant disciplinary classics. Thus they occupy a status in political science that transcends their narrow focus on trade. Finally, although each of these studies is *sui generis* with respect to its empirical focus and methodology, with respect to its guiding point of view (system, society, or state), each is broadly representative of subsequent trade studies of its analytical ilk.

This chapter examines the theoretical arguments and empirical findings of these classic works. It does so in order to set the stage (in Chapter 3) for the elaboration of an explanatory framework that integrates system, society, and state-level variables into a single analytical approach—one geared toward explaining the causal origins of America's postwar policy of world trade leadership. That said, a review of these studies does not yield a ready-made, multivariate approach; rather, it suggests the basic concepts and questions around which such an approach needs to be organized. Therefore, in addition to reviewing these works, the purpose of this chapter is to delineate the concepts and questions to which this book is addressed.

The Sphere of the International System: "State Power and the Structure of International Trade"

"State Power and the Structure of International Trade" presents an approach for explaining trade politics that focuses on the relative economic power of national states at the level of the international system. In terms of its contributions to political science the article played a pivotal role in the emergence of neo-realism as a major current within international relations theory and helped to establish a new international relations sub-field: international political economy. Broadly speaking, the article was a response to two currents within the study of international relations. First, it took aim at so-called "liberal internationalists," who argued that the post–World War II international system (particularly since the 1960s) was characterized by "complex interdependence," a phenomenon marked by expanding "contacts, coalitions, and interactions across state boundaries that are not controlled by the central foreign policy organs of government."[7] In contrast to this view, Krasner (re)asserted one of the central tenets of realist theory: the state is the central actor in world politics. The article also took aim at political scientists who argued that a nation's foreign policy largely was a reflection of its domestic politics.[8] In contrast to this view, Krasner asserted the primacy of international structures.[9]

Like subsequent system-centered studies, "State Power and the Structure of International Trade," traced the origins of national trade policies to the structures and processes of the international system. In this view, society and state factors at the domestic level play little (if any) causal role in the determination of a nation's trade policy. Rather, this policy is treated as a reflection of the relative position of a nation-state at the intersection of the world economy and the international state system. From this perspective, to know a nation's position within the international political economy is to know its trade policy.

"State Power and the Structure of International Trade" is a theoretically driven, empirically rich, and methodologically rigorous analysis of the genesis of international trading structures during the nineteenth and twentieth centuries. Krasner defines "international trading structures" as the sum total of the trade policies adopted by states within the international political economy. Thus, his central puzzle is to explain why states adopt the trade policies they do. Broadly speaking, in order to answer this question, Krasner constructed a formal, deductive theory that focused on the relationship between the distribution of economic power among states (international structure) and their trade policies (national interests). His principal hypothesis is that a state's trade policy is likely to reflect its structural position in the international political economy.

At the heart of Krasner's approach, which he calls a "state power" theory, are three basic, canonical assumptions about the nature of international relations that are at the core of neo-realism (and realism). First, states are the primary actors in international politics. Second, states are unitary actors which act rationally to "maximize national goals." Third, a state's behavior (i.e., a particular policy, or how it defines its national interest) will reflect that state's power position vis-à-vis other states in the international system. Because he dealt with an international economic issue, Krasner defined "state power" in economic terms: the relative size and level of development of a state. The larger and more developed a state, the greater its relative power. Krasner maintained that the structure of international trade (that is, the degree to which a trading system is open or closed) "is determined by the interests and power of states acting to maximize national goals."[10] Therefore, international trading structures reflect the sum total of the trade policies of the states within a given network of trade; and these policies, in turn, reflect the distribution of economic power among states within that network.

Drawing on neoclassical as well as mercantilist trade theory, Krasner posits four goals that drive state action: political power, aggregate national income, economic growth, and social stability. Given these goals, which he contends are the same for all states regardless of their domestic structures, Krasner argues that states will develop a particular preference for a liberal or a protectionist trade policy depending on their relative economic power vis-à-vis other states. Based upon this analytical matrix of interest (state goals) and power (a state's relative position), Krasner contends that six international trading structures are logically possible, each conducive to a greater or lesser degree of openness. His most important theoretical assertion, however, is that an open structure is most likely to result from a distribution of economic power among states which produces a "hegemonic system"; that is, a system within which one state, the "hegemon," is much larger and more developed than its trading partners. Within a hegemonic system, Krasner contends, there are compelling structural reasons for a hegemonic state to adopt a liberal trade policy and to use its power to take the lead in creating an open international trading structure. Conversely, periods of "hegemonic decline" are likely to generate relatively closed (protectionist) international trading structures.

Krasner tests his assertion about hegemonic systems against the history of international trading relationships among eight countries between 1820 and 1970: Denmark, France, Germany, Italy, Japan, Sweden, the United Kingdom, and the United States. Based upon a detailed analysis of changes in three variables—tariff levels, trade proportions, and regional integration—Krasner argues that during those years six distinct international trading structures can be identified: 1820–1879, a period of increasing openness; 1880–1900, a period of modest closure; 1901–1913, a period of renewed openness; 1918–1939, a period of significant closure; 1945–1960, a period of great openness; and 1960–1970, a period of continued openness.

Krasner concludes from his historical investigation that his argument about hegemonic systems "is largely, although not completely, substantiated by the empirical data."[11] This is a generous conclusion, since his hypothesis about

hegemony accurately described only three of the six trading structures he identified (1820–1879; 1880–1900; and 1945–1960). The period of increasing openness between 1820 and 1879 closely corresponds to the rise of British hegemony
in the international political economy following the Napoleonic Wars; and the
subsequent period of modest closure between 1880 and 1900 is consistent with
a decline in British hegemonic power. However, the period of renewed openness between 1901 and 1913; the period of closure between World Wars I and
II; and the period of continued openness between 1960 and 1970 do not support
his theory. In the first case (1901–1913), Krasner's theory anticipated that there
would be continued closure in the international trading structure as British power
continued to decline vis-à-vis the other states in the system. But this did not happen. On the contrary, the international trading structure became more open. In
the second case (1918–1939), his theory expected a move toward greater openness as the United States emerged from World War I as the world's dominant
economic power. Yet this did not occur. Instead, the interwar period was marked
by the development of autarkic economic empires and widespread protectionism. Finally, the period of openness following World War II (1945–1960; and
1960–1970) both confirms and confounds Krasner's theory. On the one hand, the
post–World War II period confirms his theory for the years 1945–1960, when the
United States was hegemonic and its economic power went largely unchallenged.
On the other hand, his theory fails to explain the continued (indeed increasing)
openness of the period 1960–1970, during which (Krasner argues) the relative
economic power of the United States declined.

Krasner concedes from his findings that, used in isolation, state-power theory
is an inadequate tool for explaining changes in the international trading structure (and hence the trade policies of states). There simply is not a mono-causal
relationship between the distribution of economic power among states and how
states define their national trade interests. As Krasner puts it, "The structure of
the international trading system does not move in lockstep with changes in the
distribution of potential power among states." Instead, international trading systems are initiated and ended, "not as state-power theory would predict, by close
assessments of the interests of the state at every given moment, but by external
events—usually cataclysmic ones"—such as global depression and war (341).

Krasner traces the inertia of international trading systems to domestic politics.
He argues that once states adopt particular trade policies, those policies "are pursued until a new crisis demonstrates that they are no longer feasible." He maintains that new trade policies tend to create "new social structures and institutional
arrangements" at the domestic level that prevent states from acting in accordance
with their relative economic power (342). Once these new social structures and
institutional arrangements are established, they tend to become self-perpetuat-
ing—even in the face of structural changes at the global level.

"State Power and the Structure of International Trade" suffers from three
analytical limitations. First, the article lacks a clear conception of domestic poli-

tics. Although Krasner recognizes that domestic social structures and institutional arrangements matter, he makes little attempt to systematically integrate these variables into his state-power approach. Indeed, domestic politics only appear at the end of his analysis, and then only as an exogenous factor brought in to "explain" historical deviations from his model. In the final analysis, Krasner treats domestic politics in typical neo-realist fashion. The state is simply assumed to be a rational, unitary actor which automatically seeks to maximize national goals in accordance with its structural position in the international system. The possibility that "national goals" might be influenced by the pattern of society–state relationships at the domestic level is all but ignored.

The second analytical limitation of Krasner's article is his concept of "hegemony," which is suspect analytically. The problem here is twofold. First, there is no agreed-upon definition of what it means for a state to be hegemonic. In particular, there is confusion concerning whether hegemony refers to an objective attribute of a state (e.g., the relative size and development of its economy); or if it refers to its political behavior (e.g., taking the lead [or not] in the promotion of an open world trading system).[12] In part, this confusion is rooted in the etymology of the word itself, for hegemony can mean both supremacy as well as leadership. It is possible, therefore, to identify a state as hegemonic in the sense of supremacy with respect to some objective factor(s), while at the same time determining that its political behavior does not reflect its supremacy. Indeed, drawing upon Krasner's "state power" theory, what are we to make of the period 1918–1939, when (he claims) the United States was hegemonic in the objective sense, but not in the behavioral sense (think of the rejection of the League of Nations and the Smoot-Hawley Act). By the same token, what are we to make of the period 1960–1970, when (Krasner asserts) the United States was objectively in a state of hegemonic decline but continued to exercise world trade leadership? If a state is hegemonic in the objective sense, but does not act like a hegemon, what is it? By the same token, if a state acts like a hegemon, but is not in the objective sense, what are we dealing with?[13]

The second problem with the concept of hegemony is that there are no agreed-upon criteria about how to measure its objective (non-behavioral) features. Krasner, for example, uses four measures: per capita income; aggregate economic size (GDP); world trade shares; and foreign investment. David A. Lake, on the other hand, uses only two measures: aggregate economic size (measured in terms of world trade shares); and labor productivity. What is more, regardless of the measures used, there is no objective standard against which to determine when a state crosses into or falls out of the realm of being hegemonic. Krasner, for example, never even attempts to identify an objective standard. Instead, his evaluation is intuitive and post hoc. He simply looks at England's relative position in the period 1820–1879, declares it to be hegemonic and then uses this baseline to evaluate the relative position of the United States in the periods 1918–1939, 1945–1960, and 1960–1970. For his part, Lake develops an objective standard based on relative size and level of productivity, but in so doing he establishes categories where even a slight change in either of these variables alters whether or not he considers a state to be hegemonic.[14] Are we to believe that a change of 1 percent (or less) in a nation's share of world trade or productivity is all that it takes for a state to move in and out of the realm of being a hegemon? Rather than getting bogged down in these analytical conundrums, it is better, in my view, to discard the concept of hegemony altogether.[15] This does not mean that the relative position of the United States in the international political economy should be of no concern in our analysis of the causal origins of the nation's postwar policy of world trade leadership. It simply suggests that we set aside the analytical straightjacket of hegemony in favor of a more inductive approach—one that looks at the historically specific modalities of American structural power within the postwar world trading system.

Finally, "State Power and the Structure of International Trade" fails to account for the interactions among states. Here the problem is twofold. First, the trade and economic policies of states influence one another. This is especially true of the largest and most developed states. There is no better example of this inter-subjective relationship than the trade wars of the 1930s. Furthermore, since World War II the trade and economic policies of the largest and most developed states have been a major external driver of America's exercise of world trade leadership, especially the efforts of the United States to steer other nations toward GATT/WTO-consistent practices. The second problem has a bearing on Krasner's finding that since the early 1960s the world trading system has remained open, despite America's supposed hegemonic decline. More specifically, the existence of the GATT/WTO regime has tied member states into a network of binding free trade agreements which remain operative despite changes in the distribution of economic power among them. Moreover, the existence of this regime has provided a common point of reference for states around which to organize their otherwise unilateral and inward-looking trade and economic policies.[16]

Notwithstanding these analytical limitations, there is no reason to throw all of Krasner's analysis out with the bathwater. Indeed, it is precisely the problematic nature of Krasner's argument that invites us to reconsider the impact of the international political economy and America's position within it on the pattern of politics responsible for the triumph of globalism. In particular, it invites us to re-conceptualize the concept of hegemony, without losing sight of the possibility that the structures and processes of the international political economy (including America's relative economic position, the inter-subjective interaction of states, and the GATT/WTO regime) have played an important causal role in the triumph of globalism. It also invites us to problematize the relationship between these external forces and society–state relationships at the domestic level. Thus, we may ask: what was the impact of the international political economy on the pattern of domestic politics responsible for America's postwar policy of world trade leadership?

The Sphere of Domestic Politics: *Politics, Pressures and the Tariff* and *American Business & Public Policy*

While "State Power and the Structure of International Trade" is cast at the international level and explores the relationship between a state's relative position in the international political economy and how it defines its national trade interest, the studies by E. E. Schattschneider and Bauer, Pool, and Dexter are cast at the domestic level and inquire into the influence of society and state forces in trade politics and policy-making. Yet, although both of these domestically oriented studies focus on the society–state relationship, they reach radically different conclusions. While *Politics, Pressures and the Tariff* traces American trade policy to the power and interests of economic groups and their pattern of mobilization into the political process (society), *American Business & Public Policy* traces it to the political behavior of public officials operating within differentially empowered and organized national state institutions (state). If we are to examine the influence of society and state forces on America's national policy of world trade leadership, it is necessary to come to grips with this division. Even more, it is necessary to resolve it. Clearly, the first step in moving toward such a resolution is to examine what the authors had to say about the role of society and state forces in American trade politics and policy-making.

Politics, Pressures and the Tariff

Politics, Pressures and the Tariff was in the vanguard of the so-called "revolt against formalism," which swept political science in the 1920s and the 1930s. As is well known, formalism was an approach to the study of politics that focused on constitutional doctrine, statutory authority, and the formal attributes and arrangements of state institutions; and it had been the main current within political science since well before the founding of the discipline in 1903. Although a few studies broke out of the formalist mode, such as Woodrow Wilson's *Congressional Government*, J. Allen Smith's *The Spirit of American Government*, and Arthur F. Bentley's *The Process of Government*, most lacked a clear conception of political process and treated state institutions as little more than formal legal categories, separate and distinct from the actual workings of politics.[17] The focus was not on government as it is, but on government as it was supposed to be, leading to what Bentley called "a dead political science."[18] *Politics, Pressures and the Tariff* took direct aim at formalism by focusing on the behavior of economic groups in the political process. In so doing, it played a pivotal role in moving the "group approach" into the mainstream of political science. Indeed, it "set the tone for a whole generation of political writing on pressure groups."[19]

Like subsequent society-centered studies, *Politics, Pressures and the Tariff* traces the origin of trade policy to the political behavior of economic groups in the political process; specifically, to their trade-related policy preferences and their pattern of mobilization into politics. In this view, state institutions and public officials exercise little autonomy in politics. Indeed, to the extent that they achieve any efficacy at all, it is to shape, channel, and mediate group conflict, and to translate group demands into public policy. From this vantage point, to know the policy preferences of economic groups, and to describe their pattern of mobilization into politics, is to explain the origins of policy.

Politics, Pressures and the Tariff examines the political behavior of economic groups in the formation of the Tariff Act of 1930 (the so-called Smoot-Hawley Act). Smoot-Hawley was the latest in a long line of tariff acts promulgated by the Republican Party which were designed to protect American producers from foreign competition by equalizing the cost of production between domestic and foreign firms. In this scheme, tariffs were adjusted so as to raise the price of imports to a level that eliminated price competition in the American market. Although some of Smoot-Hawley's rates were set on the floors of the House and the Senate, most were determined in the two trade committees in Congress (the House Committee on Ways and Means and the Senate Committee on Finance), which, as part of their process for determining rates, held public hearings to solicit advice from citizens with an economic interest in the policy. In the course of these hearings nearly 20,000 pages of public testimony were generated; and this testimony provided Schattschneider with his main data source.

Schattschneider's study is guided by two assumptions: that a connection exists between economic interest and group political behavior; and that public policy is the result of "effective demands" by groups upon the government. Given these assumptions, the point of his analysis was to determine the nature of the connection between interest and behavior, as well as the way group demands are shaped and modified in the political process. "To take for granted that interests and behavior are identical is to assume too much and to explain too little." The task is to "measure the strength of this drive in politics, to observe its direction and variability, and to note the manner in which it is deflected and controlled." As for "effective demands," the expression "implies that many of the claims urged upon the government are ineffective." One needed to ask: "Of the myriad of interests affected by this policy, which were able to make demands that gained recognition in the law?" Therefore, "if it is true that demands largely determine public policy, it follows that policies can be explained in terms of the processes by which pressures are shaped and modified. Policies become intelligible when considered in connection with the sequences of causes and effects by which some demands are made effective while others are neutralized."[20]

Pursuant to these assumptions, *Politics, Pressures and the Tariff* examines two aspects of the tariff-making process: how tariffs are made; and the political behavior of economic groups in the process. The first inquiry was necessary in order to determine the ways in which the legislative procedures of the two congressional trade committees affected the role of economic groups in the tariff-making process. This was a crucial consideration, for if the committees acted freely—

according to their own ideas and principles—then an investigation into the political behavior of economic groups in the tariff-making process would be unnecessary. As it turned out, however, the testimony contained in the public record showed little in the way of policy-making autonomy on the part of the two committees. Rather, *Politics, Pressures and the Tariff* details a policy-making process within which the House Committee on Ways and Means and the Senate Committee on Finance all but handed control over tariff making to the economic groups that showed up to testify. The two committees abdicated their sovereign power over the rate-setting process and established "a free private enterprise in pressure politics" (31).

How could the committees allow this to happen? The answer was found in the form of the tariff legislation itself. More specifically, the Tariff Act of 1930 set rates on thousands of separate items in an attempt to eliminate price competition in the American market by equalizing the cost of production between foreign and domestic producers. The item-by-item approach undermined the autonomy of the committees because it focused their attention on the adjudication of thousands of individual rates, with the result that committee members were overworked and prevented from considering broader and more fundamental questions of national policy. Furthermore, due to the number of tariff rates the committees had to set, the volume of persons who sought a hearing before them, and the pressure of the legislative timetable, they were forced to conduct their hearings in extreme haste. As a result, they had little time to check the veracity of the testimony they received; or to examine the representative character of the groups they heard from. Consequently, the role of the committees was reduced to little more than bargaining with witnesses over the details of specific rates.

The cost-of-production formula undermined the autonomy of the committees because it was impossible to administer. Indeed, this approach to tariff-making required the committees to gather detailed information about domestic and foreign production costs for each of the thousands of items contained in the legislation. Even if the committees possessed an independent means of ascertaining those costs (which they did not), determining rates according to this formula would have presented an enormous, if not impossible task. As it was, because the committees lacked an independent means of collecting this data, they were forced to rely on whatever cost information self-interested witnesses were willing to provide them. This posed a significant problem, for the groups that showed up to testify considered their cost information to be confidential. What is more, if they did provide information on production costs they often manipulated it so as to prevent their domestic and foreign rivals from gaining competitive advantages, as well as to make the best case for increased tariffs. Furthermore, domestic producers often had no idea about the production costs of their foreign competitors, or if they did have information it was largely based on rumor. As a result, "statistics became the handmaiden of the subconscious process of wish fulfillment" (68).

The committees' ability to independently and objectively determine tariff rates "collapsed at this point" (71).

The practical result of the committees' loss of policy-making autonomy was that they granted tariff increases to every economic group that showed up and requested them. It was only by providing "protection all around" that the committees were able to claim legitimacy for the policy, for they had no objective criteria for granting tariff increases to some producers but not to others. Thus, the tariff took on the character of a private right, and "a system under which rights have accrued forecloses debate as to its merits and leaves Congress no more than the task of administering and adjudicating the details [of the policy]" (71).

If the two trade committees abdicated their sovereign power over the tariff-setting process, what were the real causal forces behind the nation's high tariff policy? The answer was the pattern of group mobilization into the hearings process. And here *Politics, Pressures and the Tariff* argues that this pattern was highly uneven. Although tariff legislation affected the economic interests of most Americans, the groups that showed up to testify represented only a tiny fraction of those affected by it. The most dominant segment of American society represented in the hearings process was business; and among business firms and associations, the hearings were dominated by small-scale, domestically oriented producers demanding higher tariffs. Producer groups seeking lower tariffs, or who were interested in debating the overall merits of the policy, either did not testify, or were swamped by protectionist firms in the hearings process (as was the case with importers). Indeed, so biased were the hearings in favor of protection that even the opponents of higher tariffs accepted protectionism in principle (109). "To manage pressures," Schattschneider concludes, "is to govern; to let pressures run wild is to abdicate" (293).

From the point of view of explaining the origins of America's postwar policy of world trade leadership, *Politics, Pressures and the Tariff* suffers from two analytical limitations. First, the book possesses an underdeveloped view of the state. In particular, it contains little explanatory information concerning the motives and interests of the public officials engaged in the tariff revision of 1929–1930. As E. Pendleton Herring remarks in his review of the book: "What the author does not go into fully is *why* Congress listened so sympathetically to those who sought a higher tariff."[21] Indeed, although, at numerous points in the text, *Politics, Pressures and the Tariff* alludes to a complex and mutually reinforcing relationship between members of Congress and protectionist business groups, the book never examines this relationship in any detail. As a result, *Politics, Pressures and the Tariff* paints an overly one-sided picture of trade politics; and falls prey to the charge of economic determinism, especially with respect to the relationship between business and the state. As Schattschneider describes the business–state relationship, "Influence is the possession of those who have established their supremacy in the invisible empires outside of what is ordinarily known as government. From this point of view the function of pressure politics is to reconcile formal political democracy and economic autocracy. If the overloads of business are not masters of the state, they seem at least to negotiate with it as equals."[22]

The book's second limitation is its finding that the pattern of group mobilization into the hearings process was highly uneven, for it fails to provide a compelling explanation as to why this was so. Indeed, *Politics, Pressures and the Tariff* lists nearly fifty different factors contributing to this pattern, including access to information concerning the legislation; excessive faith in the tariff as an economic cure-all; political organization and psychology; sectionalism; habitual activity; and the routines of business administration (123–125). At no point does the book attempt to discern some underlying cause of the pattern it describes. Particularly absent is any consideration of how the position of a group in the economic structure might affect its trade policy preferences and its pattern of mobilization into politics. As a result, the book's attempt to identify a connection between interest and behavior falls short; and its admonition that its long list of factors conditioning the interest–behavior relationship "shows that the relation is not simple," gets us nowhere (125). Indeed, if the connection between interest and behavior is to be taken seriously, the relationship needs to be spelled out in detail. And this requires an analytical approach that anchors group political behavior in the trade-related structure of the American and world economies.[23]

It is impossible to read *Politics, Pressures and the Tariff* and not be impressed with the extent to which economic groups (especially business firms and associations) influenced the process of tariff-making in the Trade Act of 1930. Although the book slights the role of the state in the tariff-making process, and fails to provide a compelling explanation of the relationship between economic interest and group political behavior, it nonetheless invites us to consider and problematize the causal influence of economic groups in our inquiry into the origins of America's postwar policy of world trade leadership. In particular, the book's analytical limitations suggest that we re-traverse the terrain first mapped out in *Politics, Pressures and the Tariff*, but with a tighter focus on the interest–behavior relationship, and with more sensitivity to the possibility that the state and public officials may play a creative, dynamic, and efficacious causal role in trade politics and policy-making. Thus, we may ask: which economic groups (if any) became involved in the formulation and enactment of the four crucial trade statutes at the legislative core of the triumph of globalism; and what was the relationship between their trade-related economic interests, their policy preferences, their pattern of mobilization into politics, and their relationship to the state and public officials?

American Business & Public Policy

American Business & Public Policy played a pivotal role in the so-called "behavioral revolution," which swept political science in the 1950s and 1960s. Not only did the authors employ the latest behavioral research techniques in a combination and on a scale not seen before, but their work exemplified the type of "value neutral," team-based social science which became a hallmark of behaviorism.[24] Just as important, the book was in the forefront of the (re)discovery that state institutions, processes, and public officials play a dynamic and efficacious role in politics.[25] Indeed, *American Business & Public Policy* foreshadowed what David Easton has called the "return-to-the-state" movement of the 1970s and the 1980s, and one might add, the "new institutionalism" that followed in its wake.[26]

Like subsequent state-centered studies, *American Business & Public Policy* traces the origins of trade policy to the ideas, interests, and political behavior of public officials operating according to formal rules, processes, and procedures within differentially organized and empowered state institutions. In this view, society-based groups rarely make an appearance; and when they do it is usually in the role of supporters of policies whose origins are found at the level of the state. From this perspective, to know the policy preferences of public officials, and to discern their institutionally conditioned patterns of behavior, is to explain the policy itself.

American Business & Public Policy picks up where *Politics, Pressures and the Tariff* left off. Indeed, the authors saw their book as a direct reply to Schattschneider, and "a dissent from [his] position."[27] Focused on an investigation into the politics surrounding the formulation and enactment of the RTAA of 1954, the RTAA of 1955, and to a lesser degree the TEA of 1962, *American Business & Public Policy* set out to "test accepted theories of pressure groups and decision-making" by studying "the flow of communications to and within the groups involved in the foreign [trade] policy decision-making process" (xx, 5). More specifically, the book examines the relationship between business and Congress and asks the question: "How closely do the policies adopted [by Congress] reflect the wishes and interests of the business community?" (3).

American Business & Public Policy adopts a twofold approach for answering this question. One, focused on the local level, probes the business–Congress relationship in eight congressional districts. The other, focused on the national level, investigates the business–Congress relationship on Capitol Hill. At the district level, *American Business & Public Policy* found little support for the thesis that members of Congress are the handmaidens of business. Indeed, business was not very involved in trade politics and policy-making and rarely tried to influence members of Congress. Moreover, in many instances members of Congress received few, if any, direct communications from business about trade policy, or they received conflicting communications, both of which freed them up to follow their own policy preferences on the issue. Furthermore, once a member had made up his mind on the issue, and that policy position became known, communications from businesses with a different point of view tended to dry up. In the main, protectionists communicated with protectionists; free traders communicated with free traders. Perhaps most surprisingly, the authors found that large corporations were often reluctant to use their economic power to influence members of Congress at the district level for fear that it might lead to retaliation on more important issues—a phenomenon they referred to as "corporate restraint" (317).

Consistent with their district-level studies, at the national level, Bauer, Pool, and Dexter found that Congress and its members were relatively free from business pressures. In particular, after surveying a wide variety of business groups and lobbies, the authors concluded that these associations tended to be poorly financed, under staffed, ill-managed, squeezed for time, unable to engage in long-range planning, generally "out of contact with Congress, and at best only marginally effective in supporting tendencies and measures which already had behind them considerable Congressional impetus from other sources" (324). As was the case at the district level, business groups and lobbies tended to communicate only with members who already agreed with them. What is more, these associations often assumed the character of a "service bureau" for their supporters in Congress. They were the "source to which a congressman would turn for facts he needed or to which his assistant would telephone to line up witnesses for a hearing" (324–325). Indeed, the "direction of influence [between business and Congress] was almost the reverse of what is usually assumed" (357). Business groups and lobbies were far more often used by members of Congress than members of Congress were used, or "pressured," by these groups.

What accounted for the relative freedom of members of Congress from business groups and lobbies? Bauer, Pool, and Dexter argued the answer was found in two institutional features of Congress: the relationship between individual members and their districts (or states); and the internal organization of Congress itself. At the district level, *American Business & Public Policy* identified six factors that made members of Congress relatively free agents in the trade policy-making process. First, and most important, there was usually more than one possible winning electoral coalition within a district or state and thus more than one way to get elected. As a result, members of Congress had significant latitude in deciding whom they would represent and how. "A congressman must respond in what appears to be a serious and constructive way to the problems of his constituents, but he is free to be leader instead of led in deciding what response is appropriate to the problem. He must be attentive to the views of his petitioners, but attention is not agreement" (316). Second, because members of Congress worked on a wide variety of issues, they were often in the position to take an unpopular stand on any single issue without fear of substantially weakening their base of support. Third, once members of Congress made their views known on trade, opposition communications tended to dry up. Fourth, most members of Congress had only a slight notion as to the preferences of their constituents with respect to trade, thus they often operated in the dark and were consequently in the position to follow their own policy preferences. Fifth, because members of Congress were usually overworked, communications from constituents were forced to compete for their time and attention, which diluted the effectiveness of those communications. Finally, in most cases, constituents who communicated with a member of Congress only expected a fair hearing, not a definitive course of action; and while members usually sought to allay the concerns of those who appealed to them, how they did so was up to them.

The policy-making process within Congress also contributed to the autonomy of its members from business pressures. In particular, congressional policy-making procedures were so complex that it was easy for a member to "obfuscate where he stands on any issue and what he has done about it" (424). Indeed, in some instances, it was possible for a member to go on record as both an opponent *and* a supporter of the same bill. Furthermore, members of Congress often were able to engage in vote trading (log-rolling) without much regard to constituent or group preferences. Finally, while party discipline was weak in Congress, congressional party leaders, particularly in the House, were able to exercise significant influence with rank-and-file members. Indeed, Bauer, Pool, and Dexter found that if members of Congress felt any pressure at all, it was from congressional party leaders, or the administration, not from business groups or their constituents. Pressure to vote "the party line," or "with the President," often overrode constituent or group demands.

In sum, Bauer, Pool, and Dexter found that while Congress and its members were not completely free to do as they pleased when formulating trade policy, neither were they the captives of business groups or their constituents. Members of Congress could, and often did, play a dynamic, creative, and efficacious role in trade politics.

> Congress is not a passive body, registering already-existent public views forced on its attention by public pressures. Congress, second only to the President, is, rather the major institution for initiating and creating political issues and projecting them into a national civic debate. Congressmen are often the leaders in that debate. (478)

The authors conclude: "The people supposed to make decisions, officeholders, often really do make decisions" (487).

From the point of view of explaining the origins of America's postwar policy of world trade leadership, *American Business & Public Policy* suffers from two analytical limitations. First, although the book succeeds brilliantly in challenging the view that public officials are merely the handmaidens of business interests, Bauer, Pool, and Dexter have almost nothing to say about where the policy preferences of members of Congress come from. As Schattschneider put it in his review of the book,

> Perhaps . . . the authors have been too successful in driving away the wolf packs assailing Congress, because they seem to have left themselves without an adequate dynamics of politics. One is reminded of Thurber's mother who admonished him not to 'go driving around town without any gasoline in your tank' . . . . The trouble is that the authors leave Congress floating through space, rotating on its own axis, like the moon.[28]

Most importantly, the authors failed to grasp the import of their findings with respect to the way business groups and lobbies did in fact influence congressional policy-making. More specifically, Bauer, Pool, and Dexter argued that by far the most active society-based group in trade politics was business. As the group with "the most interest and the most voice in the shaping of foreign trade policy," business dominated the flow of communications from society to state.[29] As the authors observed, business groups and lobbies served as "gatekeepers in the communications process," organizing and channeling communications from their members to Congress (328). Through activities such as public meetings and conferences; the stimulation of letters, articles, and speeches; and providing testimony before congressional committees, these organizations generated and disseminated information concerning the trade policy preferences of their members. Indeed, they succeeded in arrogating to themselves "the role of authoritative spokesmen for particular sides and interests" (359). Since members of Congress tended to respond to communications they perceived as legitimate, and business groups and lobbies were typically viewed as legitimate, we have to conclude from the evidence that the flow of business communications had at least some effect on Congress and its members. But what that effect might have been we do not know, for *American Business & Public Policy* never follows it up. As a result, the book presents an overly state-centered view of trade politics that makes the same mistake as Schattschneider, only in reverse: while the latter under-theorized the state, the former under-theorized society.

The second limitation of *American Business & Public Policy* is found in its failure to more fully investigate the role of the president (and the executive branch more generally) in the trade policy-making process. Indeed, in a book of nearly 500 pages, fewer than 20 are dedicated to an analysis of the politics of the presidency. This is an egregious oversight; for ever since the enactment of the RTAA of 1934, the president had been at the institutional center of the trade policy-making process. Furthermore, Bauer, Pool, and Dexter traced their findings concerning the attenuated relationship between business and Congress precisely to the institutional dynamics of the president-centered trade policy-making process. This process, they argued, reduced the power of Congress in trade politics by placing the major decisions on trade in the hands of executive branch administrators, which had the effect of reducing business appeals to the national legislature. More specifically, the president-centred trade policy-making process has allowed Congress to free "itself from much local pressure by yielding to the executive branch the power of setting specific [tariff] rates."

> The individual representative can placate a local industry by writing to the Tariff Commission about an escape-clause proceeding or to the Committee on Reciprocity Information when a trade agreement is about to be negotiated. But letters are cheap. He can also make a speech on the floor of Congress or before a trade association. Having done his bit for local industry in this way, he is not necessarily called upon to try to translate local interests into the law of the land. . . . This means that the individual business appeals to Congress only for an intermediate goal, namely, that general

rules be framed in ways likely to result in favorable action on later petitions. That fact reduces the frequency and urgency of appeals to the congressman. By thus passing the buck, Congress has reduced its own power. (247, 455–456)

In addition to giving short-shrift to the political and institutional role of the presidency in the post-1934 trade policy-making process, Bauer, Pool, and Dexter fail to grasp the import of what they do in fact discover about the relationship between business and the executive branch.[30] More specifically, the authors found that during the Eisenhower and Kennedy Administrations a close working relationship existed between the White House and two economic groups dominated by the nation's largest and most internationally oriented corporations: the Committee for a National Trade Policy (CNTP), and the International Chamber of Commerce (ICC). The CNTP and the ICC played leading roles in organizing the business community to communicate to Congress in support of President Eisenhower's and President Kennedy's trade liberalization programs. In fact, so close were the working relationships between these organizations and the White House staff that members of the Eisenhower and Kennedy administrations considered them to be the principal lobbying and propaganda arms of the White House in its efforts to win congressional approval for new trade legislation. Yet despite finding this relationship, Bauer, Pool, and Dexter never explore it in any detail. Most importantly, they fail to adequately examine the operational modalities of this relationship; why it cut across party lines and administrations; what impact it might have had on the president-centered trade policy-making process; and how it might have influenced the content of trade policy.

There can be no gainsaying the finding in *American Business & Public Policy*, that the state and public officials play a significant and influential role in trade politics and policy making. However, because Bauer, Pool, and Dexter failed to adequately consider the impact of economic groups on the trade policy-making process, it is impossible to determine the precise nature of the causal role played by the state and public officials in politics—a problem greatly magnified by the fact that the authors expend little energy on an analysis of the president (and the executive branch more generally). Nonetheless, *American Business & Public Policy* invites us to explore the proposition that the state has been a dynamic and efficacious force in postwar American trade politics. In particular, it invites us to ask: what role was played by the state and public officials in the pattern of politics that produced the triumph of globalism (particularly the role of the president, the executive branch, and Congress and its members); and what was the relationship between these institutions and public officials and economic groups?

Recasting the Society–State Relationship

What accounts for the radically different findings of *Politics, Pressures and the Tariff* and *American Business & Public Policy*? The answer provided by Bauer, Pool, and

Dexter—that it was the result of a shift of policy-making power from Congress to the President—is only one interpretation. Another is provided by Theodore J. Lowi in his classic *World Politics* review of *American Business & Public Policy*, where he attempted to square the circle by arguing that the authors of these studies examined different "policy types"—each with its own distinct pattern of society–state relationships.[31] My own view is much more prosaic: the books simply highlighted different causal variables—society in one case, the state in the other. The view that the radically different findings of *Politics, Pressures and the Tariff* and *American Business & Public Policy* are matters of analytical emphasis has a significant bearing on the construction of a framework for explaining America's postwar policy of world trade leadership. For it suggests that, rather than casting the society–state relationship as an either-or proposition, or a zero-sum game, we focus on the nature of the transactions between the two, making sure to give equal analytical weight to both sides.

Conclusion: An Agenda for Research

The pioneering works on trade advanced three broad theoretical claims: that the political behavior of economic groups determines trade policy (Schattschneider); that trade policy is the product of the political behavior of public officials operating within differentially organized and empowered state institutions (Bauer, Pool, and Dexter); and that a nation's trade policy reflects the structures and processes of the international political economy and the relative position of a state within them (Krasner). Broadly speaking, there are two ways to view these claims, each of which calls for a very different analytical agenda. One is to treat them as mutually exclusive. Pursuant to this interpretation, the object of research would be to determine which of the three perspectives better explains the pattern of politics that produced the triumph of globalism. One way to do this would be to tell the explanatory story from each point of view and then to evaluate which perspective provides a more compelling account.[32] Thus, we might begin with an analysis that focuses on the structures and processes of the international political economy; move to one that focuses on the political behavior of economic groups; and conclude with an analysis that focuses on the political behavior of public officials. Having taken stock of each account, we would be in the position to evaluate how much the phenomenon under investigation is explained by each, and thereby be in the position to assert that one perspective is superior to the others. The problem with this approach is that it would not contribute much (if at all) to political science trade theory; for regardless of which point of view was deemed superior, our findings would merely recapitulate one of the three dominant perspectives, and serve only to reinforce the existing theoretical divisions in the literature.

I believe a more fruitful way to read the arguments and findings of the pioneering trade studies is to treat their points of view as distinct yet complementary; that is, they emphasized different aspects (or features) of trade politics. Thus, rather than advancing competing theoretical perspectives, the pioneering trade studies highlighted different causal variables. Reading the pioneering trade studies in this way suggests a research strategy that integrates system, society, and state into a single macro-analytic framework—one that allows for an empirically based exploration into the relationships among them. More specifically, it suggests the construction of a model of trade politics that combines the elaboration of a plausible hypothesis concerning the relationship among these variables that can serve as a guide for a concrete, historically specific investigation into the pattern of politics that has resulted in America's postwar policy of world trade leadership. Approached in this way, our exploration into the wellsprings of the triumph of globalism can contribute to the development of political science trade theory by transcending extant analytical divisions among system, society, state.

Drawing upon the arguments and findings of the three pioneering trade studies, we are now in the position to pose the central questions that will guide the construction of a multivariate framework for explaining the causal origins of America's postwar policy of world trade leadership (and hence the triumph of globalism). How have the structures and processes of the international political economy—and the relative position of the United States within them—influenced the pattern of domestic politics responsible for the nation's postwar policy of world trade leadership? Which economic groups became involved in the formulation and enactment of the four crucial trade statutes at the legislative core of the triumph of globalism; and what was the relationship between their trade-related economic interests, their policy preferences, and their pattern of mobilization into trade politics? What role was played by state institutions and public officials—especially the president, the executive branch, and Congress and its members—in the politics that produced the four crucial trade acts? And what was the relationship among these system, society, and state-level variables?

Given these questions, we are now in the position to advance the book's guiding hypothesis: America's postwar policy of world trade leadership has rested on a pattern of domestic society–state relationships anchored in the nation's superpower position in world trade—a pattern I call "superpower trade politics."

Notes

1 As David A. Lake put it in the conclusion to his system-centered study of American trade politics, "The task still before us is to integrate domestic and international, statist and society-centered explanations." David A. Lake, *Power, Protection and Free Trade: International Sources of U.S. Commercial Strategy, 1887–1939* (Ithaca, NY: Cornell University Press, 1988), 228.

2 Ibid.

3 Helen V. Milner, *Resisting Protectionism: Global Industries and the Politics of International Trade* (Princeton: Princeton University Press, 1988).

4 I. M. Destler, *American Trade Politics*, 2nd ed. (Washington, D.C.: Institute for International Economics, 1992).

5 Viewed in this light, the analytical approach deployed in this study seeks to overcome what J. David Singer has called, "the level of analysis problem" in international

relations. J. David Singer, "The Level of Analysis Problem in International Relations," *World Politics*, 14 (1) (October 1961): 77–92.

6　Stephen D. Krasner, "State Power and the Structure of International Trade," *World Politics*, 28 (3) (April 1976): 317–347; E. E. Schattschneider, *Politics, Pressures and the Tariff: A Study of Free Private Enterprise in Pressure Politics, as Shown in the 1929–1930 Revision of the Tariff* (New York: Prentice-Hall, 1935); Raymond A. Bauer, Ithiel de Sola Pool, and Lewis Anthony Dexter, *American Business & Public Policy: The Politics of Foreign Trade*, 2nd ed. (Chicago: Aldine-Atherton, 1972).

7　Joseph S. Nye and Robert O. Keohane, "Transnational Relations and World Politics: An Introduction," *International Organization*, 25 (3) (Summer 1971), 331. For its part, liberal internationalism emerged in the 1970s as a response to the "scientific" realism of the 1960s, as well as to the "classical realism" of the 1940s and 1950s. See Hedley Bull, "International Theory: the Case for a Classical Approach," in John R. Howard, ed., *An Overview of International Studies* (New York: MSS Information Corporation, 1972).

8　See, for example, James N. Rosenau, ed., *Domestic Sources of American Foreign Policy* (New York: The Free Press, 1967).

9　By far the most insightful analysis of the contributions of Krasner's article to the study of international politics is Robert O. Keohane, "Problematic Lucidity: Stephen Krasner's 'State Power and International Trade,'" *World Politics*, 50 (1) (October 1997): 150–170.

10　Krasner, "State Power," 317.

11　Ibid., 341.

12　The closest one comes to an agreed-upon definition of hegemony is provided by Robert O. Keohane, who defines a hegemon as a state that possess "the ability and willingness . . . to make and enforce [international] rules." Furthermore, he defines a hegemonic system as one in which "leadership is exercised by a single state." This definition raises two interpretive questions. What does "ability" mean and how are we to measure it? Keohane's answer that ability rests on a "preponderance of material resources" begs the question. For what does "preponderance" mean; and because different analysts look at different objective factors, what material resources are we to consider? See Robert O. Keohane, *After Hegemony: Cooperation and Discord in the World Political Economy* (Princeton: Princeton University Press, 1984), 38, 39, 32.

13　For a more detailed critique of structural theories of trade politics, see Timothy J. McKeown, "The Limitations of 'Structural' Theories of Commercial Policy," *International Organization*, 40 (1) (Winter 1986): 43–64. For an analysis of America's continued domination of the world economy, despite its supposed relative decline, see Susan Strange, "Still an Extraordinary Power: America's role in a Global Monetary System," in R. Lombra and W. Witte, eds., *The Political Economy of Domestic and International Monetary Policy* (Ames: Iowa State University Press, 1982).

14　See Lake, *Power, Protection, and Free Trade*, 230.

15　The concept of "hegemony" in international relations theory has been critiqued from many quarters. See, for example, Susan Strange, "The Persistent Myth of Lost Hegemony," *International Organization*, 41 (4) (Autumn 1987): 551–574; Duncan Snidal, "The Limits of Hegemonic Stability Theory," *International Organization*, 39 (4) (Autumn 1985): 579–614; and Timothy McKeown, "Hegemonic Stability Theory and Nineteenth Century Tariff Levels in Europe," *International Organization*, 37 (1) (December 1983): 73–91.

16　In a subsequent work, *International Regimes*, Krasner suggests just this sort of explanation for the persistence of an open world trading system since 1960. See Stephen D. Krasner, ed., *International Regimes* (Ithaca, NY: Cornell University Press, 1981). In the introduction to this book, Krasner defines international regimes as "principles, norms, rules, and decision-making procedures around which [state] expectations converge in a given issue area." Krasner maintains that international regimes have the power to mold the behavior of otherwise power-maximizing states, leading them to adopt or maintain policies which might be out of step with their structural position in the world economy. From this perspective, the continued openness of the postwar world trading system in the face of America's (supposed) hegemonic decline can be at least partially explained with reference to the GATT/WTO, which provides a common political framework for its members in the development of their trade policies. The existence of the GATT/WTO regime has been particularly important for the exercise of American world trade leadership; for it has provided the United States with an international rallying point around which to organize its drive for global free trade.

17 Woodrow Wilson, *Congressional Government: A Study in American Politics* (New York: Houghton Mifflin Company, 1885); J. Allen Smith, *The Spirit of American Government* (New York: The Macmillan Company, 1907); and Arthur F. Bentley, *The Process of Government: A Study of Social Pressures* (Chicago: University of Chicago Press, 1908).

18 Ibid., 162.

19 Bauer, Pool, and Dexter, *American Business & Public Policy*, 25.

20 Schattschneider, *Politics, Pressures and the Tariff*, 4–5.

21 E. Pendleton Herring, Book Review, "Politics, Pressures and the Tariff," *American Political Science Review*, 30 (2) (April 1936): 374–375.

22 Schattschneider, *Politics, Pressures and the Tariff*, 287.

23 Examples of studies that problematize this relationship include, Milner, *Resisting Protectionism*; I. M. Destler, John Odell, and Kimberly Ann Elliot, *Anti-Protection: Changing Forces in United States Trade Politics* (Washington, D.C.: Institute for International Economics, 1987); Ronald Rogowski, *Commerce and Coalitions: How Trade Affects Domestic Political Alignments* (Princeton: Princeton University Press, 1990); and Michael J. Hiscox, *International Trade and Political Conflict: Commerce, Coalitions, and Mobility* (Princeton: Princeton University Press, 2001).

24 Some ten years in the making, *American Business & Public Policy* was produced under the auspices of the Center for International Studies at MIT with primary funding from the Ford Foundation. In addition to the book's authors (two political scientists and a social psychologist), more than a dozen social scientists worked on the project. The rich and varied sources used in *American Business & Public Policy* include eight detailed "community studies" of carefully selected congressional districts; statistical analysis of survey-generated interview data from the heads of 903 business corporations; 500 participant interviews with members of Congress and their staffs, members of the executive branch, interest group leaders and lobbyists, and journalists; analysis of public opinion data from Gallup, Roper, the National Opinion Research Center, and the Survey Research Center at the University of Michigan; and thick descriptive analysis of legislative and interest-group activities.

25 The view that the state was a dynamic and efficacious actor within the political process largely was lost on the first several generations of academic political scientists. Although the institutional formalists focused on state institutions, their work lacked a concept of the state and public officials as *actors*. For their part, the group theorists who emerged to challenge institutional formalism tended to neglect state institutions and public officials altogether; or if they did focus on the state it was usually seen to play a predominantly passive role in the political process.

26 David Easton, "The Political System Besieged by the State," *Political Theory*, 9 (3) (August 1981): 303–325.

27 Bauer, Pool, and Dexter, *American Business & Public Policy*, 25.

28 E. E. Schattschneider, Book Review, "American Business & Public Policy," *Public Opinion Quarterly*, 29 (2) (Summer 1965): 343–344.

29 Bauer, Pool, and Dexter, *American Business & Public Policy*, 5.

30 See ibid., Chapter 26, "The CNTP—Spokesman for Reciprocal Trade," 375–387.

31 See Theodore J. Lowi, "American Business, Public Policy, Case-Studies, and Political Theory," *World Politics*, 16 (4) (July 1964): 677–715.
32 This is the explanatory strategy used by Peter Gourevitch, *Politics in Hard Times: Comparative Responses to International Economic Crises* (Ithaca, NY: Cornell University Press, 1986); John S. Odell, *U.S. International Monetary Policy: Markets, Power, and Ideas as Sources of Change* (Princeton: Princeton University Press, 1982); and Graham Allison, *Essence of Decision: Explaining the Cuban Missile Crisis* (New York: Little, Brown and Co., 1971).

3

SUPERPOWER TRADE POLITICS

If trade in itself is by no means the decisive factor in political expansion, the economic structure in general does co-determine the extent and manner of political expansion.

Max Weber (1904)

The principal explanatory argument presented in this book is that America's postwar policy of world trade leadership (and hence the triumph of globalism) has been the product of a historically distinct pattern of domestic politics anchored in America's superpower position within the evolving postwar world trading system. My analytical focus, therefore, is on the ways in which America's superpower position has been translated into domestic trade politics. And here I argue that this position has generated a structural bias in U.S. society and state that is global in orientation. In the final analysis, it is how this structural bias has come together in American trade politics that accounts for the nation's postwar policy of world trade leadership.

This chapter begins with an examination of America's superpower position within the evolving postwar world trading system. This is followed by an exploration of how this position has generated a globally oriented, structural bias in American society and state. Finally, in its conclusion, this chapter presents an overview of the pattern of domestic politics responsible for the triumph of globalism—a pattern I call "superpower trade politics."

The Superpower Structure of the Postwar World Trading System

There is no agreed-upon definition of what it means for a nation to be a superpower; or of what standards of measurement and comparison are appropriate for determining this status. However, Max Weber once defined a "great power" as a state that possesses the capacity to "ascribe to itself and usurp an interest in political and economic processes . . . [that] . . . encompass the whole surface of the planet."[1] It follows, therefore, that a "superpower" can be defined as a state that possesses comparatively more power than the great powers. A superpower is not merely the greatest of the great powers: it occupies a position above them. Thus, to identify the United States as a superpower in world trade is to locate its dominant position in relation to the other leading trading nations.

Two aspects of America's superpower status in the postwar world trading system have had a decisive impact on the pattern of domestic trade politics responsible for the nation's postwar policy of world trade leadership. One is the nation's position in the trade-related structure of the postwar world economy. The other is the nation's position in the trade-related structure of the postwar international state system. Although these features of America's superpower status are inextricably interconnected, for our purpose it is necessary to treat them as analytically distinct. This is because the economic and political aspects of America's superpower position have had independent and differential effects on the pattern of politics responsible for the triumph of globalism. On the one hand, the nation's economic supremacy in the postwar world trading system has generated a global bias in the trade-related structure of its domestic economy. On the other hand, the nation's political supremacy within this system has been the source of a global bias in the trade-related structure of the American national state. The first has affected the pattern of group mobilization into the trade policy-making process. The second has affected the trade-related operation of national state institutions.

Superpower Trade Politics: Global Economic Foundations

There is nearly universal agreement among students of international relations that World War II produced an epochal transformation in the international system, marked by a seismic shift in the distribution of power among the world's leading nations. At the center of this transformation was the emergence of the United States as an economic superpower. Indeed, it is well known that World War II catapulted the United States to a position of economic preeminence among the great powers not seen since Great Britain emerged victorious from the Napoleonic Wars, with its industrial revolution in full swing. Although the war disorganized or destroyed the economies of Great Britain, Germany, France, Italy, and Japan, the United States emerged from the conflagration with its economy fully intact and operating at historically high levels of production. The magnitude and speed of this breathtaking transformation is documented in Figure 3.1, which compares U.S. GDP to the combined GDPs of the five other prewar powers.

Within the specialist discourse on international political economy, America's towering position in the immediate postwar period is routinely described as one of "hegemony." In turn, the nation's supposed fall from its hegemonic position

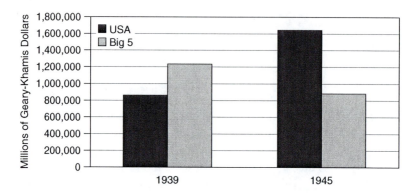

FIGURE 3.1 War-Induced Changes in the Distribution of GDP among the United States and the Big Five, 1939–1945

Source: Angus Maddison, "Historical Statistics of the World Economy," Table 2: GDP Levels, 1 AD–2008 AD. www.ggdc.net/maddison/Historical.../horizontal-file_02-2010.xls (accessed March 15, 2013).

has framed decades of scholarly debate concerning its consequences for American trade policy and the political organization of international trading relationships. Yet, with respect to America's position within the postwar world trading system, it is far too easy to overestimate the extent of this fall, or its qualitative effects. Although America's relative economic power may have declined over the postwar period, the nation remains something much more than one among many economic "great powers," or even *primus inter pares*. By any fair estimation, at least through the end of the twentieth century, the United States was the only world trade superpower at the economic level.[2]

America's status as a world trade superpower at the economic level can be discerned by making quantitative comparisons between the United States and the other leading capitalist nations along a series of economic dimensions: gross domestic product; value added in manufacturing; share of the world's largest corporations; and world trade shares.[3] Each of these indicators measures a different aspect of trade-related economic power. The first is the broadest, and provides an overall measure of a nation's ability, in principle, to produce exports and consume imports. The second indicator measures the position of a nation's manufacturing sector in the international division of labor. The third indicator measures the position of a nation's largest corporations in the global production structure. Finally, the fourth indicator measures a nation's actual importance as a world supplier (exports) and consumer (imports).

Tables 3.1–3.3 compare America's relative economic position vis-à-vis the other leading capitalist nations along the dimensions of gross domestic product, value added in manufacturing, and share of the world's largest corporations. A similar story is told in each case: although the United States is not as preponderant

TABLE 3.1 Percent World GDP, Selected Years, 1950–2000

	1950	1960	1970	1980	1990	2000
USA	27	24	22	21	21	22
Japan	3	4	7	8	9	7
Germany	5	7	6	6	5	4
England	7	5	4	4	3	3
France	4	4	4	4	4	3
Italy	3	4	4	4	3	3
Total	49	48	47	47	44	42

Source: Angus Maddison, "Historical Statistics of the World Economy," Table 2: GDP Levels, 1 AD–2008 AD. www.ggdc.net/maddison/Historical.../horizontal-file_02-2010.xls (accessed March 15, 2013). Author's calculations.

TABLE 3.2 Value Added in Manufacturing as a Percent of World Total, Selected Years, 1970–2000

	1970	1980	1990	2000
USA	27	22	22	25
Japan	13	14	17	15
Germany	13	11	10	9
England	7	5	5	4
France	5	5	4	4
Italy	4	6	5	5
Total	69	63	63	62

Source: United Nations, "National Accounts Main Database." http://unstats.un.org/unsd/snaama/selbasicFast.asp (accessed March 15, 2013). Author's calculations.

TABLE 3.3 Distribution of World's Largest Corporations, Selected Years, 1960–2000

	1960	1970	1980	1990	2000
USA	176	260	218	164	186
Japan	11	51	67	111	104
Germany	22	26	38	30	34
England	29	46	54	43	35
France	11	21	28	30	35
Italy	4	7	8	7	8
Other	23	49	87	115	98
N=	(276)	(460)	(500)	(500)	(500)

Source: *Fortune Magazine*, "The Fortune Directory of the Largest U.S. Industrial Corporations," July 1961; "The Fortune Directory of the 100 Largest Industrial Corporations Outside the United States," August 1961; "The Fortune Directory of the 500 Largest Industrial Corporations," May 1971; "The 200 Largest Industrial Companies Outside the U.S.," August 1971; "The 500 Largest Industrials," May 4, 1981; "The Foreign 500," August 10, 1981; "The World's Biggest Industrial Corporations," July 29, 1991; "The World's Largest Corporations," July 23, 2001. Author's count. Note: for the years 1960–1990, industrial corporations only; for 2000, all corporations (including financials).

as it once was, at the end of the twentieth century the nation continued to hold a commanding lead across these three measures. In terms of GDP, in 2000 the United States was three times larger than the next largest nation (Japan), and its GDP was greater than the gross domestic products of Japan, Germany, England, France, and Italy combined. Perhaps most striking, in 2000 America's share of the total GDP of all the countries in Table 3.1 (including the United States) was only slightly less than its share of the total in 1950 (52 and 55 percent respectively). Thus, while in absolute terms America's GDP in 2000 accounted for somewhat less of the world total than it did in 1950, in terms of its relative size compared to the other leading capitalist nations it was virtually unchanged.

With respect to value added in manufacturing, in 2000 the United States remained the most important global industrial producer by far, accounting for 25 percent of global manufacturing value added, two-thirds greater than Japan, the next largest manufacturing nation, and more than twice as large as Germany, the third largest manufacturing nation. Although Table 3.2 does not go back to 1950 it shows that in terms of the total manufacturing value added of all the countries in the table (including the United States) America's share in 2000 (40 percent) was virtually unchanged from 1970 (39 percent). Thus, after a dip in the years 1970–1990, by century's end the United States was just as dominant in terms of its share of value added in manufacturing relative to the other leading capitalist countries as it had been thirty years earlier, and only slightly less dominant in terms of its share of the world total.

Finally, in 2000 the United States was home to 186 of the world's largest 500 corporations, more than three-quarters more than Japan, the nation with the second most companies, and more than the total of Germany, England, France, and Italy combined. Although this represented a significant change from 1960, the United States remained by far the most dominant nation in terms of its share of the world's largest corporations. Furthermore, although not captured in Table 3.3, it is noteworthy that by 2005 America's share of the world's largest corporations radically expanded from its 2000 level relative to the nation with the second most companies (Japan). In that year, the United States was home to 176 of the world's largest corporations, more than twice as many as Japan, which was home to 81.[4]

Table 3.4 zeros in on international trade. Table 3.4 documents America's leading position in the postwar world trading system in terms of world exports and imports. As can be seen, in the period from 1950 to 2000, the United States was the world's most important trading nation. With respect to exports, while the nation's lead diminished somewhat over the course of the postwar period, at century's end the United States nonetheless exported nearly one third more value in goods and services than the world's second largest exporter (Germany), which gave the nation nearly the same lead it held over the world's second largest exporter in 1950 (England). With respect to imports, it might be thought that America's out-sized position as the world's leading importing nation in 2000 is

TABLE 3.4 World Trade Shares, Selected Years, 1950–2000

	1950	1960	1970	1980	1990	2000
Percent World Exports						
USA	17	16	14	11	13	13
Japan	1	3	6	6	8	7
Germany	3	9	11	9	11	8
England	10	8	6	6	6	5
France	5	5	6	7	7	5
Italy	2	3	4	4	5	4
Total	38	44	47	43	50	42
Percent World Imports						
USA	15	12	13	12	14	18
Japan	2	3	6	7	7	6
Germany	4	7	9	9	10	8
England	11	10	7	6	6	5
France	5	5	6	7	7	5
Italy	2	3	5	5	5	4
Total	40	40	46	46	49	46

Source: World Trade Organization (WTO), Statistics Database, "Time Series on International Trade," http://stat.wto.org/Home/WSDBHome.aspx?Language=E (accessed March 15, 2013). Author's calculations. Note: For the years 1950–1970, merchandise trade only; for the years 1980–2000, merchandise and services trade.

an indication of weakness. But this is not necessarily the case. First, America's share of world imports in 2000 was only slightly higher than it was in 1950, when the nation was at the apex of its postwar international economic power. More importantly, as Albert O. Hirschman argued in his seminal text, *National Power and the Structure of Foreign Trade*, the size of a nation's market for imports is a potential power resource vis-à-vis other states.[5] This is because the importing nation is in the position to inflict damage on the domestic economies of the states that export to it by cutting off their access to its market (or threatening to do so). The larger the domestic market of the importing nation, and the more imports it actually consumes, the greater its potential power to inflict damage. Conversely, "the offer to open up one's huge [domestic] market to other exporters, in return for concessions or deference, can be an effective means of influence."[6] Indeed, perhaps more than any other factor, it has been America's large domestic market and the nation's capacity to absorb imports that has been the most important power resource used by the United States in its construction of the postwar world trading system. For American leadership in the creation, maintenance, and expansion of the GATT/WTO regime has rested on the nation's willingness to open its domestic market to other exporters in return for market-opening initiatives of their own.

In sum, despite more than fifty years of change in the distribution of economic power among the world's leading trading nations, at the end of the twentieth century the United States remained by far the most dominant nation within the world trading system. Whether measured in terms of GDP, value added in manufacturing, share of the world's largest corporations, or share of world trade, America's position in the postwar world economy was unrivaled. From the end of World War II through the end of the twentieth century, it was arguably the sole superpower in world trade at the economic level. Thus, we can say that over the course of the postwar period (at least through 2000) the superpower structure of the world trading system, and America's leading position within it, was an invariant (or structural) feature affecting the pattern of domestic politics responsible for the nation's policy of world trade leadership.

Superpower Trade Politics: Global Political Foundations

World War II did more than catapult the United States to a position of unrivalled preeminence in the world economy. It also generated a political vacuum in international trading relationships.

It is well known that during the nineteenth century Great Britain served as the pivot of a global economic order based on an international gold standard and a relatively open world trading system.[7] World War I shook this order to its foundations, and while efforts were made to restore it in the 1920s, they largely failed. Indeed, these efforts were abandoned within a few years of the onset of the global depression. In their place emerged a headlong rush by the great powers to create autarkic national economies or international economic empires, which led to the fragmentation of international trade into a number of more or less distinct subsystems, each one centered on a single great power.[8] World War II came down like a hammer on this "twenty years crisis" in world economic order, eliminating the capacity of all nations save the United States to exercise political influence at the level of global trading relationships. Although each country retained its sovereign capacity to block free trade at its borders, no country but the United States had the power to induce others to participate in the creation of a new international regime for world trade.

The United States seized this opportunity and took the sole leadership role in the construction of an open world trading system—a role it has maintained ever since. Indeed, the defining characteristic of American world trade leadership since World War II has been the nation's capacity to rally other national states, especially the great powers, around its global trade project. Although it is true that over the course of the postwar period other major trading nations have shown a capacity to exercise political power *within* the world trade regime— even using its rules to gain victories over the United States—America nonetheless has dominated the construction and amendment of the rules themselves. And it has been this regime-creating power that allows us to identify the United

States as the sole superpower at the political level within the postwar world trading system.

As a practical matter, the United States has approached its construction of the postwar world trading system in the manner of an alliance leader, positioning itself at the forefront of an expanding group of national states that have agreed to cooperate in a common global project. Although the United States has sometimes resorted to threats and coercion to maintain or expand the world trade alliance, its typical mode of system management has been marked by cooperation and appeals to the common trade interests of all. Indeed, America's construction of the post-war world trading system has been based on a series of *invitations* for other nations to join it in moving the project forward. These invitations have taken the form of periodic calls by the United States for other nations to join it in multilateral nego-tiations designed to strengthen and expand the scale and scope of the system, as well as to deepen the degree of trade liberalization among its participants.[9] At the core of these invitations has been America's offer to (further) open its domestic market to the exports of its trading partners in return for market-opening com-mitments of their own. As mentioned in the previous section, the capacity of the United States to exercise leadership in this fashion has rested on its possession of the largest domestic market in the world, as well as on its status as the world's largest importer.

Since World War II the United States has initiated and brought to successful conclusion eight multilateral trade rounds (see Table 1.1)—four of which are widely regarded as watersheds in the development of the GATT/WTO regime: the first Geneva Round (1947); the Kennedy Round (1964–1967); the Tokyo Round (1973–1979); and the Uruguay Round (1986–1994).[10] In addition to expanding the scale and scope of the world trading system, and deepening the degree of trade liberalization among its members, each of these watershed trade rounds was initiated by the United States to address specific trade-related chal-lenges to the overall health and maintenance of the system; and these challenges served as the chief stimuli for the formulation and enactment of the four crucial trade acts at the legislative core of the triumph of globalism.

The first Geneva Round was America's response to its emergence as an eco-nomic superpower at the end of World War II and the concomitant generation of a political vacuum in international trading relationships. It was at the end of World War II that the United States went global and came forward with a plan for the management of postwar international trading relationships. This plan was embodied in the GATT, which established a multilateral regime for freer world trade.[11] This assertion of world trade leadership was made possible through the enactment of the RTAA of 1945.

America's initiation of the Kennedy Round was a response to the emergence of the EEC as a major trading power. Although the United States had encouraged the formation of the EEC as part of its economic reconstruction efforts in postwar Western Europe, the creation of the Common Market involved the construction of a Common External Tariff (CXT) and the inauguration of a common agricultural policy (CAP), both of which raised fear in the United States that the EEC would adopt an inward-looking, regional trade policy—one that could fracture the world trading system into competing economic blocks; or short of that, introduce a high degree of discrimination into world trade. The Kennedy Round was designed by the United States to forge a free trade-oriented "Atlantic Partnership" between itself and the EEC, one that would strengthen the GATT by deepening the degree of trade liberalization between the two economic areas, while at the same time steering the EEC toward an outward-looking, GATT-centered trade policy.[12] This assertion of world trade leadership was predicated upon the enactment of the TEA of 1962.

The United States launched the Tokyo Round to deal with a host of challenges that emerged in the wake of the Kennedy Round. Some of these challenges grew out of the Kennedy Round itself, especially its success in reducing tariff levels among industrialized countries to their lowest levels in history. The diminution of tariffs as a major barrier to trade in most manufactured products shifted attention to so-called nontariff barriers to trade (NTBs). Although some NTBs were of long standing (perhaps most importantly in agriculture), many were of recent vintage and designed to mitigate the increased liberalization brought about by the Kennedy Round's tariff cuts; ease national economic adjustment to a rapid rise in oil prices; promote domestic employment at a time of spreading stagflation; and deal with the international monetary disorder caused by the collapse of the Bretton Woods system. Perhaps the most pernicious of these non-tariff distortions to trade was the use of state-sponsored export subsidies to gain global market share; the imposition of import quotas; and the negotiation and implementation of so-called orderly marketing agreements (OMAs) and voluntary export restraints (VERs) to slow the pace of import penetration.

Beyond these challenges, but not unrelated to them, was the continuing problem of the European Community's status in the GATT (especially in light of its enlargement in 1973) and the emergence of Japan as a major trading power. With respect to the EEC, four aspects of its trade and economic policy posed problems for the GATT: the protectionist nature of its common agricultural policy; its expanding use of preferential trade agreements with non-Community countries and dependent territories; its discriminatory and protectionist treatment of Japanese exports, which led Japan to concentrate on the American market; and Community enlargement itself, which again raised the specter of a protectionist turn in its trade policy. With respect to Japan, two aspects of its economic policy caused concern for the United States: its slow pace of import liberalization; and the activist role of its "developmental state"—both of which allowed Japan to take advantage of the increasing export opportunities afforded to it by its participation in the GATT, while keeping its domestic market relatively closed to the exports of its trading partners. Although the United States had tolerated Japan's status as a free rider (even encouraged it) during the first two postwar decades, by the early 1970s Japan's new-found economic power and the rapid expansion of its exports made its free-rider status destabilizing for the GATT regime, especially by raising questions about "unfair competition" within the system. In initiating the Tokyo Round, the principal strategic objective of the United States was to forge a "trilateral partnership" between itself, an enlarged European Community, and a more muscular Japan—one that would coax Japan into adopting trade and economic policies more in line with its new-found economic power, continue to steer the EEC toward a GATT-centered trade policy, and deepen the degree of trade liberalization among the three economic areas at the core of the regime.[13] The ability of the United States to launch the Tokyo Round was anchored in the enactment of the Trade Act of 1974.

The United States launched the Uruguay Round in order to expand GATT disciplines to cover new sectors of the global economy, such as services, trade-related investment, intellectual property rights, and agriculture; to institutionalize a new, binding dispute settlement system; to strengthen the GATT's operational machinery; and to further liberalize trade in traditional areas such as tariffs and quotas. From the American point of view, the need for a wholesale reform of the GATT was rooted in the regime's incapacity to deal with a growing array of problems. These included the spreading use of export subsidies, dumping, and industrial targeting to help domestic manufacturers in an increasingly competitive world economy; the bilateral settlement of trade disputes because of the largely ineffectual nature of the GATT's dispute settlement system; the continued use of orderly marketing agreements and voluntary export restraints which in effect took major industrial sectors (including textiles and clothing, ships, steel, and automobiles) outside the GATT; the protectionist nature of domestic agricultural policies and the lack of a comprehensive GATT agreement on agricultural trade; the growing importance of services trade and trade-related investment in the world economy, neither of which was covered in the GATT; and the need to more fully integrate developing countries into the regime.

Alongside these issues were the perennial problems of the European Community and Japan, which continued to engage in many of the trade-distorting practices the United States attempted to deal with in the Tokyo Round. For the European Community these practices included the continued protectionist nature of its common agricultural policy; its continued use of preferential trade agreements; its continued discrimination against Japanese exports; and the use of state-sponsored industrial targeting by its member states. For Japan, the problem remained its low level of imports (relative to exports); and the continued role of its "developmental state" in perpetuating this problem. In addition to these ongoing challenges was a new one: the meteoric rise of a handful of newly industrialized countries (NICs). Although policy specifics differed from one NIC to the next, as a group these nations (most importantly Brazil, Mexico, Taiwan, South Korea, and South Africa), pursued trade and economic policies that encouraged exports while curtailing competitive imports, and used GATT rules regarding "differential and more favorable treatment" of developing countries to avoid moving toward freer trade. Since the NICs had radically expanded their exports between the 1970s and the 1980s, and went from large trade deficits to large trade surpluses, their use of state intervention to promote industrial development undermined confidence in the GATT's capacity to enforce discipline among its members (as did the trade-distorting practices of the European Community and Japan); and it continued to raise questions about "unfair trade" within the system. The Uruguay Round was America's attempt to institute a "new multilateralism" within the world trading system—one that would strengthen the GATT as an international organization, make it more relevant to the new trade realities of a rapidly internationalizing world economy, and encourage the European Community, Japan, and the NICs to assume responsibilities for the management of the regime commensurate with their economic power.[14] The capacity of the United States to launch and participate in the Uruguay Round was made possible by the enactment of the OTCA of 1988.

Whatever may be said about changes in America's relative economic power since World War II or how it has approached its management of the world trading system, its capacity to exercise world trade leadership at the political level (defined as its singular role in initiating GATT trade rounds) was unabated during the first five postwar decades. And this unabated capacity is *prima facie* evidence of the nation's status as the sole superpower in world trade at the level of state-to-state relations. Indeed, scholars who embrace the concept of hegemony posit that it may be said to exist in any international system within which "one state is powerful enough to maintain the essential rules governing interstate relations, and [is] willing to do so."[15] More specifically, a hegemonic state is one that is able to exercise "leadership in maintaining a regime," and is in the structural position to "play the dominant role in constructing new rules."[16] Viewed in this light, it is beyond question that America's capacity to exercise political leadership within the GATT/WTO system was just as hegemonic in initiating the last international trade round of the twentieth century (the 1986–1994 Uruguay Round), which created the WTO, as it was in initiating the first (the 1947 Geneva Round), which created the GATT.

In sum, just as the United States has occupied the sole superpower position within the postwar world trading system at the economic level, so too has it occupied the sole superpower position at the level of interstate relations—a position marked by the enduring capacity of the United States to exercise leadership in the creation, maintenance, and expansion of an international regime for freer world trade. Thus, just as we can speak of a superpower structure at the economic level, so too can we identify a superpower structure at the level of interstate relations. And just as America's superpower position within the world trading system at the economic level was an invariant feature affecting the pattern of domestic politics responsible for the nation's policy of world trade leadership, so too was the nation's superpower position at the political level.

The Superpower Structure in American Trade Politics

Thus far I have been treating the United States as a unitary actor. To do so, however, is to engage in the fallacy of composition. For the United States is not a unitary actor; and the impact of the nation's superpower position in the post-war world trading system falls unevenly on American society and state. More specifically, America's position as a world trade superpower has generated a deep structure of globally oriented economic and political power within U.S. society and state, one that has played to the economic power and interests of the nation's largest and most internationally oriented corporations, as well as to the political power and interests of the president of the United States. In the final analysis, it has been the mobilization of this globally oriented structure of power and interest in American society and state that has resulted in a national policy of world trade leadership (and hence the triumph of globalism). In order to account for this pattern it is first necessary to understand how this deep structure of globally oriented economic and political power has affected American society and state.

The Superpower Structure in American Society

America's position as a world trade superpower at the economic level has been the source of a globally oriented structure within American society. At the apex of this structure are the nation's largest and most internationally oriented corporations, investment banks, and corporate law firms.

It should go without saying that the American economy is not composed of an endless series of coordinate business units making equal contributions to national income and foreign trade; rather, it is dominated by a handful of giant corporations. In 2000, 20 percent of American business firms were corporations, yet these firms accounted for 87 percent of all business receipts.[17] Furthermore, among the nation's corporations the top one third of one percent (.003) accounted for 91 percent of corporate assets; 64 percent of corporate receipts; and 73 percent of corporate profits.[18] A similar pattern is found in the distribution of firms participating in foreign trade. While in 2000, 1 percent of American firms were engaged in exporting (246,452 exporting firms in total), the top 2,000 of these firms accounted for 78 percent of U.S. exports, while the top 100 alone accounted for 39 percent.[19] Not surprisingly, the most important exporters were multinational corporations (defined as firms exporting to fifty or more countries). While in 2000 these firms made up only 7 percent of known exporters, they accounted for 68 percent of U.S. exports.[20]

Not only are the nation's largest corporations the most active participants in foreign trade, but as a group they are more export oriented than the American economy as a whole. While in 1999, total U.S. exports amounted to 8 percent of U.S. GDP, total multinational corporation (MNC) exports amounted to 20 percent of MNC gross product.[21] Furthermore, as Table 3.5 shows, while the

TABLE 3.5 U.S. Merchandise Trade Balance, Total, Multinational Corporations, and Non-Multinational Corporations, Selected Years, 1966–1999 (Millions of Dollars)

	Total U.S. Merchandise Trade Balance	Trade Balance of Multinational Corporations	U.S. Trade Balance Excluding Multinational Corporation Trade
1966	3,824	5,291	-1,467
1970	2,164	7,619	-5,455
1977	-29,097	15,087	-44,18
1982	-31,666	42,615	-74,281
1989	-110,386	35,189	-145,575
1994	-151,000	87,684	-238,684
1999	-328,821	63,791	-392,612

Sources: US Department of Commerce, "U.S. Foreign Trade Associated with U.S. Multinational Corporations," *Survey of Current Business*, December 1972, Table 1, 21; "U.S. Merchandise Trade Associated with U.S. Multinational Corporations," *Survey of Current Business*, May 1986, Table 1, 56; "Operations of U.S. Multinational Companies," *Survey of Current Business*, March 2002, Table 14, 39 (Author's calculations).

Note: It should be noted that these data reflect the trade pattern of all multinational corporations (MNCs) operating in the United States—both domestically owned MNCs as well as the U.S. affiliates of foreign-owned MNCs. That said, according to Department of Commerce data, U.S. affiliates of foreign-owned MNCs account for the bulk of MNC-associated U.S. imports, while domestically owned MNCs account for the bulk of MNC-associated U.S. exports. As a result, Table 3.5 significantly *understates* the positive trade balance of MNCs that are domestically owned.

American economy as a whole began to experience a growing trade deficit in the 1970s, the trade balance of the nation's MNCs has been consistently positive, reflecting their dominant position in the world economy.

It is often remarked that the benefits of free trade are diffuse, falling principally to consumers who gain access to less-expensive goods and services produced by more efficient foreign business firms. However, while it is true that free trade contributes to lower-cost goods and services, it is patently false that its benefits are diffuse. For the benefits of free trade fall disproportionately to domestic economic groups who are in the position to reap the profits from it. And in the United States in the postwar period, it has been the nation's largest and most internationally oriented corporations that have had the most to gain. Indeed, since 1945 America's policy of world trade leadership has first and foremost served the collective economic interests of the nation's largest and most internationally oriented corporations.[22]

Given their interest in free trade, it should come as no surprise to find that the nation's largest and most internationally oriented corporations, their leaders, and their political organizations, have been active participants in postwar American trade politics. Indeed, since World War II these business firms, their leaders, and their political organizations have been intimately involved in trade politics; and it is this involvement that has given practical political expression to the superpower structure in American society. What, then, have been the operational modalities of this involvement?

Broadly speaking, corporate involvement in postwar American trade politics has taken four forms. First, corporate leaders have routinely been recruited into the executive branch of the American state to help formulate the nation's trade policy as well as to coordinate the legislative campaigns needed to secure enactment of administration trade bills in Congress. Second, elite policy-planning organizations such as the Council on Foreign Relations (CFR) and the Committee for Economic Development (CED) have played a special role in trade policy formation, serving as the leading society-based groups to which executive branch officials have turned for research and analysis on America's national trade interests as well as for policy proposals for asserting this interest. These organizations also have served as sites for the recruitment of executive-branch trade officials. Third, corporate participation in postwar American trade politics also has involved the formation of special-interest lobby groups, whose efforts have focused on persuading members of Congress to enact executive-branch trade proposals. In the main, these groups have been of two types: they either have been organized to promote freer trade in general, such as the CNTP and the Emergency Committee for American Trade (ECAT); or they have been organized to promote the free trade interests of particular sectors and industries. Finally, individual corporations have become involved in trade politics through direct lobbying efforts by the firms themselves.

Although the nation's largest and most internationally oriented corporations have been the most ubiquitous society-based players in postwar American trade politics, they have not been the only actors. Small and medium-sized firms, agricultural producers, and workers, acting through peak associations such as the U.S. Chamber of Commerce, the American Farm Bureau Federation (AFBF), and the AFL-CIO (American Federation of Labor and Congress of Industrial Organizations) have played important roles in lobbying Congress to advance the trade policy preferences of their members; so too have more narrowly focused associations of business, agriculture, and labor organized along sector, industry, or product lines. However, unlike the nation's largest corporations, which have been in the vanguard of the movement for freer trade, these mass-based business, agriculture, and labor organizations have not been uniformly in support of a world trade leadership role for the United States. Although small and medium-sized exporting businesses and export-oriented agricultural producers (acting through their organizations) generally have lined up in favor of freer trade, those facing or fearing increased foreign competition in the American market have not. For its part, organized labor has at times been a supporter of freer trade, but at other times it has not. Prior to the merger of the AFL and the CIO in 1955, the former was an opponent of freer trade, while the latter was a supporter—a phenomenon that reflected the different bases of the two organizations: the former rooted in industries dominated by craft workers, who were more vulnerable to import competition; the latter rooted in the mass-production industries, many of which possessed an interest in exporting. After the merger and through the mid-1960s, the AFL-CIO was a supporter of freer trade, but since then it has been one of its most ardent opponents. In the main, organized labor supported freer trade when it was seen as directly contributing to jobs and income; it was an opponent when freer trade was seen as undermining jobs and income.

This division between supporters and opponents of freer trade has been the main source of the contentious nature of postwar American trade politics at the level of American society. Indeed, each of the crucial trade acts at the legislative core of the triumph of globalism was opposed by a shifting array of business, agriculture, and labor organizations whose members believed that freer trade would compromise their economic wellbeing. The existence of this opposition, and the fact that it was unsuccessful in preventing the enactment of the four crucial trade acts, allows us to conceptualize postwar American trade politics at the level of society as one of domination; specifically, the domination of free trade over protectionist interests. And given America's superpower status at the economic level, this domination has first and foremost reflected the power and interests of the nation's largest and most internationally oriented corporations (albeit with the support of export-oriented business, agriculture, and labor groups).

Although the domination of postwar American trade politics at the level of American society first and foremost reflects the superpower position of the nation's largest and most internationally oriented corporations, it reflects as well their unique pattern of mobilization into trade politics. Like the mass-based organizations of business, agriculture, and labor, the nation's largest and most internationally oriented corporations make their interests felt by lobbying Congress. However, unlike the mass-based organizations of business, agriculture, and labor whose main contact with the American state is through congressional lobbying efforts, the nation's largest and most internationally oriented corporations have possessed a special relationship with the executive branch. As mentioned above, the leaders of these giant business enterprises routinely have been recruited into the executive branch to help in the formulation of the nation's trade policy as well as to help in the coordination of the legislative campaigns needed to secure the enactment of administration trade bills in Congress. Furthermore, time and again elite policy-planning organizations, such as the CFR and the CED, have been tapped by executive branch officials for research and analysis on America's national trade interest, as well as for policy proposals for asserting this interest at the global level. Whether through the direct recruitment of corporate leaders, or through the activities of elite policy-planning organizations, no other sector of American society has enjoyed such a close working relationship with the executive branch in the field of trade as have the nation's largest and most internationally oriented corporations. And it has been this special relationship with the executive branch that has provided the nation's giant business firms with their most important political resource in asserting their interests in postwar American trade politics.

The Superpower Structure in the American State

America's position as a world trade superpower at the level of interstate relations has been the source of a globally oriented structure of power within the American state. At the apex of this structure has been the president of the United States.

Within America's constitutional system the president, rather than Congress, is empowered to conduct the nation's foreign affairs. In addition to his being commander-in-chief of the military, Article II of the Constitution empowers the president to enter into international negotiations, make binding executive agreements, appoint and receive ambassadors, and recognize foreign governments. Pursuant to these powers, since the earliest days of the Republic the executive branch has been understood to exercise plenary control over the conduct of the nation's foreign relations. Indeed, as future Chief Justice John Marshall famously declared: "The President is the sole organ of the nation in its external relations, and its sole representative with foreign nations," a point of view given constitutional legitimacy by the Supreme Court in its 1936 *Curtiss-Wright* decision.[23] As the Court put it, "In this vast external realm, with its important, complicated, delicate and manifold problems, the President alone has the power to speak or listen as a representative of the nation. He makes treaties with the advice and consent of the Senate; but he alone negotiates. Into the field of negotiation the Senate cannot intrude; and Congress itself is powerless to invade it."[24]

As a result of its plenary authority over foreign relations, "[t]he power of the President is at its zenith under the Constitution when the President is directing" the external affairs of the nation.[25] Yet, as Alexis de Tocqueville trenchantly observed, the capacity of the president to exercise his foreign affairs power requires that he have something to exercise it on; and this is a function of the nation's position in the international system. Noting that, "It is generally in its relations with foreign powers that the executive power of a nation has the chance to display skill and strength," Tocqueville argued that the relative isolation of the United States within the international state system during the early 1800s contributed to the relative weakness of the president within America's constitutional system, especially when compared to France, which had been at the center of great-power rivalries for centuries. Although the U.S. Constitution granted the president "almost royal prerogatives" in foreign affairs, America's position on the periphery of the international state system meant that the chief executive had little opportunity to exercise them.

> [T]he President of the United States is commander-in-chief of the army, but that army consists of six thousand soldiers; he commands the navy, but the navy has only a few ships; he conducts the Union's relations with foreign nations, but the Union has no neighbors . . . and its interests are seldom in contact with those of the other nations of the globe.

As a result, the constitution allowed the president "to be strong, but circumstances have made him weak." Conversely, Tocqueville argued, as the United States emerged as a great power, as he believed it would, the power of the president within America's constitutional system would increase accordingly. "If the Union's existence were constantly menaced, and if its great interests were continually interwoven with those of other powerful nations, one would see the prestige of the executive growing, because of what was expected from it and of what it did."[26]

Furthermore, Weber argued that states tend to compete for honor, prestige, and glory; and that, in this competition it is the big political communities that are the natural exponents of "pretensions to prestige."[27] He went on to say, however, that *within* a state, such pretensions are not evenly distributed; rather, the individuals and groups "who hold the power to steer common conduct within a polity will most strongly instill themselves with [the] idealistic fervor of power prestige." By virtue of the president's position as the person in charge of steering the common conduct of the United States in its external relations, the emergence of the United States as a world trade superpower made the president the epicenter of a globally oriented structure of power within the American state.

With respect to trade policy, throughout most of American history, the president took a back seat to Congress. Trade policy was domestic policy, and Congress jealously guarded its Article I Section 8 power to "regulate commerce with foreign nations" from presidential encroachment. Although the president's power in trade began to increase incrementally with America's rise as a great economic power toward the end of the nineteenth century, it was not until the enactment of the RTAA of 1934 that Congress saw fit to delegate, for three years, its Article I, Section 8 trade powers to the president for the purpose of negotiating and implementing binding international trade agreements.[28] Yet, while the RTAA of 1934 marked a major change in the role of the president in trade politics, it was a highly partisan emergency measure, submitted by a New Deal president to a New Deal Congress over the nearly unanimous opposition of congressional Republicans. Furthermore, although the act enhanced presidential power by authorizing the chief executive to negotiate binding international trade agreements, it was not cast as part of a broader foreign policy, but rather as a domestic policy designed to increase American exports at a time of great and rising protectionism in the world market.

It was America's entrance into World War II and its subsequent emergence as an economic superpower that transformed the RTAA into a routine instrument of foreign policy (a policy of world trade leadership). Furthermore, by virtue of the president's position as the person in charge of the conduct of the nation's foreign affairs, the emergence of the United States as a nation with the capacity to shape the international system (rather than just reacting to it) fundamentally altered the balance of power between Congress and the executive branch in the field of trade. Put simply, as long as the president was able to cast trade policy as a matter of global affairs, the trade policy-making process would assume a globally oriented bias in favor of the executive branch—a bias anchored in the president's plenary foreign affairs power, which was given practical effect by the external position of the United States as a world trade superpower.

Since World War II, presidents of both parties have treated the nation's trade policy as an instrument of foreign policy: a policy designed to promote the creation, maintenance, and expansion of an open world trading system. And by virtue of the president's plenary power in foreign affairs, the chief executive has been the principal animating force in the formulation of the nation's policy of world trade leadership. Indeed, the promulgation of the nation's postwar policy of world trade leadership has been executive altogether.

Although the executive branch has been the epicenter of the nation's postwar policy of world trade leadership, Article I Section 8 of the Constitution makes Congress a powerful and ubiquitous player in trade politics. It does so because, while the Constitution vests the president with the power to negotiate international trade agreements, if those agreements make changes to U.S. domestic law (including trade law) they cannot take effect unless specifically authorized by Congress. As a result, to the extent that America's presidentially determined policy of world trade leadership requires specific grants of trade policy-making authority from Congress, or congressional approval of already negotiated agreements, the president must convince the national legislature that freer trade is in the national interest. And while the president's plenary powers in foreign affairs bias the trade policy-making process toward the executive branch, the participation of Congress in trade politics has been the source of significant challenges to presidential leadership.

The origins of this institutional conflict are not hard to find. In contrast to the president, whose Article II powers give the chief executive an outward-looking orientation, Congress is a profoundly inward-looking institution. Its members are elected from local districts and states; and while individual members may develop a national or international perspective, their electoral fortunes are tied to their local constituencies. As a result, Congress is an internally oriented institution, one that is responsive to the entreaties of domestic groups whose economic interests are threatened by a national policy of world trade leadership. As former Secretary of State Dean Acheson put it: one of the chief concerns of the president, "the world beyond our boundaries—[is] to most members of the Congress only a troublesome intrusion into their chief interest—the internal affairs of the country, and especially of the particular parts of it they represent." This was especially true with respect to trade, where, regardless of the party composition of Congress, "the sea was always rough . . . [for] . . . trade more often appears as a threat of foreign competition than as potential markets for American goods."[29] Given the inward-looking orientation of Congress, and its susceptibility to protectionist pressures, it is not surprising that over the course of the postwar period the national legislature has been the source of significant challenges to presidential leadership in trade. Indeed, just as the chief conflict within postwar American trade politics at the level of society has been between free trade-oriented and protectionist economic groups, the principal conflict at the level of the American state has been between an outward-looking executive branch promoting a national policy of world trade leadership and an inward-looking Congress sensitive to the concerns of domestic economic groups who face or fear foreign competition and demand protection, as well as those who believe the nation's trading partners are unfairly blocking their exports on world markets and demand unilateral solutions.

In point of fact, since World War II Congress has been the source of nearly every feature of American trade policy that smacks of parochialism and protectionism. It also has been unilateralist, using its constitutional authority over trade as a tool to coerce concessions from other countries by threatening to close the American market to their exports. It has railed against the protectionist trade practices of other countries while supporting such practices in the United States. It has shown little restraint in flouting the rules of the world trading system when it has deemed such action to be in the national interest, even while castigating other nations when they have done the same. It has provided protection to important sectors of the American economy while demanding that such protections be dismantled abroad. And it has forced more than one president to serve as an accomplice in the commission of these acts. Most importantly, it has resisted nearly every effort by postwar presidents to secure congressional enactment of trade bills empowering the executive branch to enter into international trade agreements, or to enact the results of a global trade round.

Yet, while losing many battles with Congress, over the course of the postwar period the president has won the war. For the central feature of postwar American trade policy has been the exercise by the United States of a world trade leadership role in the creation, maintenance, and expansion of an open world trading system. And this result has hinged on a pattern of domestic politics anchored in the nation's superpower position in world trade.

Superpower Trade Politics

America's postwar policy of world trade leadership has reflected the superpower structure in U.S. society and state, which has undergirded a pattern of power and politics marked by the domination of the trade policy-making process by the nation's largest and most internationally oriented corporations and the president of the United States. This pattern of "superpower trade politics" has displayed three principal characteristics. First, the trade acts at the legislative core of the triumph of globalism were externally driven. They were designed to allow the United States to leverage its superpower position in world trade to respond to challenges to the overall health and maintenance of the world trading system through the initiation of international trade rounds. Second, the formulation and drafting of these trade statutes (or at least their negotiating authorities) was executive altogether; and it involved a close working relationship between the executive branch and internationally oriented corporate elites and their organizations. Third, the enactment of these statutes involved a concerted effort on the part of the president and his corporate allies to convince Congress to support administration trade proposals (or at least their negotiating authorities). The success of these efforts themselves rested on three factors.

First, due to the president's plenary powers in foreign affairs, executive branch trade officials were able to advance a regime-centered global trade policy as a matter of national interest, which softened the local and parochial orientation of Congress by enhancing the position of the president in the legislative process. Second, the president did not face off against Congress without domestic allies. Not only did the nation's largest and most internationally oriented corporations lobby Congress in support of presidential trade bills, but so too did small and medium-sized exporting firms, export-oriented agricultural producers, and (at times) organized labor. Presidential mobilization of these export-oriented groups formed a powerful counterweight to the lobbying efforts of economic groups demanding protection or other forms of trade-distorting practices. That Congress was receptive to the entreaties of these export-oriented groups flowed naturally from the same institutional factors that made it sensitive to the entreaties of protectionist groups: its fragmented and decentralized institutional design. Finally, the president was able to blunt the sharp edge of congressional resistance to administration trade proposals by making special and strategic concessions to protectionist economic groups and their supporters in Congress both within and outside the framework of trade bills. With respect to concessions made within the framework of trade bills, the president has conceded to Congress the promulgation of domestically oriented trade laws designed to respond to fair and unfair foreign competition in the American market; or to pressure the nation's trading partners to unilaterally open their markets to the exports of particular U.S. industries.[30] With respect to presidential concessions made outside the framework of trade bills, the chief executive has negotiated various quota or market-opening agreements with the nation's trading partners designed to protect or expand the export markets for particular industries. Although protectionist in nature, these concessions (both within and outside the framework of trade bills) can be viewed as movements within free trade; for their purpose was to help gain congressional acceptance of new, globally oriented negotiating authority for the president.[31]

In sum, the genesis of the four crucial trade acts at the legislative core of the triumph of globalism exhibited a similar pattern. First, America's position as the sole superpower in world trade generated a globally oriented confluence of power and interests between the nation's largest and most internationally oriented corporations and the president; and allowed the United States to exercise leadership in the creation, maintenance, and expansion of an open world trading system. Second, the chief stimuli for the policy-making activities of this superpower alliance were external in origin, anchored in the evolution of the postwar world trading system itself. Third, the four crucial trade acts at the legislative core of the triumph of globalism were enacted by an otherwise protectionist and nationalist Congress as a result of legislative campaigns waged by the executive branch that advanced a globally oriented view of the national trade interest; that mobilized export-oriented domestic producers to lobby Congress; and that made strategic concessions to protectionist groups and their supporters in Congress both within and outside the framework of administration trade bills. It is to a detailed examination of this pattern of superpower trade politics in the formulation and enactment of the RTAA of 1945, the TEA of 1962, the TA of 1974, and the OTCA of 1988 that we now turn.

Notes

1 Max Weber, *Economy and Society*, Vol. II, ed. Guenther Roth and Claus Wittich (Berkeley: University of California Press, 1978), 912.
2 It may be asked why I discard the appellation "hegemony" in favor of "superpower"? The answer is not merely one of linguistics. As noted in Chapter 2, the concept of hegemony is mired in decades of debate concerning both its economic foundations and its political effects. Although this debate has generated a wide-ranging literature, it nonetheless has failed to resolve the central theoretical conundrum outlined in the preceding chapter: the disconnect between historical situations when a state that is hegemonic in the economic sphere does not act like a hegemon in the political sphere; and situations in which a state acts like a hegemon in the political sphere but is not hegemonic in the economic sphere. The former was the case of the United States during the interwar period; the latter was the case of Great Britain in the late nineteenth century through World War I. My use of the term "superpower" is designed to clear the conceptual field by treating American structural power in the postwar period as *sui generis*—and not as an example of what is often cast as a trans-historical phenomenon (hegemony). By this I mean that my use of the term superpower is meant to be historically specific: anchored in the unique configuration of American structural power at both the economic and the political levels in the years since World War II—and only with respect to its power within the world trading system. For once one gets beyond theoretical generalities and embraces historical particulars, the economic underpinnings and the political manifestations of America's exercise of world trade leadership in the postwar world trading system cannot be meaningfully compared to any other country at any other time or in any other issue area. For example, beyond generalities can we really say that the economic foundations and political characteristics of Great Britain's structural power in the wake of the Napoleonic Wars and America's structural power in the wake of World War II were the same? I think not. Among other things, England did not launch an international regulatory authority for the management of world trade on a global basis. Indeed, as the London *Economist* put it in the closing days of World War II, when the United States advanced its plan for a new world trading system: "Let there be no mistake about it, the policy put forward by the [Americans] is revolutionary. It is a genuinely new conception of world order." Cited in Richard Gardner, *Sterling–Dollar Diplomacy* (New York: McGraw-Hill, 1969), 1. Beyond this, I use the term superpower more as an organizing principle than as a fully developed theoretical concept. In so doing it is my intent (or hope) to be better able to grasp the historically specific structural modalities of America's exercise of world trade leadership than if I use the trans-historical concept of hegemony. In the end, we need to call

America's unique position in the postwar world trading system something; and if the concept of hegemony is problematic, the use of the term superpower seems as good a candidate as any.

3 As mentioned in the previous chapter, Stephen D. Krasner uses four measures to determine the relative economic power of nations in world trade: per capita income, aggregate economic size, world trade shares, and foreign investment. David A. Lake uses two: labor productivity and world trade shares. Thus, my measures incorporate three of these—aggregate economic size, foreign investment (measured in terms of share of the world's multinational corporations), and world trade shares. Per capita income and labor productivity seem to me to be suspect analytically. If we were to measure relative economic power via per capita income we would have to conclude that in 2000 the structural power of the United States ($35,040) was less than that of Switzerland ($35,720) and substantially lower than Monaco ($75,642), Liechtenstein ($75,606), the Cayman Islands ($56,658), Bermuda ($55,388), Luxembourg ($46,544), and San Marino ($40,883). Indeed, in 2000 only Japan makes it into the top ten countries in terms of per capita income ($37,633), while the United Kingdom ($25,040), Germany ($22,907), and France ($21,828) are down the list. See United Nations Economic Statistics, Per Capita GDP at Current Prices, U.S. Dollars, http://unstats. un.org/unsd/snaama/dnllist.asp (accessed August 20, 2013). Labor productivity yields somewhat similar results. Among the top ten countries in 2000, America's labor productivity ranked second, behind Luxembourg, and just ahead of Belgium, Ireland, and Italy. See Eustat, Labour Productivity by Employee, Country, and Year, http://www.eustat.es/elementos/ele0002500/tbl0002544_i.html#axzz2cYSsHhA3 (accessed August 20, 2013).

4 *Fortune Magazine*, http://money.cnn.com/magazines/fortune/global500/2005/index. html (accessed March 15, 2013).

5 Albert O. Hirschman, *National Power and the Structure of Foreign Trade* (Berkeley: University of California Press, 1945). As Hirschman explains: "the power to interrupt commercial or financial relations with any country, considered as an attribute of national sovereignty, is the root cause of the influence or power position which a country acquires in other countries, just as it is the root cause of the 'dependence on trade'," 16.

6 Robert O. Keohane, *After Hegemony: Cooperation and Discord in the World Political Economy* (Princeton: Princeton University Press, 1984), 33.

7 Clair Wilcox, *A Charter for World Trade* (New York: Macmillan Company, 1949).

8 Karl Polanyi, *The Great Transformation: the Political and Economic Origins of Our Time* (Boston: Beacon Press, 1957); Douglas A. Irwin, "Multilateral and Bilateral Trade Policies in the World Trading System: An Historical Perspective," in Jamie de Melo and Arvind Panagariya, eds., *New Dimensions in Regional Integration* (New York: Cambridge University Press, 1993).

9 The idea that the United States has approached its management of the postwar world trading system in the manner of an alliance leader is widely accepted by students of the postwar world trading system. See, for example, Ernest H. Preeg, *Traders and Diplomats: An Analysis of the Kennedy Round of Negotiations under the General Agreement on Tariffs and Trade* (Washington, D.C.: Brookings Institution, 1970); Andrew Shonfield, "International Economic Relations of the Western World: An Overall View," in Andrew Shonfield, ed., *International Economic Relations of the Western World, 1959–1971*, Vol. 1 (London: Oxford University Press, 1976); Gilbert R. Winham, *International Trade and the Tokyo Round Negotiation* (Princeton: Princeton University Press, 1986); and John Croome, *Reshaping the World Trading System* (Geneva: WTO Publications, 1995).

10 David A. Deese, *World Trade Politics: Power, Principles, and Leadership* (New York: Routledge, 2008); Croome, *Reshaping the World Trading System*; Ernest H. Preeg, *Traders in a Brave New World: the Uruguay Round and the Future of the International*

Trading System (Chicago: University of Chicago Press, 1995); Patrick Low, *Trading Free: the GATT and U.S. Trade Policy* (Washington, D.C.: Twentieth Century Club, 1993); Miriam Camps and William Diebold, Jr., *The New Multilateralism: Can the World Trading System Be Saved?* (New York: Council on Foreign Relations, 1986); Winham, *International Trade and the Tokyo Round*; and Preeg, *Traders and Diplomats*.

11 See Wilcox, *A Charter for World Trade*.

12 See Preeg, *Traders and Diplomats*.

13 See Winham, *International Trade and the Tokyo Round*.

14 See Camps and Diebold, *The New Multilateralism*. It should not be thought that the United States was immune from implementing trade-distorting policies and practices of its own. Indeed, this was not the case. For example, in 1955 the United States secured a GATT waiver exempting its agricultural policy from free trade rules. Furthermore, throughout the postwar period scores of anti-dumping and countervailing duty decisions placed high tariffs on selected foreign imports. In the 1960s and 1970s the United States negotiated an array of orderly marketing agreements and voluntary export restraints for sectors such as textiles and clothing, steel, and automobiles. And in the 1980s the United States resorted to unilateral market opening schemes on a bilateral basis which threatened to limit access to the American market to trading partners who the United States believed discriminated against American exports. Thus, in addition to pushing its trading partners to liberalize their trade practices through the initiation of GATT trade rounds, U.S. negotiators also used the rounds to rein in the protectionist and unilateral policies of the United States.

15 Robert O. Keohane and Joseph S. Nye, *Power and Interdependence*, 2nd ed. (Boston: Scott, Foresman and Company, 1989), 44.

16 Ibid.

17 United States Census Bureau, *Statistical Abstract of the United States 2003* (Washington, D.C.: Government Printing Office, 2004), Table No. 732, p. 495 (author's calculations.)

18 Internal Revenue Service, *Tax Statistics 2000*, www.irs.gov/uac/SOI-Tax-Stats-Table-3-Corporation-Returns-With-Net-Income (accessed April 15, 2013) (author's calculations.)

19 Census Bureau, U.S. Department of Commerce, *A Profile of U.S. Exporting Companies, 2000–2001* (Washington, D.C.: GPO), Table 2b, 14 (author's calculations).

20 Ibid., Table 4b, p. 20.

21 "Operations of U.S. Multinational Companies," *Survey of Current Business*, March 2002, Table 1, 25 and Table 14, 39 (author's calculations).

22 Of course, the global free trade interest of MNCs is reinforced by the fact that many of their foreign affiliates export to third-country markets. In 1999, for example, 25 percent of the gross product of U.S. MNCs was produced by their majority-owned foreign affiliates; and 34 percent of the sales of these affiliates were exports to third-country markets. See "Operations of U.S. Multinational Companies," Table 1, 25 and Table 13, 38.

23 Cited in, John C. Woo, *The President's Constitutional Authority to Conduct Military Operations against Terrorists and Nations Supporting Them*, September 25, 2001, http://www.justice.gov/olc/warpowers925.htm (accessed April 24, 2013), 5.

24 *United States v. Curtiss-Wright Export Corporation*, 299 U.S. 304 (1936).

25 John C. Yoo, Memorandum Opinion, 2.

26 Alex de Tocqueville, *Democracy in America*, J. P. Mayer, ed. (New York: Harper Perennial, 1966), 126.

27 Max Weber, *Economy and Society*, Vol. II (Berkeley: University of California Press, 1978), 922.

28 See David A. Lake, *Power, Protection and Free Trade: International Sources of U.S. Commercial Policy, 1887–1939* (Ithaca, NY: Cornell University Press, 1988).

29 Dean Acheson, *Present at the Creation: My Years in the State Department* (New York: W. W. Norton and Company, 1987), 99.
30 The most important fair trade laws are the escape clause and adjustment assistance. The most important unfair trade laws are those dealing with dumping and export subsidization; as well as Section 301, which places pressure on the president to take unilateral trade opening actions against foreign governments which engage in practices that unfairly limit U.S. exports to their markets. It is important to note, however, that in all these cases it is left up to the president to accept or reject the petitions of domestic producers.
31 These actions typically took the form of various quota schemes; Voluntary Export Restraint (VER) agreements; and Section 301 actions designed to pressure foreign governments to unilaterally open their markets to the exports of particular U.S. industries.

PART III
Historical Cases

4

GOING GLOBAL

The Reciprocal Trade Agreements Act of 1945

> This is no longer a question on which Republicans and Democrats should divide. The logic of events and our clear and pressing national interest must override our party controversies . . . . The point in history at which we stand is full of promise and danger. The world will either move toward unity and widely shared prosperity or it will move apart into necessarily competing economic blocs. We have a chance, we citizens of the United States, to use our influence in favor of a more united and cooperating world. Whether we do so will determine, as far as it is in our power, the kind of lives our grandchildren can live.
>
> *Franklin D. Roosevelt (1945)*

The RTAA of 1945 initiated America's postwar drive to construct an open world trading system and marked the first major shift of trade-related policy-making power from Congress to the president for the purpose of exercising world trade leadership. A response to America's emergence as a world trade superpower and a war-generated vacuum in international trading relationships, the RTAA of 1945 was the product of a six-year postwar policy-planning alliance between the New York-based CFR and the United States Department of State. At the statutory heart of the act was congressional authorization for the president to enter into binding international trade agreements for a period of three years and to reduce American tariffs by up to 50 percent of their 1945 rates in exchange for reciprocal concessions from other countries. Although the RTAA of 1945 did not authorize the president to launch a new international regime for world trade, American negotiators used the act's tariff-cutting power to do just that. The result was the GATT, which began a process of transferring trade policy-making power from the domestic to the global level.[1]

The Global Challenge: A New World Trading System

The origin of the RTAA of 1945 is found in the most sweeping change in the modern world system of capitalism and states since England rode its industrial revolution to world economic supremacy in the wake of its victory over France in the Napoleonic Wars. This change was the meteoric rise of the United States to superpower status during World War II.

It is well known that in the century prior to World War I Great Britain played a special role in pioneering a relatively open world economic order, which, while punctuated by periodic depressions and financial crises, contributed to a period of rapid global economic growth and a century of relative peace among the great powers of Europe.[2] This British-led order was badly shaken by World War I, and efforts to restore it in the 1920s met with only limited success. Although at the end of World War I, "world leadership was offered, by almost unanimous consent, to the United States,"[3] the nation was unprepared to assume the leadership role exercised by Great Britain during the nineteenth century. Instead of playing a positive role in the reconstruction of an open world economic order, the United States rejected the Treaty of Versailles, demanded repayment of Allied war debts, returned to its traditional high-tariff policy, and provided only lukewarm support for a series of conferences organized by the League of Nations which attempted to lay the foundations for the restoration of an open world trading system.[4]

America's failure to assume the mantle of global economic leadership in the wake of World War I did not cause the global depression of the 1930s, the origins of which remain the subject of much debate.[5] It did, however, inject a large measure of instability into international economic relationships. Thus, when the disaster finally struck, the nations of the world were left with no place to turn except to self-help and the creation of autarkic national economies and empires. The first to move was the United States, which in 1930 raised its tariffs to their highest levels in history; and four years later, from behind its high tariff walls, instituted a bi-lateral, reciprocal trade policy designed to increase American exports by offering foreign nations lower tariffs in exchange for market-opening concessions of their own.[6]

With its invasion of Manchuria in 1931, Japan began its bid to construct a regional economic bloc in Asia, an imperial program of military and economic conquest that would lead to the creation of a Greater East Asia Co-Prosperity Sphere.[7] In 1932, Great Britain abandoned its commitment to free trade by raising its tariffs and establishing an Imperial Preference System within the Commonwealth that discriminated against the outside world.[8] In 1933, following the seizure of power by the Nazi Party, Germany began to erect a bi-lateral system of managed trade with its weaker neighbors to the south and east, which by the end of 1940 had blossomed into a continent-wide military and economic empire.[9] France (before its invasion by Nazi Germany) and Italy also entered the fray: the former by constructing a gold-bloc trading system among a small group of northwestern European nations; the latter by embarking on a program of military and economic conquest that pulled into its orbit parts of northern Africa, eastern and southern Europe, and France.[10]

World War II consigned the twenty years' crisis in international economic order, and the multi-polar organization of the world economy it generated, to the dustbin of history. The Axis Powers were swept from the field; and with them went their various regional schemes of economic autarky, managed trade, and military conquest. In 1940, the French gold-bloc trading system had crumbled with the Nazi invasion; and as part of its Mutual Aid Agreement with the United States, in 1943 Great Britain had agreed—at least in principle—to dismantle its Imperial Preference System as part of an American-led effort to establish an open world trading system at the end of hostilities. Emerging from the war with its economy fully intact and operating at historically high levels of production—in a world position that Dean Acheson likened to that of God "in the first chapter of Genesis"[11]—only the United States possessed the power to step into the breach with a program for collective action among states in the economic field.

This war-induced transformation in the global position of the United States generated a crisis in American foreign policy, which opened the door for an unprecedented postwar foreign policy planning alliance between the nation's leading private foreign policy organization and the lead department within the American state responsible for the management of the nation's external affairs: the New York-based CFR and the United States Department of State. America's new global trade policy, and its codification in the RTAA of 1945, grew out of the wartime work of this globally oriented, private-public partnership.

The Formulation of the RTAA of 1945

While high-ranking State Department officials were involved in the creation of the CFR during World War I and the two organizations enjoyed a cordial relationship during the interwar period,[12] it was not until the outbreak of World War II that an opportunity emerged for the institutionalization of this relationship.

Germany's invasion of Poland on September 1, 1939, presented foreign policy elites in the United States with a profound problem: how to determine America's national interest in the rapidly changing international environment and in the eventual peace settlement. Ultimate responsibility for answering these questions fell to the president, but they fell as well to the Department of State. Yet, in September 1939 the Department was wholly unprepared to answer these questions; for it lacked the funds and institutional capacity to engage in foreign policy research and analysis. Indeed, as Dean Acheson saw it, as late as 1941 the State Department "was closer to its nineteenth-century predecessors in both what it did and how the work was done," than to the department that would emerge in 1945. More specifically, "most matters that concerned the Department arose from specific incidents or problems and then evolved into policies, rather than beginning as matters of broad decision and ending in specific action."[13] It is not surprising then, that when, on September 12, 1939, CFR leaders proposed to State Department officials that the two organizations join forces "to develop . . . long-range concepts of American foreign policy . . . and a foreign policy strategy for the United States,"[14] Secretary of State Cordell Hull "forthwith accepted."[15] For in the two decades since its inception as an informal dinner club of 100 globally oriented financial, corporate, and legal elites, the CFR had grown into the foremost private foreign policy organization in the United States, with a well-funded program of internal study groups on U.S. foreign policy and international affairs.[16] The offer of help from the CFR therefore pointed the way forward for the State Department at a moment of profound, systemically generated, institutional crisis. And over the next three months, personnel from the two organizations worked in strict secrecy to develop a plan for coordinated action.

By late December 1939, it had been agreed that overall responsibility for what became known as the "War and Peace Studies" would rest with a small steering committee of CFR leaders chaired by the organization's president, Norman H. Davis, a New York investment banker. The project would be divided into a number of study groups, each organized around a specific foreign policy problem; and participants would be chosen by CFR and State Department leaders. The study groups would be staffed by CFR employees, and the project's base of operations would be at CFR headquarters in New York City. Operationally, the study groups would engage in a program of research and analysis within their spheres of competence and, based upon this work, they would draft formal memoranda for the State Department, which would include specific foreign policy recommendations. These memoranda, which would be marked "confidential" and not made public, would be forwarded via the project's Steering Committee to Cordell Hull or his designates in the department.[17] The United States' new global trade policy was the product of the War and Peace Studies' Economic and Financial Group, which was dominated by central bankers, international financial capitalists, and globally oriented nonbank corporate directors.[18]

The trade policy work of the Economic and Financial Group passed through two distinct stages. The first was exploratory and corresponded to the interregnum between the outbreak of war in Europe and the Japanese attack on Pearl Harbor. During this phase, the Group focused on defining the United States' national trade interest and the main lines of approach for a globally oriented postwar trade policy. And here the Group determined that the national trade interest of the United States lay in a large and growing volume of international trade, which was seen as necessary for the promotion of high levels of domestic production, employment, and consumption in the postwar period. Yet, given the collapse of the world economy during the 1930s, and the concomitant rise of international trade barriers, the problem was how to achieve global trade expansion. The Group answered this question by arguing that what was required was U.S. global leadership in the elaboration of "new policies and new international arrangements" that would bind states into a worldwide free trade system that would operate according to a single set of rules.[19] At the core of these new arrangements needed to be a frontal assault on one of the features of national sovereignty that had contributed to the autarkic policies of the 1930s: the capacity of states to unilaterally regulate their cross-border trade flows. A "more closely integrated world economic order," the Group believed, "will almost certainly require some restrictions on sovereignty." Indeed, "[n]ational self-determination [must] be qualified and limited," for states must "solve economic problems . . . as economic problems, regardless of national boundaries."[20] Furthermore, if the United States was to take the lead in the construction of such a system, it was incumbent upon the nation to limit its own trade sovereignty after the war, but to do so within the context of providing global leadership in the construction of "new international institutions" and "schemes of international economic cooperation."[21]

Once the United States entered the war as a full-scale belligerent, the Economic and Financial Group turned its attention to the preparation of concrete postwar plans. By summer 1942 its thinking had evolved along two lines. In Memorandum E-B 55, "International Control of Trade Policies," the Group advanced a proposal for the creation of an International Trade Authority (ITA), the purpose of which was to provide a common set of rules for world trade, police the trade policies of its members, enforce trade agreements negotiated under its auspices, and act as a break on national economic self-determination.[22] Although recognizing the need for gradualism and flexibility in the operation of the ITA, the Group nonetheless was clear that its ultimate objectives were "universal free trade," and the "transfer of [trade policy-making] power by sovereign states . . . to an international, or, more accurately, to a federal authority."

> Experience shows that we cannot rely upon the separate action of national states to adopt tariff policies which, in the long run, will further either their own interest or that of the community of nations; the effect of their policies may prove quite the opposite. But the free flow of international trade is of such vital importance to all nations . . . that no nation should be able by its independent and arbitrary action to interrupt trade or divert it into unproductive channels. Hence . . . international control of trade policies must be established.[23]

E-B 55 provided the conceptual framework for the GATT, which would be negotiated pursuant to the tariff-cutting authorities of the RTAA of 1945.

The second proposal by the Economic and Financial Group concerned the RTAA itself. In Memorandum E-B 57, "Possible Revisions of the Trade Agreements Act," the Group argued that the basis for America's new global trade policy should be an established legal instrument: the reciprocal trade agreements program initiated by Secretary of State Cordell Hull in 1934.[24] Yet the Group believed that in its existing form the Hull program was inadequate to the task. In order to serve as a tool for U.S. global leadership in the field of trade, the RTAA required substantial modification. Whereas in the original RTAA of 1934 Congress delegated its Article I Section 8 power to "regulate commerce with foreign nations" to the president for a period of three years, the Group argued that the time limits on this authority should be "abolished entirely"[25]—that is, the president should be granted standing authority to negotiate international trade agreements without the involvement of Congress. However, recognizing that it was unlikely that Congress would consent to such a fundamental reorganization of constitutional power, or if it did so consent that the Supreme Court would uphold the authorization, the Group instead recommended that an attempt be made to lengthen the three years' authority to at least five. The Group also recommended that Congress provide the president with the power to make "an unlimited cut" in U.S. tariffs, in effect allowing the United States to move to free trade all at once; but short of that, new legislation should empower the president to cut U.S. tariffs by up to 50 percent of their prevailing rates—a power that Congress had granted only once before: in the original RTAA of 1934.[26] Finally, the Group argued that a new preamble should be inserted into the act "setting forth the constructive uses of the program in building a postwar world economy."[27] Memorandum E-B 57 laid the conceptual ground for the RTAA of 1945.

While the Economic and Financial Group took the lead in the conceptual formulation of the United States' new global trade policy, the State Department exercised leadership in translating the Group's work into practical policy instruments, in coordinating the postwar trade policy agenda of the executive branch, and in building support for this agenda within Congress and U.S. society. In these efforts, the State Department's chief strategist and organizer was its Secretary, Cordell Hull, who worked closely with a senior team of advisors drawn from the Department and the CFR.[28] This senior team became known as the "Informal Agenda Group" and was responsible for planning, selecting, and guiding the Department's postwar work "toward a final inclusive pattern of recommended policy."[29] Because the Department was "the chief agency of government to engage in postwar planning,"[30] the men of the Informal Agenda Group dominated this field within the executive branch. Indeed, President Roosevelt (FDR) referred to them as "my postwar advisors."[31]

Hull's work to position the Department of State to play the leading role in postwar foreign policy preparation (including trade policy) began shortly after the initiation of the War and Peace Studies. However, it was not until the Japanese attack on Pearl Harbor that his efforts swung into high gear. Within days of the attack, FDR approved a proposal from Hull to establish an interdepartmental Presidential Advisory Committee on Post-War Foreign Policy (ACPFP), funded with emergency appropriations from the Bureau of the Budget—the first allocation made by the Roosevelt administration for the purpose of postwar foreign policy planning.[32] The purpose of the ACPFP was to act as the central coordinating body for all executive branch action aimed at the "preparation for this country's effective participation in the solution of the vast and complicated problems of international relations which will confront [it] and the world after the final defeat of the forces of aggression." From 1942 to 1944, the ACPFP served as "the authorized superior structure" for all postwar foreign policy planning within the executive branch.[33]

Chaired by Hull, with his authority flowing directly from the president, eight of the ACPFP's initial members were members of the CFR who were deeply involved in the War and Peace Studies, including CFR leaders Davis, Taylor, and Bowman. With the creation of the ACPFP, arrangements were made to strengthen the relationship between the War and Peace Studies and the postwar preparations of the State Department at the working level. As part of the ACPFP's structure, Hull established a new Division of Special Research within the Department to serve as the ACPFP's technical arm; and CFR staff working as research secretaries for the War and Peace Studies were brought into the Department on a part-time basis: an "arrangement [that] made it easier for the Council to select the problems particularly in need of study and to fix a timetable for dealing with them to best advantage."[34]

It was within the framework of the ACPFP that State Department staff began to study and discuss the trade policy work of the War and Peace Studies' Economic and Financial Group. Initially, this effort was exploratory in nature and coordinated by two economic subcommittees. However, as the work of those subcommittees moved to technical considerations, they were folded into a single Committee on Post-War Foreign Economic Policy (CPFEP). Chaired by CFR Board Director and former CEO of the United States Steel Corporation, Myron C. Taylor, the CPFEP functioned as part of the larger ACPFP but was given cabinet-level status—the only subcommittee of the ACPFP elevated to that position.[35] It was under the aegis of the so-called "Taylor Committee" that the Economic and Financial Group's Memorandum E-B 55, "International Control of Trade Policies," was translated into the technical blueprint for the State Department's postwar initiative for a "multilateral convention on commercial policy"—including the creation of an international trade organization.[36] Indeed, in both conception and design, the plans put forward by the Taylor Committee's Special Committee on Relaxation of Trade Barriers was a detailed and technical elaboration of E-B 55, which had been transmitted to the State Department by the War and Peace Studies Steering Committee more than a year earlier.

In addition to moving the work of the War and Peace Studies into the State Department, Hull used the ACPFP to position the Department to dominate postwar foreign policy preparation within the executive branch; to build non–partisan agreement on the Department's postwar foreign policies between the executive and Congress; and to develop "an informed public opinion" in the "support of such policies."[37] In pursuit of these objectives, early in 1942 Hull began to expand the ACPFP's membership to make it more representative of the political and economic interests that would need to support State's postwar plans if they were to bear fruit. Toward this end, the ACPFP came to include high-ranking officials from the Departments of Treasury, Commerce, Agriculture, and War and Navy; the Joint Chiefs of Staff; the War Production Board; the Office of War Mobilization; the Federal Reserve System; the Office of the Attorney General; the U.S. Tariff Commission; and the White House Office. Fifteen members of Congress were added to the Committee: nine Democrats and six Republicans, including two each from the Senate Foreign Relations Committee and the House Committee on Foreign Affairs. Rounding out the expanded ACPFP were representatives from the American Federation of Labor (AFL), the Congress of Industrial Organizations (CIO), the United Automobile Workers (UAW), and the U.S. Chamber of Commerce.[38]

While the inclusion of executive branch departments, bureaus, and agencies was designed to secure the Department of State's leadership in the preparation of postwar foreign policy within the executive branch, the participation of members of Congress and officials from the AFL, the CIO, the UAW, and the Chamber of Commerce was meant to build "a unified national view of basic foreign policy."[39] Therefore, in addition to securing a coordinating role for the State Department within the executive branch, Hull used the expanded ACPFP to educate strategically placed individuals concerning America's new role in world affairs and the State Department's evolving postwar plans; and he hoped that these individuals would use their influence as leaders in their own realms to build support for those plans. In particular, he sought to avoid having the Department's program dragged into the "battleground of [domestic] politics."[40]

The ACPFP was phased out by the end of 1943 as the State Department began to move toward the elaboration of more definitive plans for postwar action. In the economic field, the Taylor Committee was replaced in April 1944 by a new interdepartmental Executive Committee on Economic Foreign Policy (ECEFP).[41] Chaired by Assistant Secretary of State Dean Acheson, the ECEFP took its direction from the Informal Agenda Group.[42] It was under the auspices of the ECEFP that the RTAA of 1945 was drafted by working-level State Department personnel in February and March 1945. The legislation they produced closely followed the thinking presented to the Department by the Economic and Financial Group in Memorandum E-B 57, "Possible Revisions of the Trade Agreements Act," nearly three years earlier.

In a series of reports produced for the ECEFP, State Department technical staff outlined their thinking on the new trade bill.[43] They argued that a new RTAA should extend the president's trade-negotiating authority for an indefinite period of time; however, since such a grant was not likely to meet with congressional approval, the new bill should simply ask for a traditional extension of three years. It was further suggested that a significant increase in the president's authority to cut tariffs be the centerpiece of the new legislation, but by how much was not specified. Finally, they argued that a new section should be added to the RTAA outlining the legislation's use in allowing the United States to launch a new world trading system. The leadership of the ECEFP agreed with the three-year time limit and determined that the president should be authorized to cut tariffs by up to 50 percent of their prevailing rates, as originally suggested in E-B 57. However, after discussions with congressional leaders it was decided that the inclusion of a new section relating the bill to U.S. leadership in the creation of a new world trading system should be abandoned for fear that it would generate needless opposition.[44] Not only was this section not required for the State Department to actually embark upon such a project, but the Department already had informed Congress that it intended to use the new legislation "to seek an early understanding with the leading trading nations, indeed with as many nations as possible, for the effective and substantial reduction of all kinds of barriers to trade."[45]

The Enactment of the RTAA of 1945

Congressional enactment of the RTAA of 1945 was not inevitable. Although the Democratic Party held substantial majorities in both houses of Congress and the ECEFP had scaled back what the State Department and the CFR wanted in new trade legislation (permanent standing authority for the president to reduce U.S. tariffs to zero through international trade negotiations), State Department personnel were doubtful about the bill's prospects in Congress. Most importantly, they were concerned about the willingness of Congress to consent to the bill's new 50 percent tariff-cutting authority. As one member of the State Department's drafting team put it: "the fight [on] this point will be hard."[46] Yet the State Department had one thing going for it: America's new-found position as a superpower in world trade. This new global reality gave the Department a twofold political advantage in its confrontation with Congress: first, it enabled the Department to mobilize support for the administration's trade bill among domestic economic groups with an interest in export expansion (and thereby counter protectionist pressures in Congress); and second, it enabled the Department to couch the administration's trade bill in terms of foreign policy (and thereby weight the legislative process toward the executive branch). The introduction of these elements into the trade policy-making process in Congress generated a globally oriented bias in its legislative proceedings—a bias that reflected the mobilization of the superpower structure in American society and state, and that played to the interests of the CFR and the Department of State.

The State Department's campaign to mobilize domestic support for the administration's trade bill began in earnest in May 1944: approximately one year before its introduction into Congress. During that year, and into the spring of 1945, Secretary of State Cordell Hull turned the State Department into an engine of public relations designed to build broad-based support for a new world trade leadership role for the United States, anchored in a new conception of the national trade interest. The basic theme of the campaign, which was driven home by State Department personnel in scores of radio broadcasts and in-person appearances at national and local business and civic organizations across the country, was first articulated by Hull in a press release that declared May 21–27, 1944, "National Foreign Trade Week."

> Leadership toward a new system of international trade and other economic affairs will devolve very largely upon the United States because of our great economic strength. We should assume this leadership, and the responsibility that goes with it, primarily for reasons of pure national self-interest. We ourselves cannot live in prosperity and security in our own country while people in other countries are suffering want and being driven to despair by economic hardship. If we are to have jobs for all our workers and markets for all our goods people in other countries must likewise have opportunity to produce to their maximum capacity and to pay us, with the fruits of their efforts, for the things we want to sell to them.[47]

In addition to its own efforts, the State Department received the help of numerous business and civic organizations at the national and local levels, which flooded the country with pamphlets explaining the United States' new global trade policy and espousing the administration's view of the national trade interest. So well orchestrated was the State Department's campaign that one member of Congress charged that it was an exercise in "super-propaganda," turning the Department into "a vast public pressure group to destroy our constitutional process."[48]

While the State Department's campaign of "super-propaganda" was designed to create an "informed public opinion," and thereby soften up members of Congress prior to the introduction of the administration's trade bill, the real work of translating this campaign into legislative majorities occurred within Congress itself. And here Cordell Hull placed Assistant Secretary of State, Dean Acheson, in command of mobilizing America's new superpower status in world trade into legislative majorities.[49] In this he was aided by the Department's first Assistant Secretary of State for Economic Affairs, William L. Clayton. Known in Washington and business circles as "Mr. Cotton," Clayton was brought on board specifically for the purpose of helping to gain congressional approval of the administration's new global trade policy.[50] He was uniquely suited to the task. Clayton was Southern gentry with deep connections to the nation's corporate capitalist elite. In addition to being the founder of the world's largest cotton merchandizing firm, he was a founder of the CFR affiliate in Houston, Texas, and a member of the CFR, the BAC, and the CED.[51] Given his social and economic background, Clayton was able to appeal to members of Congress from the South (where cotton was the leading cash crop), as well as to members from industrial districts and states which were home to the nation's largest corporations. While Acheson worked in the background, it was Clayton who led the charge for the RTAA of 1945 in Congress; specifically, by appearing as the State Department's lead witness before the two committees with jurisdiction over trade: the House Committee on Ways and Means and the Senate Committee on Finance.

The Democratic Party leadership in both the House and the Senate was only too happy to turn the legislative process over to Acheson and Clayton. The "leadership in both houses helped those who helped themselves," recalled Acheson, and "[s]elf-help included not only the basic committee work, the hearings, and work with the committee staffs on their reports, but the initial canvassing of members' voting predilections."[52] Acheson and Clayton worked closely with the House and Senate leadership to establish a timeline for the administration's trade bill that worked to their perceived advantage. They prepared and distributed economic studies for every member of Congress detailing the contributions exports made to production and employment in their districts and states; they took charge of lining up witnesses to appear in support of the administration's trade bill at the hearings of the two congressional trade committees; they helped committee staff to prepare their reports on the bill; they lobbied every member of Congress individually in their offices; and when all else failed they distributed political favors to shore up wavering supporters or to buy off wavering opponents. In effect, the State Department took control of the legislative process in Congress, harnessing all the resources at its command to rally support for America's new global trade policy.

In its efforts to construct a legislative majority, the most important resource the State Department had at its command was the president himself; most importantly, the president's status as the nation's foreign policy leader and his ability to articulate a unified conception of the national interest. The "Constitution makes the President the piano player of foreign policy," declared Acheson, and in the final analysis it was up to the president to make the case for a new global trade policy.[53] Therefore, Acheson opened the State Department's legislative campaign on March 26, 1945, by distributing to every member of Congress a message from FDR urging "extension of the reciprocal trade agreements program." Penned by Acheson, the president's message set out the rationale for the new policy in the broadest terms of national interest—at once world historic and pragmatic.

> The coming total defeat of our enemies, and of the philosophy of conflict and aggression which they have represented, gives us a new chance and a better chance than we have ever had to bring about conditions under which the nations of the world substitute cooperation and sound business principles for warfare in economic relations.[54]

Arguing that "[i]t is essential that we move forward aggressively and make the most of this opportunity," the president's message concluded with a call for members of Congress to set aside differences of party and section, to reject special-interest pleas, and to act in the national interest.

The first test for the administration's trade bill (H.R. 2652) came in the House Committee on Ways and Means, which convened public hearings on the legislation from April 18 to May 14, 1945. Because the majority members of the Committee had signaled their intention to support the bill from the start—as long as the State Department "helped itself" by conducting a vigorous legislative campaign—the Department used the hearings as a platform to make its case to the full House.[55] In the context of the public hearings of the Ways and Means Committee, self-help meant demonstrating that the administration's new global trade policy enjoyed the support of broad sectors of American society, which was immediately forthcoming. Indeed, in addition to the BAC and the CED, which represented the economic interests of the nation's largest and most internationally oriented corporations, unqualified support for H.R. 2652 came from the United States Chamber of Commerce, the AFBF, and the CIO, many of whose members stood to gain from increased U.S. exports.[56] Coupled with the arguments of FDR (courtesy of Acheson) and the testimony of William L. Clayton and other administration officials (especially those from the Departments of Commerce and Agriculture), the Democratic majority on the Ways and Means Committee was persuaded that the new global trade policy promulgated by the State Department was, indeed, in the national interest.[57]

Republicans were not so convinced. Deeply distrustful of an aggrandizement of presidential power and fearing that the administration's new global trade policy would undermine the American economy by encouraging a flood of imports into the domestic market, the minority members of the Ways and Means Committee threw their support to a coalition of business, labor, and farm groups who testified against H.R. 2652. At the core of this coalition, led by the National Association of Manufacturers (NAM), the American Wage-Earners Protective Conference of the AFL, the National Grange, and the American Protective Tariff League, were capitalists and workers from labor-intensive industries who faced or feared increased foreign competition in the American market, farmers producing products that enjoyed historically high rates of tariff protection, and certain extractive industries.[58] In their minority report on H.R. 3240 (the former H.R. 2652), Republicans charged the majority members of the Committee with supporting a trade policy that sold out the U.S. economy and that was "a travesty upon the principles of free, representative government."[59]

> We do not charge the majority members of the committee with promoting [nefarious] objectives, but we do contend that in reporting out the bill they have bowed to the demands of the State Department and have been over-reached by the soft talk of world planners and globocrats who, we believe, would put the American worker, the American farmer, and the American businessman on the international auction block. It is most unfortunate that the majority members of the committee have thus been persuaded that the destiny of the United States lies on foreign soil.[60]

Having been defeated in their attempt to kill the administration's trade bill in committee, Republican members of Ways and Means moved to challenge the bill on the floor of the House. Much to the chagrin of the State Department, which had accepted the determination of the Rules Committee that it was safe to send its bill to the floor under an open rule, when Republicans held a party caucus on May 22, 1945, to organize for the floor fight, they were joined by Democrats representing the interests of fruit and vegetable farmers from California and Florida; furniture makers from Rhode Island; independent oil producers from Texas; and mining interests from Utah and West Virginia.[61] Startled by these defections and fearing more to come, Acheson beseeched President Truman to submit a letter to the House stressing his support for the bill "in which he lays his political head on the block with ours."[62] Written by Acheson, Truman's letter was read to the full House by Speaker Sam Rayburn "with great dramatic effect."[63] Designed to counter arguments that the bill would cause harm to domestic producers, the president's letter declared, "I have had drawn to my attention statements to the effect that this increased authority might be used in such a way as to endanger or 'trade out' segments of American industry, American agriculture, and American labor. No such action was taken under President Roosevelt and Cordell Hull, and no such action will take place under my Presidency."[64] This promise, of course, was political subterfuge, for the "trading out" of segments of U.S. industry, agriculture, and labor was a constituent feature of the State Department's global trade program. Indeed, it was vital to its success.[65]

Truman's assurances notwithstanding, sixteen amendments were offered on the floor of the House which threatened to kill or compromise the legislation. And in the closing minutes of debate Minnesota Republican Harold Knutson, who believed the bill would "break down the [protective] system that has made America great and prosperous," exercised his prerogative as ranking minority member on Ways and Means to call for a vote recommitting the bill to the Committee with instructions to report back the existing act for a period of two years.[66] However, all of these challenges failed; and following the defeat of the Knutson motion, the House voted to pass H.R. 3240, 239–153. On final passage, 205 Democrats, 33 Republicans, and 1 American Labor Party member voted in the affirmative. The core strength of the Democratic vote came from members representing the export interests of Southern cotton and tobacco farmers as well as industrial capitalists and labor unions concentrated in manufacturing districts spread across the Northeast, Midwest, and Far West. Not surprisingly, the thirty-three Republican defectors (one-fifth of those voting) came from districts in states with large industrial or agricultural export interests.[67]

While Democrats on the Ways and Means Committee closed ranks around the administration's trade bill, the same was not true of the majority on the Senate Finance Committee. After taking public testimony from the same business, labor, and farm groups that had appeared before Ways and Means, the ranking minority member on Finance, arch-protectionist Robert A. Taft, introduced a motion in closed session to strike the 50 percent tariff-cutting authority from the House bill. This motion was designed to gut the administration's trade bill, rendering it incapable of serving as a tool for world trade leadership. Indeed, as Acting Secretary of State Joseph C. Grew stated: the motion made the bill "an empty symbol of our hopes for cooperation with the rest of the world in [the] economic field." While Democrats outnumbered Republicans on the Committee, three broke party ranks in order to protect textile and mining interests in their respective states (Rhode Island, Massachusetts, and Colorado) and voted to support Taft's motion, which passed the Committee 10–9.[68]

Taft led the charge against the administration's new global trade policy on the Senate floor, recapitulating the arguments made by Republicans in the House that enactment of H.R. 3240 would result in "having . . . people driven out of work" and in trade policy-making by "executive fiat."[69] Senate Democratic leaders responded to these charges by reading that portion of Truman's letter to the House that gave his assurance that U.S. industry, labor, and agriculture would not be "traded out" in international trade negotiations; and by pointing out that the Supreme Court had upheld the constitutionality of the RTAA program since its inception in 1934.[70] These pronouncements notwithstanding, after the full Senate voted to reject the Finance Committee's bill and substitute the House bill in its place, Democratic and Republican opponents of H.R. 3240 introduced a series of amendments that sought to severely restrict the capacity of the president to unilaterally determine the national trade interest; as well as to protect specific domestic producers from foreign competition.[71]

All of these measures were voted down; and after seven days of debate, the Senate passed the legislation, 54–21. As in the House, Democratic support for the measure came from Southern states with strong export interests in cotton and tobacco and industrial states in the Northeast, Midwest, and Far West. The Republican Party split down the middle, with defectors coming from states with significant agricultural and industrial export interests.[72] Thus, after six years of planning and preparation in and around the executive branch, a year-long campaign of public education, and three months of intense legislative work on Capitol Hill, the State Department had its trade bill and the United States had a new global trade policy.

Conclusion: The Triumph of Globalism in the RTAA of 1945

The RTAA of 1945 was the first trade act of the postwar period which shifted trade policy-making authority from Congress to the president for the purpose of exercising world trade leadership. And it was pursuant to the act's tariff-cutting power that the State Department negotiated the GATT, thereby consummating a further transfer of trade policy-making authority from the American state to an international regime for the management of world trade.

This chapter has shown that America's new global trade policy was first and foremost a reaction to external events: the emergence of the United States as an economic superpower at the end of World War II and the concomitant generation of a political vacuum at the level of international trading relationships. Taken together, these external phenomena set the stage for a pattern of domestic politics that made possible a global turn in U.S. trade policy. At the core of this pattern was the formulation of a new American trade policy through a postwar policy planning alliance between the New York-based CFR and the U.S. Department of State. This globally oriented partnership was unambiguously anchored in America's superpower position in world trade, for it fused the economic interests of the nation's largest and most internationally oriented corporations, investment banks, and corporate law firms with the foreign policy interests of the executive branch.

Yet the CFR–State Department alliance was not able to implement its postwar plans without convincing Congress to delegate its Article I Section 8 power to "regulate commerce with foreign nations" to the president. Consequently, the State Department worked to mobilize America's new-found position as a world trade superpower into the legislative process. It did so in two ways: first, it mobilized support for the administration's trade bill among domestic economic groups with an interest in export expansion; and second, it couched the administration's trade bill in terms of foreign policy. The introduction of these elements into the trade policy-making process in Congress generated a global bias in its legislative proceedings and created the domestic political foundations for the enactment of the RTAA of 1945. Viewed in this light, the triumph of globalism in the RTAA of 1945 reflected a pattern of domestic politics anchored in the nation's superpower position in world trade—a pattern that reflected the domination of the trade policy-making process by the nation's largest and most internationally oriented corporations, investment banks, and corporate law firms and the executive branch of the American state.

Notes

1 The Truman administration launched the GATT and committed the United States to its binding rules and regulations by executive agreement, using the president's constitutional powers as chief of state to enter into such an agreement without congressional assent. The chief means to this end-run around Congress was a specially designed legal instrument, the Protocol of Provisional Application. Rather than setting up the GATT as a full-fledged international organization comprised of members, the global trade authority was negotiated and entered into in the form of a provisional international agreement among Contracting Parties. Although GATT was not legally binding on Congress, it *was* legally binding on the president.

2 Karl Polanyi, *The Great Transformation: The Political and Economic Origins of Our Time* (Boston: Beacon Press, 1944), 3–19.

3 E. H. Carr, *The Twenty Years' Crisis: 1919–39* (New York: Harper Collins, 1946), 234.

4 Clair Wilcox, *A Charter for World Trade* (New York: The Macmillan Company, 1949), 5–7.

5 See, for example, Heinz W. Arndt, *The Economic Lessons of the Nineteen-Thirties* (London: Oxford University Press, 1944); Charles P. Kindleberger, *The World in Depression, 1929–39* (Berkeley: University of California Press, 1986); and William E. Stoneman and Frank Freidel, eds., *A History of Economic Analysis of the Great Depression in America* (New York: Taylor & Francis, 1979).

6 David A. Lake, *Power, Protection, and Free Trade: International Sources of U.S. Commercial Strategy 1887–1939* (Ithaca, NY: Cornell University Press, 1988), 193–212.

7 William G. Beasley, *Japanese Imperialism, 1894–1945* (New York: Oxford University Press, 1987).

8 Lake, *Power, Protection, and Free Trade*, 189.

9 Albert O. Hirschman, *National Power and the Structure of Foreign Trade* (Berkeley: University of California Press, 1981).

10 Barry Eichengreen and Douglas A. Irwin, "Trade Blocs, Currency Blocs and the Reorientation of World Trade in the 1930s," *Journal of International Economics*, 38 (February 1995): 1–24.

11 Dean Acheson, *Present at the Creation: My Years in the State Department* (New York: W. W. Norton & Company, 1969), xvii.

12 Laurence H. Shoup and William Minter, *Imperial Brain Trust: The Council on Foreign Relations and United States Foreign Policy* (New York: Monthly Review Press, 1977), 11–28; Michael Wala, *The Council on Foreign Relations and American Foreign Policy in the Early Cold War* (Providence: Berghahn, 1994), 1–30.

13 Acheson, *Present at the Creation*, 15.

14 Wala, *The Council on Foreign Relations*, 30.

15 Cordell Hull, *The Memoirs of Cordell Hull*, Vol. II (New York: The Macmillan Company, 1948), 1625.

16 Robert D. Schulzinger, *The Wise Men of Foreign Affairs: the History of the Council on Foreign Relations* (New York: Columbia University Press, 1984), 30; Shoup and Minter, *Imperial Brain Trust*, 14–28; Wala, *The Council on Foreign Relations*, 15–30. While not strictly a business organization, the by-invitation-only membership of the CFR included many high-ranking officials from the nation's largest and most internationally oriented corporations, investment banks, and services companies (especially corporate law firms). In 1945, for example, more than half of the organization's nearly 700 members were corporation board members, investment bankers, and corporate lawyers. Among the remaining members—in descending order—were: educators, government officials, journalists and authors, economists, and representatives of organized labor (two) and national farm organizations (one). Included in the CFR's business membership were leaders from: General Motors; Westinghouse Electric Company; International Business Machines (IBM); Curtis-Wright Corporation; General Electric Company; United States Steel Corporation; National Cash Register Corporation; International Paper Company; Rockwell Manufacturing; Douglas Aircraft; Lockheed; Standard Oil; Chase National Bank; J. P. Morgan and Company; National City Bank of New York; Kuhn, Loeb and Company; Dillon, Read, and Company; First National Bank of New York; Bankers Trust Company; Goldman, Sachs and Company; Morgan, Stanley and Company; Guarantee Trust of New York; and Chemical Bank. See Council on Foreign Relations, *By-Laws with a List of Officers and Members* (New York: Council on Foreign Relations, January 1946).

17 Council on Foreign Relations, *The War and Peace Studies of the Council on Foreign Relations* (New York: Council on Foreign Relations, 1946); Shoup and Minter, *Imperial Brain Trust*, 118–125; Wala, *The Council on Foreign Relations*, 30–33.

18 Council on Foreign Relations, *The War and Peace Studies of the Council on Foreign Relations*, Appendix A. Among the economic elites who participated in the Economic and

Financial Group, the involvement of Ralph E. Flanders was especially significant. In addition to being President of the Federal Reserve Bank of Boston, Flanders was a Vice President of the Business Advisory Council (BAC), and a Trustee of the CED—organizations founded in 1933 and 1942, respectively, to represent the economic interests of America's largest and most internationally oriented corporations in matters of public policy. Flanders' participation in the Economic and Financial Group ensured not only that the interests of the BAC and the CED were represented in the formulation of America's new global trade policy, but that the evolution of the thinking of the Economic and Financial Group (if not its formal memoranda) was communicated to them.

19 Council on Foreign Relations, *Studies of American Interests in the War and the Peace*, Economic and Financial Group, Memorandum E-B 36, "Economic War Aims: Main Line of Approach" (New York: Council on Foreign Relations, 1941), 5.

20 Council on Foreign Relations, *Studies of American Interests in the War and the Peace*, Economic and Financial Group, Memorandum E-B 32, "Economic War Aims: General Considerations" (New York: Council on Foreign Relations, 1941), 13.

21 Economic and Financial Group, "Economic War Aims: Main Line of Approach," 5.

22 Council on Foreign Relations, *Studies of American Interests in the War and the Peace*, Economic and Financial Group, Memorandum E-B 55, "International Control of Trade Policies" (New York: Council on Foreign Relations, 1942), 1–4.

23 Ibid., 6–7.

24 Council on Foreign Relations, *Studies of American Interests in the War and the Peace*, Economic and Financial Group, Memorandum E-B 57, "Possible Revisions of the Trade Agreements Act" (New York: Council on Foreign Relations, 1942), 3.

25 Ibid., 4.

26 Ibid., 7.

27 Ibid., 8.

28 This senior team included: Undersecretary of State, Sumner Wells, a long-time CFR member; investment banker, CFR President, and Chairman of the War and Peace Studies, Norman H. Davis; CFR Board Director and Treasurer and former CEO of the United States Steel Corporation, Myron C. Taylor; and Vice Chairman of the War and Peace Studies Steering Committee and CFR Board Director, Johns Hopkins University President, Isaiah Bowman.

29 Harley A. Notter, *Postwar Foreign Policy Preparation, 1939–1945* (Washington, D.C.: GPO, 1949), 169.

30 E. F. Penrose, *Economic Planning for the Peace* (Princeton: Princeton University Press, 1953), 39.

31 Notter, *Postwar Foreign Policy*, 172.

32 Ibid., 63–64.

33 Ibid., 154.

34 Council on Foreign Relations, *The War and Peace Studies*, 6.

35 Notter, *Postwar Foreign Policy*, 138–140.

36 Ibid., 622–624.

37 Ibid., 95.

38 Ibid., 71–78. It is important to point out that the inclusion of these new members was on a purely consultative basis. They did not participate in policy making.

39 Ibid., 75.

40 Hull, *Memoirs*, 1656.

41 Notter, *Postwar Foreign Policy*, 219.

42 By mid-1944, the Informal Agenda Group had changed its name to the Post-War Programs Committee and had added a new member to its elite roster: Edward R. Stettinius, Jr., Cordell Hull's new Undersecretary of State. A CFR member, Stettinius was the former Vice Chairman of General Motors and Senior Administrator of U.S. Steel.

Thus, at the time the RTAA of 1945 was drafted the ECEFP was taking its direction from a senior group in the State Department comprised of Cordell Hull; Norman H. Davis; Myron C. Taylor; Isaiah Bowman; and Edward R. Stettinius, Jr.

43 National Archives. Committee on Trade Agreements and Committee on Trade Barriers, 1945, *Legislative Program for Renewal and Expansion of Trade Agreements Authority and for Multilateral Negotiations*, February 6, International Trade Files, Box 101, Trade Barrier Minutes; National Archives, Executive Committee on Economic Foreign Policy, 1945, *Legislative Program on Trade Barriers*, February 8, Interdepartmental and Intradepartmental Committees, Box 47, ECEFP Docs.; National Archives, *Objectives of a Legislative Program on Trade Barriers*, March 2, Interdepartmental and Intradepartmental Committees, Box 47, ECEFP Docs.; National Archives, *Minutes of the Meeting of the Executive Committee on Economic Foreign Policy*, March 9, Interdepartmental and Intradepartmental Committees, Box 57, ECEFP Minutes; National Archives, *Minutes of the Meeting of the Executive Committee on Economic Foreign Policy*, March 16, Interdepartmental and Intradepartmental Committees, Box 57, ECEFP Minutes.

44 National Archives. Executive Committee on Economic Foreign Policy, *Minutes of the Meeting of the Executive Committee on Economic Foreign Policy*.

45 Notter, *Postwar Foreign Policy*, 359.

46 National Archives. William A. Fowler, Executive Committee on Economic Foreign Policy, 1945, *Legislative Program on Trade Barriers*, February 8, Interdepartmental and Intradepartmental Committees, ECEFP Docs., Box 47.

47 Cordell Hull, "National Foreign Trade Week," *Department of State Bulletin* 10 (256) 1944, 480.

48 U.S. Congress. House. Robert A. Taft, *1945 Extension of the Reciprocal Trade Agreements Act: Hearings before the Committee on Ways and Means*, U.S. House of Representatives, 79th Cong. 1st sess. on H.R. 2652, superseded by H.R. 324, 1637.

49 Acheson, *Present at the Creation*, 106–109.

50 U.S. Congress. House. Committee on Ways and Means, *Foreign Trade Agreements, Report from the Committee on Ways and Means to Accompany H.R. 3240*, U.S. House of Representatives, 79th Cong., 1st sess., 19.

51 As mentioned earlier, the BAC and the CED were founded in 1933 and 1942 respectively to represent the interests of the nation's largest and most internationally oriented corporations in matters of public policy. Between them they counted among their membership more than 200 of the nation's largest financial, commercial, transportation, and service companies.

52 Acheson, *Present at the Creation*, 98.

53 Ibid., 85.

54 U.S. Congress. House. *Message from the President of the United States urging Extension of the Reciprocal Trade Agreements Program*, U.S. House of Representatives, 79th Cong., 1st sess., March 26, 1945, Document No. 124, 3.

55 Congressional Quarterly, "Extension of Reciprocal Trade Agreements," *Congressional Quarterly Annual Report* (Washington, D.C.: CQ Press, 1945), 311.

56 Committee on Ways and Means, *1945 Extension of the Reciprocal Trade Agreements Act*.

57 As the Committee's Majority Report declared: "The committee has . . . had the benefit of the views of a representative cross section of practically all of the interests of the country which would be affected by this legislation. Although a simple numerical count indicates more witnesses in opposition than those favoring the program, when account is taken of the interests represented by all the witnesses and the number of people for whom they spoke, the testimony is overwhelmingly in favor of passage of the bill" (14).

58 Committee on Ways and Means, *1945 Extension of the Reciprocal Trade Agreements Act*.

59 Committee on Ways and Means, *Foreign Trade Agreements, Report*, 6.

60 Committee on Ways and Means, *1945 Extension of the Reciprocal Trade Agreements Act*, 4.

61 Congressional Quarterly, "Extension of Reciprocal Trade Agreements," 312.
62 Acheson, *Present at the Creation*, 107.
63 Ibid.
64 Cited in Congressional Quarterly, "Extension of Reciprocal Trade Agreements," 315.
65 The Economic and Financial Group of the War and Peace Studies Project was fully cognizant of the fact that its global trade program would require a fundamental altera- tion in the trade-related aspects of the nation's production structure. In particular, the Group was aware that the international economic processes set in motion by its program would drive uncompetitive firms and industries out of business—leading to a hollowing-out of the nation's economy in certain lines of production. As the Group put it in Memorandum E-B 76, "Persons attached to protected industries are naturally loathe to face the necessity of shifting into other lines of production, and yet many of them must do so if a program for trade barrier reduction is to accomplish really significant economic results." See Council on Foreign Relations, *Studies of American Interests in the War and the Peace*, Economic and Financial Group, Memorandum E-B 76, "Coupling Economic Adaptation with Trade Policy" (New York: Council on Foreign Relations, 1945), 1.
66 Since the existing RTAA of 1943 contained no tariff-cutting authority, this would have killed the administration's new global trade program.
67 Congressional Quarterly, "Extension of Reciprocal Trade Agreements," 308–309.
68 Ibid., 315.
69 Ibid.
70 Ibid., 315–316.
71 Ibid., 315–317.
72 Ibid., 305.

5

ATLANTIC PARTNERSHIP

The Trade Expansion Act of 1962

Our supreme economic challenge at this moment . . . is the task of achieving maximum interaction and cooperation between the expanding industrial societies of North America and Western Europe . . . . Our ability to meet this challenge depends in large measure upon the manner in which these two great industrial systems of the Atlantic develop and utilize their vast resources and upon the politics and practices which guide their trade with each [other] and with the rest of the world. We are determined that the United States shall adopt policies which will enable us to meet this challenge, and thereby resume our proper role of leadership in the development of a dynamic and prosperous free-world economy.

John F. Kennedy (1961)

The TEA of 1962 marked the second major assertion of American world trade leadership in the postwar period and initiated a higher stage in the triumph of globalism in American trade politics. A response to the emergence of the EEC as a major trading power, and designed to steer the EEC toward a low-tariff, GATT-centered trade policy, the TEA granted the president more authority to roll back U.S. tariff barriers through multilateral negotiations than any trade act since the RTAA of 1945. Indeed, compared to the RTAA of 1945, the TEA radically expanded presidential power in the field of trade. Most importantly, the act empowered the president, for a period of five years, to cut American tariffs by 50 percent of their prevailing rates, reduce to zero tariffs of 5 percent or less, and to eliminate tariffs completely on economic sectors where the combined total of European Economic Community and U.S. exports were 80 percent or more of the world total (the so-called dominant supplier provision). It was under the auspices of the TEA of 1962 that the United States launched the second watershed trade round in GATT history—the Kennedy Round of Multilateral Negotiations, which reduced most tariffs among advanced industrial countries to their lowest levels in history, and resulted in a near-doubling of the countries participating in the regime.

The origins of the TEA are to be found in a global trade policy planning alliance between the CFR and CED and the Department of State—an alliance that reflected the superpower structure in American society and state. Not only was this superpower alliance responsible for the formulation of the Kennedy Administration's trade bill, its participants coordinated the campaign for the enactment of the TEA by Congress. Their success in this effort was—first and foremost—a product of America's superpower position within the GATT regime; for this status enabled the architects of the TEA to cast the legislation in systemic terms, as vital to the national interest at a critical juncture in the development of the postwar world trading system. In particular, it enabled them to mobilize domestic economic groups with an interest in export expansion, and their supporters in Congress, around a new free trade initiative, one designed to forge an "Atlantic Partnership" with the EEC for the purpose of expanding the scale and scope of the GATT regime, and the degree of trade liberalization within it. And while enactment of the TEA was eased by a number of concessions to protectionist economic groups and their supporters in Congress, none of these actions fundamentally threatened the overriding objectives of the legislation.

The Global Challenge: The Rise of the European Economic Community

The principal objective of the TEA of 1962 was to respond to the creation of the EEC. The EEC was the natural outgrowth of America's efforts in the 1940s and 1950s to foster Western European economic integration as part of the nation's effort to rebuild the war-torn world economy and to create a liberal international economic order. One of the first steps in this direction was taken in 1947 when seventeen Western European states formed the Organization for European Economic Cooperation (OEEC) to allocate Marshall Plan aid and to coordinate their reconstruction efforts. Although the OEEC had no power over its member states, it served as a forum within which member countries could address their international payments and trade problems in a formal and ongoing manner. Within the first few years of its operation, the OEEC developed the European Payments Union and a code of trade liberalization to help restore commerce among its members. Coupled with Marshall Plan aid, these efforts fostered the recovery of Western Europe.[1]

With the OEEC in full swing, in 1950 the French foreign minister, Robert Schuman, proposed that France and West Germany pool their coal and steel resources in a new organization which other European nations could join. The idea behind the proposal was to create a regional authority to manage a unified coal and steel market among member states similar to that which existed in the United States. After almost two years of discussion, in 1952 six OEEC members, with the full backing of the United States, decided to move forward with the formation of the European Coal and Steel Community (ECSC): France, West Germany, Italy, Belgium, the Netherlands, and Luxembourg. The ECSC established a single market for coal and steel among its members and moved rapidly to abolish all tariffs and quotas on these products. A key ingredient in the ECSC's success was its management by a supranational commission which exercised control over the coal and steel markets in all six countries.

From the start, the ECSC was seen by its members as the first step toward fuller economic integration; and by 1955 the six ECSC nations were discussing the formation of a more far-reaching economic union. The result was the Treaty of Rome, which came into force on January 1, 1958. Signed by the six ECSC nations, and endorsed by the United States, the Treaty of Rome established the EEC. The EEC was modeled directly on the ECSC, although its economic reach was much greater. At the economic core of the EEC was the goal of moving toward a single common market for goods, capital, services, and labor among its members. The Treaty of Rome also contemplated the harmonization of various national policies which directly affected commerce within the EEC, including exchange restrictions, subsidies, taxation, and business law. The Treaty also called for the creation of a common transportation policy, a common agricultural policy, and a number of financial institutions designed to promote economic development and adjustment. The EEC was managed by a Commission and Council of Ministers comprised of representatives from the six member states. While any member of the EEC could exercise a veto over its policy through the Council of Ministers, the Community was designed to function as a supranational authority. Its ultimate objective was to turn its members as effectively as possible into a single economic unit.

Although the United States supported the creation of the EEC, the Community presented three problems for the GATT-centered world trading system. By far the most important was the formation of the Community's CXT. While the EEC's internal policy was clear—movement toward free trade among its members—its external trade policy remained an open question. It was not at all clear by the early 1960s if the EEC would impose high external tariffs in an attempt to reduce foreign competition and establish a Western European protectionist trade bloc, or if it would join with the United States in promoting an open world trading system centered on the GATT. If the EEC were to reject an outward-looking trade policy and retreat within a high tariff wall, it would severely damage America's efforts to promote an international regime of freer trade. Moreover, it would limit U.S exports to the EEC (the nation's second largest export market in 1960), and divert many exports heading to the EEC from non-members to the United States. This was particularly true of Japan, which suffered severe discrimination at the hands of the Europeans.

These were not remote possibilities. Indeed, by 1960 the disruptive impact of the EEC on the world trading system already was being felt; for in that year, after failing to negotiate terms of admission to the Common Market that it could accept, Great Britain organized a rival European Free Trade Association (EFTA), which created an exclusive free trade zone between itself, its Commonwealth territories and states, and six European nations: Austria, Switzerland, Portugal, Denmark, Norway, and Sweden. While the EFTA did not establish a common external tariff for its members, and thus was not a trading bloc in the full sense, it did raise the specter of rival trading blocs on either side of the English Channel—a development that could fragment the GATT, as well as challenge Western European economic integration.

The second major problem posed by the EEC to the world trading system was the creation of its CAP. The CAP was initially contemplated in the Treaty of Rome and promulgated in concrete proposals in 1960. The foremost goal of the CAP was to make the EEC as self-sufficient in agriculture as possible. At the heart of the CAP was a system of price supports, variable levies, and export subsidies. Price supports were designed to keep farmers on the land by giving them direct cash payments from the EEC. Variable levies (usually in the form of quotas or very high tariffs) were designed to moderate or eliminate foreign agricultural competition in targeted EEC markets. And export subsidies were used to reduce the selling price of many EEC agricultural products on world markets. Although many GATT nations, including the United States, supported programs designed to promote their agricultural sectors, the CAP was a particularly protectionist and discriminatory arrangement. Not only did it undermine the efforts of more efficient agricultural producers to sell in the Common Market, it undermined their efforts to sell in world markets as well.

The final problem posed by the EEC was its negotiation of a network of trade agreements with its "Associated Territories"—mainly the current and former colonies of its members located in Africa. Because these agreements provided preferential access to the Common Market by associated territories and states, and were negotiated on a bilateral basis outside the framework of the GATT, they challenged the regime's principles of nondiscrimination and multilateralism. As a practical matter, their effects fell most heavily upon producers of agricultural products and raw materials in other parts of the developing world, particularly Latin America.

These problems notwithstanding, the rise of the EEC also generated opportunities for the liberalization and expansion of the GATT-centered world trading system. At the time the EEC was founded, the rate of economic growth for its six members was nearly twice as fast as for the United States; and its drive toward internal free trade was likely to act as a spur to this growth. Both of these factors meant that the EEC's capacity to absorb imports was growing rapidly; indeed, so fast was this growth that even with higher tariffs, imports into the EEC were projected to increase over time as a result of rising demand. Yet if the EEC could be steered toward a more liberal trade policy, one that resolved the major problems the Common Market posed for the GATT regime, its creation could be harnessed to create a more open and non-discriminatory world trading system. A general lowering of EEC tariffs would contribute to the growth of export industries in other GATT nations; and reducing or eliminating the EEC's discriminatory treatment of Japanese exports, as well as the exports of non-Associated Territories, would make the world trading system fairer and more market oriented. Perhaps most importantly, if a rapprochement could be reached between the EEC and England (one that brought England into the EEC), the political underpinnings of Western European economic integration would be strengthened, the zone of free trade in the region would be expanded, and a new trade-liberalizing force would be introduced into the Common Market that could temper the more protectionist proclivities of the French.[2]

The task of resolving the EEC's impact on the postwar world trading system fell to the United States, which by virtue of its superpower position within the GATT was the only nation with the capacity to steer the EEC toward an outward-looking and regime-consistent trade policy. The question was, how to do it? The answer was the TEA of 1962, which was designed to forge an "Atlantic Partnership" between the United States and the EEC within the framework of a new global trade round—a round geared toward expanding the scale and scope of the GATT and to more fully integrate the EEC into the regime.

The Formulation of the TEA of 1962

The origins of the TEA of 1962 are to be found in a global trade policy planning alliance between the CFR and the CED and the Department of State. And in this the CFR and the CED were the first to move.[3]

At the time when the EEC was created the ability of the United States to respond with the initiation of a major international trade round was highly constrained. The most recent trade act—the RTAA of 1958—was a meager statute. Although the act gave the president the power to enter into international trade agreements for a period of four years (the most extensive grant of such authority up to that time), it only authorized the chief executive to reduce American tariffs by up to 20 percent of their prevailing levels.[4] In addition, the act contained a congressionally sponsored "peril point" provision, which required the president to submit to the U.S. Tariff Commission a list of all items on which he planned to negotiate and required the Commission to recommend minimum rates necessary to protect domestic production of articles that competed with those on which duties were to be lowered.[5] If the president made agreements undercutting these "peril points," he had to explain to Congress his reason for doing so. Although peril points were merely advisory, State Department trade officials took them seriously; and, as a result, the 20 percent tariff-cutting authority granted in the RTAA of 1958 was applicable to only 17.5 percent of imports from nations with whom they sought to negotiate within the framework of the Dillon Round of Multilateral Trade Negotiations (1960–1961), including the newly formed EEC.[6]

As a result, the average reduction in industrial tariffs produced by the Dillon Round was only 10 percent; and that did little to dissolve the emerging system-wide impact of the EEC on the GATT regime.[7] Clearly, if the United States was to effectively respond to the rise of the EEC, the president—and through him U.S. trade negotiators—would require substantially more tariff-cutting power than Congress had authorized in the RTAA of 1958.

The problems posed by the EEC for the GATT regime, coupled with the inability of the United States to effectively respond, were not lost on the CFR and the CED. Although in the wake of the RTAA of 1958 "[i]t was conventional thinking [in the State Department] that there was no chance that the recipro-cal trade legislation could be extended once again . . . [because] . . . Congress wouldn't do it," the leaders of the CFR and the CED were undeterred.[8] Thus, in the late 1950s both organizations initiated research and policy-planning projects designed to assess the implications of the EEC for the world trading system and to push for a new trade bill with broadly expanded negotiating powers for the president.

The response of the CFR and the CED to the rise of the EEC was to join forces in a common effort to convince public officials—mainly within the execu-tive branch—that the United States should meet this development with a major new assertion of American world trade leadership. The CED took the lead in this endeavor. Early in 1958, just months after the Treaty of Rome took effect, the CED's Research and Policy Committee called together its Subcommittee on International Economic Policy to study the emergence of the EEC and to make recommendations concerning American policy toward it. This subcommittee was comprised of fourteen individuals, most of whom represented investment banks, multinational oil corporations, and a variety of industrial concerns, including: the Standard Oil Company; the Olin Mathieson Chemical Corporations; and the General Electric Company.[9] Eleven of the subcommittee's members were also members of the CFR, including investment banker Howard C. Petersen, who had chaired the subcommittee in the early 1950s. In 1961 President Kennedy would appoint Petersen to serve as his Special Assistant on International Trade Policy; and in this capacity Petersen would help direct the administration's efforts to formulate the TEA and to move the bill through Congress.

The CED's Subcommittee on International Economic Policy met continu-ously for more than a year, beginning in early 1958. During this time the group produced two authoritative reports which were the first significant investigations into the implications of the formation of the EEC on the world trading system.[10] Both of these reports saw great economic opportunities for the American and world economies if the EEC pursued an outward-looking, GATT-centered trade policy. This conclusion was rooted in the belief that the creation of the Com-mon Market would "increase the efficiency and raise the standard of living of the whole area," which would expand the EEC's global purchasing power.[11] If the EEC could be persuaded to pursue an outward-looking, GATT-centered trade policy, the subcommittee reasoned, this expanding purchasing power could serve as an engine of global economic growth, for the EEC would be able to absorb an ever-growing volume of the world's exports. At the same time, however, the subcommittee argued that a failure of the EEC to adopt such a trade policy could "solidify trade barriers between regions of the world . . . [and] . . . degenerat[e] into a new economic isolationism."[12] The subcommittee concluded that the "most constructive way to tie the Common Market into the world economy would be to reduce world barriers to trade substantially. To take the initiative in such a move should be the main response of the United States to the Common Market."[13] More specifically, the subcommittee called for "a bold new United States initiative for the reduction of trade barriers" within the framework of a new round of international trade negotiations under the auspices of the GATT.[14] This recommendation was the first articulation of the broad strategic plan that would frame the Kennedy administration's approach to the rise of the EEC; and it would be directly communicated to the president through the appointment of Howard C. Petersen as the President's Special Assistant on International Trade Policy.

In addition to the work of the CED, early in 1959 the CFR formed its own group to examine the problems posed by the EEC for the world trading system. Organized under the auspices of the CFR's Committee on Studies, the Discussion Group on U.S. Foreign Trade Policy was chaired by Alfred C. Neal, President of the CED, and included Howard C. Petersen. Neal's direction of the CFR trade policy group helped to integrate its work with that of the CED. Although Neal was not a direct participant in the CED's Subcommittee on International Economic Policies, as president of the organization he was intimately involved in all phases of its work. In 1959–1960, the CFR trade policy group met monthly, during which time more than twenty individuals—including corporate directors, corporate lawyers, and academics—participated in the group's activities. While the CFR's trade policy group did not produce a final report, one of its leaders went on to serve as President Kennedy's Under Secretary of State for Economic Affairs. This leader was international corporate lawyer George W. Ball. As Under Secretary of State for Economic Affairs, Ball would work closely with Howard C. Petersen in drafting the TEA and in managing the administration's campaign to push it through Congress.[15]

It is hard to prove a counterfactual, so it is difficult to say how the United States would have responded to the rise of the EEC if the presidential election of 1960 had gone the other way. Yet it is instructive that slightly more than a decade later the Nixon administration would champion the Trade Act of 1974, which would grant the president more international trade-negotiating authority than ever before and would allow the United States to launch the third watershed trade round of the postwar period: the Tokyo Round of Multilateral Trade Negotiations. As it was, the 1960 presidential election was won by John F. Kennedy.

Kennedy was not a doctrinaire free trader; and "[t]here was nothing crystal-clear in [his] record on trade policy."[16] Indeed, as a congressman and senator, he had defended the Massachusetts textile industry, going so far as to vote to recommit the 1949 extension of the Reciprocal Trade Agreements Act to the House Ways and Means Committee, "which might well have broken the continuity of American trade policy at a crucial time."[17] Furthermore, during his presidential campaign, Kennedy had promised the textile industry that his administration would take action to protect it from rising foreign competition in the American market. Yet, serving in Congress and running for president is not the same thing as governing from the Oval Office, especially where foreign policy is concerned. And within weeks of his election Kennedy turned to George W. Ball for guidance in the formulation of his administrations' trade policy. Ball, it will be recalled, was an international corporate lawyer and a member of the CFR's trade policy group. His law firm—Clearly, Gottlieb, Friendly, and Ball—had been associated with the CFR since World War II and had numerous foreign clients, including the Venezuelan Chamber of Commerce (composed mainly of U.S. multinational oil companies); Cuban sugar interests; the ECSC; and the EEC—for whom Ball served as its Washington attorney.[18] Most of Ball's legal work focused on trade policy. Perhaps most importantly, in the early 1950s he had helped to form the CNTP for the purpose of lobbying Congress for freer trade. Consisting of the presidents, directors, or high-ranking board members of thirty-four investment banks, industrial corporations, and corporate law firms—including the Chase National Bank, the Bank of America, the Standard Oil Company, Pitney-Bowes, IBM, the Ford Motor Company, the Gillette Company, Bechtel Corporation, and W. R. Grace and Company—the CNTP quickly became "the recognized spokesman for the freer-trade point of view" among Washington lobby groups.[19] Indeed, the CNTP worked closely with the Eisenhower Administration to help spearhead its successful campaigns to secure congressional renewal of the RTAA in 1954, 1955, and 1958.

Early in November 1960, President-elect Kennedy selected Ball to head a pre-inaugural task force to study U.S. foreign economic policy, including trade policy. In its report on trade policy, presented to Kennedy just prior to his inauguration, the so-called "Ball Committee" warned that the failure of the of the United States to confront the challenge of the EEC with a major new effort to liberalize world trade could result in the "disintegration of the Free World economy into separate trading systems."[20] The report specifically called on the president-elect to seek congressional authority to cut American tariffs by as much as 50 percent of their prevailing rates through negotiations with the EEC and other countries, within the framework of a new GATT trade round. At the same time, the report called for the creation of an adjustment assistance program for businesses and workers harmed by rising foreign competition in the American market; as well as a modified escape-clause provision allowing qualified industries to apply for temporary protection. Echoing the trade policy work of the CFR and the CED, the report of the Ball Committee formed the basis for the TEA of 1962.

Shortly following his inauguration as the 35th President of the United States, Kennedy appointed Ball to serve as his Under Secretary of State for Economic

Affairs.[21] In this capacity, Ball was charged with the task of developing the administration's strategy for dealing with the challenge of the EEC and for formulating America's response. As a first step, Ball recommended the creation of two trade-policy working groups: one in the State Department under his command to formulate general policy; the other in the White House to coordinate the day-to-day campaign for the administration's trade bill.[22] Kennedy accepted Ball's proposal; and to direct the special White House trade office he appointed a longtime CED trade policy leader, Howard C. Petersen. A Republican whose appointment helped the administration to cast its new trade policy as a bi-partisan undertaking, Petersen was a former Wall Street lawyer turned investment banker, and a member of the CFR's study group on U.S. Foreign Trade Policy. Not only was Petersen an active member of the CED's Subcommittee on International Economic Policy, he had served as that subcommittee's chairman in the early 1950s.[23]

Work on the administration's trade bill began in earnest in September 1961. During that month the Ball group in the State Department and the Petersen group in the White House began an extensive review of American trade policy. After a good deal of debate concerning the timing and scope of a new trade bill, these groups were merged into a single steering committee chaired by Howard C. Petersen.[24] This committee included top representatives from the Departments of State, Commerce, and Labor—including George W. Ball; and during December 1961, and early January 1962, its members went over every major issue raised in the Ball and Petersen groups and reached agreement on the content of an administration trade bill. The draft statute they arrived at incorporated many of the suggestions of Ball's pre-inaugural task force, and contemplated the most sweeping delegation of trade policy-making power from Congress to the president since the inauguration of the RTAA program in 1934. More specifically, the draft statute authorized the president, for a period of five years, to cut American tariffs by up to 50 percent of their 1962 rates through reciprocal trade agreements; to reduce to zero all tariffs where the combined exports of the U.S. and EEC accounted for 80 percent of the world market (designed to provide an incentive for England to join the EEC); and to reduce to zero all tariffs of 5 percent or less. The draft statute also called for the creation of an adjustment assistance program to help qualified industries and workers adjust to rising foreign competition in the American market, as well as a modified escape-clause procedure. The inclusion of the adjustment assistance and escape-clause provisions was designed to gain political support for the administration's trade bill from economic groups which generally favored freer trade, but were concerned about the domestic economic consequences of American world trade leadership. In neither case did they compromise the fundamental purpose of the legislation: the delegation of major new negotiating authority to the president for the purpose of launching a major new trade round.

The work of drafting the TEA was carried on deep within the executive branch and largely out of public view. It was paralleled, however, by a vigorous "public relations campaign to sell the bill across the country the likes of which had seldom been seen."[25] This campaign was waged on two broad fronts. One was to build a globally oriented coalition of business, labor, and farm groups that could present a united front in support of congressional enactment of the TEA. The other was to undercut potential protectionist opposition to the bill by making concessions to a number of major industries which faced or feared rising foreign competition in the American market and could make enactment of the TEA difficult.

The administration's campaign to build society-based and congressional support for the TEA was coordinated by Petersen's White House trade office, working in conjunction with Ball's office in the State Department. Broadly speaking, Ball and Petersen worked on two different tracks. On the one hand, Ball's efforts were focused on the roll-out of a high-profile campaign designed to generate broad-based public support for the administration's trade bill. On the other hand, Petersen's efforts were focused on mobilizing economic groups behind the TEA, as well as coordinating the administration's campaign to push the legislation through Congress.

The campaign for the TEA began on November 1, 1961, when Ball delivered the keynote speech at the annual National Foreign Trade Convention of the National Foreign Trade Council—an organization of the nation's largest exporting and importing companies. In his speech, "Threshold of a New Trading World," Ball set out the main themes of the administration's thinking on trade, especially as it related to the dangers and opportunities presented by the rise of the EEC to the United States and the world trading system as whole. The rise of the EEC, Ball argued, marked the dawn of "a new era" in international trading relationships, which if not properly managed could spark "an inward-looking economic nationalism"—not only in the EEC but also in the United States and across the GATT regime. However, if the United States took the lead in steering the EEC toward an outward-looking, low-tariff trade policy within the framework of the GATT, it would "bring about the kind of open trading world in which our most efficient export industries can share the potential of this new market." While Ball did not present the details of the administration's trade bill, he let it be known that "the program will represent a set of new proposals tailored to the unprecedented requirements of a radically altered trading world."[26] Yet the high point of the convention came when Ball read a message from the president which drove home the themes set out by Ball.

> Our supreme economic challenge at this moment in our history does not arise from the Sino-Soviet bloc itself. Our greatest immediate challenge is the task of achieving maximum interaction and cooperation between the expanding industrial societies of North America and Western Europe. . . . We are determined that the United States shall adopt policies which will enable us to meet this challenge, and thereby resume our proper role of leadership in the development of a dynamic and prosperous free-world economy.

It is essential that we have new tools to deal with the problems of international trade in a new and challenging world. The forging of these tools is a task that must be shared by all segments of American society—business, industry, agriculture, and labor, as well as the Government itself. I can assure you that we are prepared to take whatever steps may be necessary to protect and promote our national interests.[27]

Over the next six months, in scores of appearances before business, labor, and farm groups, members of the administration delivered the message that the rise of the EEC required a major new effort on the part of the United States to liberalize world trade. The most important interventions, however, were made by the president himself. On December 6, 1961, Kennedy appeared in person at the annual convention of the NAM, where he urged support for U.S. cooperation with the EEC for the purpose of lowering tariffs and thereby stimulating international trade and global economic growth. Declaring that "[t]he hour of decision has arrived," the president argued that the existing RTAA program "must not simply be renewed, it must be replaced."[28] While not revealing a specific piece of legislation, the president concluded that the trade issue would not be postponed until after the 1962 congressional elections.

Kennedy continued these themes the next day at the national convention of the AFL-CIO in Miami Beach, Florida, which adopted a resolution supporting the administration's trade program as long as it provided assistance or relief to workers who lost their jobs due to foreign competition.[29] Yet the president's most important intervention came in January 1962, when he made trade policy a cornerstone of his State of the Union Address. Outlining the major tariff-cutting provisions of the administration's trade bill, the president cast the legislation in terms of America's national interest in the exercise of world leadership.

But the greatest [foreign policy] challenge of all is posed by the growth of the European Common Market. Assuming the accession of the United Kingdom, there will arise across the Atlantic a trading partner behind a single external tariff similar to ours with an economy which nearly equals our own. Will we in this country adapt our thinking to these new prospects and patterns—or will we wait until events have passed us by?

This is the year to decide. The Reciprocal Trade Act is expiring. We need a new law—a bold new instrument of American trade policy. Our decision could well affect the unity of the West, the course of the Cold War, and the economic growth of our Nation for a generation to come.

Members of Congress: The United States did not rise to greatness by waiting for others to lead. This Nation is the world's foremost manufacturer, farmer, banker, consumer, and exporter. The Common Market is moving ahead at an economic growth rate twice ours. . . . The opportunity is ours—the initiative is up to us—and I believe that 1962 is the time.[30]

Alongside the administration's high-profile public relations campaign (which was coordinated by Ball), Howard C. Petersen's White House trade office undertook a feverish campaign to rally support for the TEA among society-based groups which dominated world markets and thus had a direct economic interest in the enactment of the legislation. Petersen maintained an active correspondence with more than a hundred groups, most of which were among the nation's largest and most internationally oriented corporations, including, for example: Bank of America; Chase National Bank; Chemical Bank New York Trust Company; First National City Bank; Westinghouse Electric Corporation; Whirlpool Corporation; the Proctor & Gamble Company; the Ford Motor Company; the Boeing Corporation; United Fruit Company; and Standard Oil Company.[31] His most active correspondence, however, was with the CNTP—the free trade lobby group George W. Ball helped to found in 1953. Petersen and the chairman of the CNTP, Carl J. Gilbert, Chairman of the Gillette Company and a CED Trustee, were in frequent communication to coordinate strategy. Indeed, as former Secretary of Commerce Luther Hodges recalled: the CNTP did "a very great deal from the public relations angle."[32] Petersen also maintained ongoing contacts with the CFR, the CED, the National Council of American Importers (the largest organization of U.S. importing firms), and the Foreign Economic Committee of the U.S. Chamber of Commerce (which was dominated by multinational corporations, including General Motors; the Ford Motor Company; and the Gulf Oil Corporation). Furthermore, he kept up a hectic schedule of public appearances. However, of the more than fifty speeches Petersen delivered, he gave only one each to the AFL-CIO and the NAM, and none to the AFBF, the largest farm group in America. Finally, in addition to rallying society-based support for the TEA, Petersen also coordinated the administration's legislative campaign in Congress, which included lining up witnesses to testify at the House and Senate trade hearings, as well as lobbying individual members to support the administration's trade bill.

The final aspect of the administration's campaign to mobilize support for the TEA was an attempt to diffuse potential opposition to the legislation among protectionist economic groups and their supporters in Congress. The most important initiative in this regard involved the textile industry, which by the time Kennedy took office had become the largest and most outspoken group demanding curbs on imports. Spread throughout New England and the South, the textile industry employed nearly two million workers and carried substantial weight in Congress. Indeed, by 1962, 128 members of the House of Representatives were members of an informal textile caucus, who threatened to vote against the administration's trade bill unless presidential action was taken to limit rising textile imports into the American market. Although at least one member of the Kennedy administration believed it would be possible to secure majorities in Congress without bowing to the textile industry (principally by focusing more effort on mobilizing Northeastern Republicans), the president was taking no chances.[33] Thus, in July

1961, the United States negotiated what became known as the "Short-Term Textile Arrangement," which was followed in February 1962 by a "Long-Term Arrangement" (LTA). The LTA allowed a nation threatened by cotton textile imports to freeze those imports for two years, after which time it could limit their increase to 5 percent a year.[34] While the LTA allowed an increase of 5 percent a year in cotton textile imports into the United States, the agreement was hailed by the industry and most of its supporters in Congress. As one member of the informal textile caucus in the House put it: "The Administration worked for us . . . . [N]ow we can work for the Administration on the bill."[35] In addition to textiles, President Kennedy also threw sops to the domestic (independent) oil industry; Pacific Northwest timber interests; and the carpet and glass industries. These moves by the administration deeply fractured whatever major protectionist opposition might have developed against the TEA. Indeed, as one observer put it: "the Administration's moves . . . cracks the opposition's ranks wide open."[36]

The Enactment of the TEA of 1962

With its public relations campaign in high gear, and potential protectionist opposition blunted by side-payments, President Kennedy transmitted the TEA to the House of Representatives on January 25, 1962. Although the legislation "was heavily soaped,"[37] administration trade officials geared up for a major fight in Congress. As former Secretary of Commerce Luther Hodges recalled: "The chief difficulty in all of this was how are you going to get [it] through the House and the Senate, particularly the House Ways and Means Committee."[38] That the administration succeeded was the result of two overriding factors—both anchored in America's position as a superpower in world trade. First, the legislation was sold to Congress as a matter of foreign policy (the exercise of world trade leadership in the creation of an "Atlantic Partnership" with the EEC) and as vital to America's national interests. As President Kennedy put it in his message accompanying the introduction of the TEA to Congress:

> On June 30, 1962, the negotiating authority under the last extension of the Trade Agreements Act expires. . . . A new American trade initiative is needed to meet the challenges and opportunities of a rapidly changing world economy. . . . For many years our trade legislation has enjoyed bipartisan backing from those members of both parties who recognize how essential trade is to our basic security abroad and our economic health at home. . . . The Trade Expansion Act of 1962 is designed as the expression of a nation, not of any single faction or section. . . . Our efforts to maintain the leadership of the free world thus rest, in the final analysis, on our success in this undertaking. Economic isolation and political leadership are wholly incompatible. . . . It is in [this] spirit that I recommend [the TEA] to the Congress for prompt and favorable action.[39]

The second major factor contributing to the success of the TEA in Congress was the mobilization of economic groups with an interest in freer trade to lobby Congress in support of the administration's trade bill, which was forthcoming in the public hearings of the House Committee on Ways and Means and the Senate Committee on Finance.

The House Committee on Ways and Means opened hearings on the administration's trade bill (H.R. 9900) in March 1962. And over the course of a month, the committee heard testimony from the administration as well as scores of economic groups. Although the chairman of the Ways and Means Committee, Arkansas Democrat Wilbur D. Mills, was known for having his hand on the pulse of the House, he relied heavily on the efforts of the administration to gauge support for the TEA among the rank-and-file members of that chamber. As one administration trade official recalled:

> [W]e had the best intelligence gathering network on the Hill so that we were in a position to keep a running tab of how various congressmen would vote, which was extremely helpful, particularly in working with Wilbur Mills who always wants to know what the temper of the House is. And we were able to give Mills on a weekly basis running reports on the membership of the House, which he [found to be] very reliable.[40]

During the course of its public hearings, the Ways and Means Committee heard testimony from nearly 250 witnesses, the vast majority of whom represented economic groups. From the moment the hearings opened, it was clear that the battle over the legislation would be waged between two hostile camps: an alliance of world market-oriented economic groups led by the administration; and a coalition of domestically oriented, import-sensitive groups led by the Committee's old-guard Republicans who had long been "the heart of protectionism in Congress."[41] At the core of society-based support for the TEA was an alliance between the nation's largest and most internationally oriented corporations, represented by the CED and the United States Council of the International Chamber of Commerce; export-oriented small and medium-sized businesses, represented by the U.S. Chamber of Commerce; organized labor, represented by the AFL-CIO; and the nation's peak agricultural associations—the AFBF, the National Farmers' Union (NFU), and the National Grange.[42] The favorable testimony of these groups was buttressed by testimony from numerous multinational corporations, internationally oriented business groups, and labor unions in export-oriented industrial sectors, including: the Standard Oil Company; Hewlett Packard Company; Raytheon Company; Caterpillar Tractor Company; International Telephone & Telegraph Company; United Fruit Company; Standard Fruit & Steamship Company; American Paper and Pulp Association; the Automobile Manufacturing Association; the U.S.–Japan Trade Council; the American Bankers Association; the United Auto Workers; the International Union of Electrical, Radio, and Machine Workers; and the United Steel Workers of America.[43]

Opposition to the TEA came from a coalition of business, labor, and farm groups whose members faced or feared growing foreign competition in the American market. Historically, the NAM had been the chief mouthpiece for protectionist business interests in Congress; however, for the first time since the inauguration of the reciprocal trade program in 1934, the NAM took no stand on the trade legislation—a reflection of a growing split in its ranks between multi-national corporations and exporters, and import-sensitive, domestically oriented firms. With the NAM on the sidelines, no major business group came out against the TEA; nor was there opposition from a major labor union or farm group. As a result, society-based opposition to the TEA was spearheaded by the Trade Relations Council (the former American Protective Tariff League) and the Nation-Wide Committee on Import and Export Policy. The Trade Relations Council was a business organization whose board included the presidents or CEOs of more than twenty companies, mostly from the textile and chemical industries, but also including glass, machine tools, electronics, shoes, and copper and lead. The Nation-Wide Committee on Import and Export Policy included business, labor, and farm groups representing producers in a broad range of industries, including textiles, shoes, leather, chemicals, ranching, and dairy. The Trade Relations Council and the Nation-Wide Committee on Import and Export Policy were joined in their opposition to the TEA by scores of import-sensitive business, labor, and farm groups.[44]

While the supporters of the TEA recapitulated the arguments of the administration and urged the Ways and Means Committee to report the bill to the full House with its trade-liberalizing authorities intact, opponents charged that continuation of the nation's policy of freer trade would undermine the American economy; lead to the loss of profits, jobs, and incomes for business, labor, and agriculture; encourage the shifting of U.S. production overseas; enrich other countries at America's expense; and aggrandize the power of the president vis-à-vis Congress. As the director of the Nation-Wide Committee on Import and Export Policy saw it, the administration's trade bill would lead to "the subordination of domestic economic interests to . . . considerations of foreign policy and the State Department"; would give imports "the right of eminent domain" in the American market; would lead to an "extreme concentration of power in the President"; and would put Congress "on the sidelines for five years," when its powers "would be completely atrophied."[45] The Trade Relations Council and the Nation-Wide Committee for Import and Export Policy demanded the outright rejection of the TEA and called for its substitution by a simple renewal of the RTAA of 1958 with no new trade-negotiating authority for the president. This call was echoed by many of the opponents of the TEA; and when they did not call for the outright rejection of the measure, they demanded amendments to protect them from its potentially damaging effects.[46]

One day after the close of its hearings, on April 12, 1962, the Ways and Means Committee began a series of closed executive sessions to consider the administration's trade bill. Five weeks later, the committee reached tentative agreement on a slightly amended version of the bill, which contained all the basic authorities sought by the administration. A new bill (H.R. 11970) was then drafted and introduced to the committee by Wilbur D. Mills; and on June 4 the committee voted to report the amended bill to the full House. The Committee vote on H.R. 11970 was 20–5, with all the Committee's Democrats and five Republicans voting in favor, and five Republicans opposed. The Republicans voting against the bill said they opposed the measure because "it licenses the President" to injure domestic workers and industry and "intends that this be done," and that it transforms trade policy into an instrument of foreign aid, foreign policy, and other non-trade objectives.[47] The bill, they said, "abandons the philosophy . . . that our negotiators refrain from agreeing to a reduction in duties which will bring about serious injury to . . . domestic industry."[48] For its part, the Committee's majority argued that tariff-cutting negotiations with the EEC within the framework of a new international trade round "will be of critical importance to U.S. exports," and that the president needed the trade-negotiating authority in the TEA to accomplish that goal.[49]

H.R. 11970 was brought to the floor of the House under a closed rule, which stipulated that the bill could not be amended from the floor except by members of the Committee on Ways and Means. As per House tradition, the amendment process under a closed rule usually took the form of a motion to recommit the bill back to the committee for further action. Therefore, before the TEA was brought to the floor, Illinois Republican Noah M. Mason made it known that he would exercise his prerogative as senior minority member on the Ways and Means Committee to call for a motion to recommit the bill with instructions to replace it with a simple one-year extension of the president's existing negotiating authority, with no additional power to cut American tariffs. If adopted, Mason's motion would have prevented the administration from responding to the challenge of the EEC with a major new assertion of American world trade leadership; and because of its potentially fatal consequences for the administration's trade policy, the vote on the Mason motion was the most important vote taken on the TEA. Much to the administration's benefit, on June 26, 1962, one day before the TEA was brought to the floor of the House, the Republican Policy Committee held a meeting on the bill which resulted in a split in its ranks between the liberal Northeastern and conservative Midwestern wings of the Party. As a result of this split, the House Republican Party took no position on the legislation. And on June 27, the House voted 253–171 to reject the Mason motion. The core of Republican opposition to the motion came from Northeastern states; while the core of Democratic support for the motion came from the Southern wing of the party, which represented textile and oil-producing areas. After the defeat of the Mason motion, and after eight hours of "lackluster and ill-attended" debate, the House voted to pass the TEA, 298–125.[50] On final passage, the TEA garnered the support of 218 Democrats and 80 Republicans. It was opposed by 90 Republicans and 35 Democrats.

Once the administration's trade bill was overwhelmingly approved by the House in a bi-partisan vote, action in the Senate was largely perfunctory. Indeed, once the bill passed the House, Secretary of Commerce Luther Hodges recalled: "we knew pretty generally that we had a Trade Expansion Act."[51] The administration's confidence was borne out. The Senate Committee on Finance held four weeks of hearings on the House bill and heard from the same witnesses that had testified before the House Committee on Ways and Means. H.R. 11970 was reported by the Finance Committee, with minor amendments, on September 14, 1962, after a unanimous vote of 17–0. Five days later, after a debate that was marked by absenteeism, the Senate voted to pass the amended version of the House bill as reported by the Finance Committee, 78–8. As passed by the Senate, the TEA did not differ in any major way from the bill passed by the House. No major changes were made to the bill on the Senate floor, and the amendments proposed by Finance were accepted without opposition. On final passage, fifty-six Democrats and twenty-two Republicans voted for the bill, while seven Republicans and one Democrat (Strom Thurmond from the textile-producing state of South Carolina) voted against it. The minor differences in the Senate and House versions of the bill were resolved in a one-day meeting of a conference committee; and in early October the conference committee bill was passed in House, 256–91, and in the Senate by voice vote. Looking back at the legislation that finally emerged from Congress, one administration official later recalled that "it was remarkably clean," and that the price in terms of concessions made to protectionist interests "was awfully cheap."[52]

On October 11, 1962, President Kennedy signed the TEA into law, calling the act "the most important international piece of legislation . . . affecting economics since the passage of the Marshall Plan. It marks a decisive turning point for the future of our economy, for our relations with our friends and allies, and for the prospects of free institutions and free societies everywhere."[53]

Conclusion: The Triumph of Globalism in the TEA of 1962

With the president's signature, the TEA of 1962 shifted trade policy-making power from Congress to the chief executive for the purpose of exercising world trade leadership. And it was under the authority of this statute that American trade officials negotiated the Kennedy Round of Multilateral Trade Negotiations, which resulted in a transfer of trade policy-making power from the American state to the GATT.

This chapter has argued that the Kennedy administration's trade policy was first and foremost a reaction to external events: the rise of the EEC and the challenges it presented to the world trading system. Furthermore, America's response to the emergence of the EEC was the result of a collaborative undertaking between the CED, the CFR and the Department of State, which achieved practical expression within the Kennedy administration through the efforts of Howard C. Petersen and George W. Ball. This globally oriented partnership was unambiguously anchored in America's superpower position in world trade, for it fused the economic interests of the nation's largest and most internationally oriented corporations with the foreign policy interests of the executive branch.

Yet this superpower alliance was not able to implement its trade policy without convincing Congress to delegate its Article I Section 8 power to "regulate commerce with foreign nations" to the president. Consequently, the Petersen trade office in the White House and the Ball trade office in the State Department worked to mobilize America's position as a world trade superpower into the legislative process. They did so in two ways: first, they cast the administration's trade bill in terms of foreign policy; and second, they organized a well-orchestrated campaign to mobilize globally oriented economic groups into the legislative process. As a result of these efforts, the president and his trade policy lieutenants were able to generate a globally oriented bias in the legislative process in Congress and to create the domestic political foundations for the enactment of the administration's trade bill. And while the administration made a handful of concessions to protectionist interests, these side-payments did not affect the chief objectives of the TEA. Viewed in this light, the triumph of globalism in the TEA of 1962 reflected a pattern of domestic trade politics anchored in the nation's superpower position in world trade—a pattern that expressed the power and interests of the nation's largest and most internationally oriented corporations and the executive branch of the American state.

Notes

1 Unless otherwise noted, this section draws its information from the Chase National Bank, "The New European Market: A Guide for American Businessmen" (New York: The Chase National Bank, 1962); and Thomas D. Cabot, *Common Market: Economic Foundation for a U.S. of Europe?* (New York: Committee for Economic Development, 1959).

2 Between the two big players within the EEC, the French were less free trade-oriented than the West Germans. Indeed, it was France who led the charge for the CAP, as well as for the Community's policy toward its associated territories and states.

3 It will be recalled that while not strictly a business organization, the membership of the CFR was dominated by the presidents or CEOs of some of the nation's largest and most internationally oriented investment banks, industrial corporations, and corporate service firms (particularly corporate law firms). Furthermore, in 1958 the CFR initiated a new program "for maximizing business support," which in effect created a whole new category of membership by allowing corporations, not just their leaders, to join the organization. In 1961, this Corporate Service included more than 80 participants, including: Bankers Trust Company; the Chase Manhattan Bank; the First City Bank of New York; Brown, Brothers, Harriman and Company; Ford Motor Company; General Motors; IBM; General Electric; Merck and Company; General Dynamics

Corporation; Texas Instruments; United States Steel Corporation; Mobile Oil Company; Sinclair Oil Corporation; and Standard Oil Company. See Council on Foreign Relations, *Annual Report of the Council on Foreign Relations, with List of Members and By-Laws* (New York: Council on Foreign Relations, 1961). For its part, by 1960 the CED had grown to include more than 150 corporate members, including: the National Cash Register Company; Bechtel Corporation; Inland Steel Company; United States Steel Corporation; General Dynamics; Westinghouse Electric Corporation; General Electric Corporation; Radio Corporation of America (RCA); the B. F. Goodrich Company; General Motors Corporation; Chrysler Corporation; Ford Motor Company; Caterpillar Tractor Company; Standard Oil Company; Kerr-McGee Oil Industries; American Telephone and Telegraph Company; Bank of America; First National Bank of Chicago; the First National Bank of New York; and Goldman Sachs & Company. See Committee for Economic Development, *The European Common Market and Its Meaning to the United States* (New York: Committee for Economic Development, 1959), 142–149.

4 The RTAA of 1945, it will be recalled, authorized tariff reductions by up to 50 percent.

5 Congressional Quarterly, *Special Report: The Trade Expansion Act of 1962* (Washington, D.C.: Congressional Quarterly Service, 1962), 7.

6 Alfred E. Eckes, *Opening America's Market: U.S. Foreign Trade Policy since 1776* (Chapel Hill: University of North Carolina Press, 1995), 181.

7 Ernest H. Preeg, *Traders and Diplomats: An Analysis of the Kennedy Round Negotiations under the General Agreement on Tariffs and Trade* (Washington, D.C.: The Brookings Institution, 1970), 40. As it turned out, in order to get even this meager result, State Department trade negotiators were forced to breach peril points on $76 million of U.S. imports (less than 1 percent of total U.S. imports).

8 Alfred E. Eckes, Interview with W. Michael Blumenthal, in Alfred E. Eckes, *Revisiting U.S. Trade Policy: Decisions in Perspective* (Athens: Ohio University Press, 2000), 50.

9 See Committee for Economic Development, *The European Common Market and Its Meaning to the United States*, 6.

10 Committee for Economic Development, *The European Common Market and Its Meaning to the United States*; Cabot, *Common Market*.

11 Cabot, *Common Market*, 12.

12 Ibid., 14.

13 Committee for Economic Development, *Taxes and Trade: 20 Years of CED Policy* (New York: Committee for Economic Development, 1963), 47.

14 Cabot, *Common Market*, 14.

15 Randall Hinshaw, *The European Community and American Trade* (New York: Praeger Publishers, 1964), vii–ix.

16 William Diebold, "A Watershed with Some Dry Sides: the Trade Expansion Act of 1962" (revised text provided to the author), 4.

17 Ibid., 26.

18 Raymond A. Bauer, Ithiel de Sola Pool, and Lewis A. Dexter, *American Business & Public Policy: The Politics of Foreign Trade*, 2nd ed. (Chicago: Aldine, Atherton, Inc., 1972), 324.

19 Ibid., 324; John F. Kennedy Presidential Library, Committee for a National Trade Policy, Board of Directors (February 23, 1962), Petersen Box 14, Finney File, CNTP Information Kit.

20 *The New York Times*, 8 January 1962, 1.

21 Ball's appointment generated great fanfare at the CFR, which held a special dinner in his honor on June 8, 1961. This dinner was attended by more than 50 people, most of whom were the presidents, CEOs, or other high-ranking corporate officials, representing many of the nation's largest investment banks, multinational

corporations, and corporate law firms, including: Morgan Guaranty Trust Company; Brown, Brothers, Harriman, and Company; Ford Motor Company; International Telephone and Telegraph Corporation; Westinghouse Electric Company; Singer Manufacturing Company; Phelps Dodge Corporation; IBM; Standard Oil Company; Continental Oil Company; Mobile Oil Company; and Sinclair Oil Corporation. See Columbia University Libraries Rare Book and Manuscript Library, Frank Altschul Papers, "Dinner in Honor of George W. Ball," Organizations (CFR), General Correspondence (1961).

22 Joseph Kraft, *The Grand Design: From Common Market to Atlantic Partnership* (New York: Harper and Brothers Publishers, 1964), 24–25.

23 Committee for Economic Development, *United States Tariff Policy* (New York: Committee for Economic Development, 1954); and Committee for Economic Development, *The European Common Market*.

24 Kraft, *The Grand Design*, 38–39.

25 Congressional Quarterly, *Special Report*, 2.

26 United States Department of State, "Threshold of a New Trading World," *Department of State Bulletin*, 20 November 1961.

27 Ibid., 833.

28 United States Department of State, "The Hour of Decision: A New Approach in American Trade Policy," *Department of State Bulletin*, December 25, 1961.

29 United States Department of State, "The Hour of Decision." For its part, the NAM decided not to take a stand on the administration's trade bill, which reflected divisions within its ranks between export-oriented and import-competing industries.

30 State of the Union Address: John F. Kennedy (January 11, 1962), www.infoplease. com/t/his/state-of-the-union/175.html (accessed on May 9, 2013).

31 John F. Kennedy Presidential Library, Howard C. Petersen, Chronological File, Box 1 (August 1961–September 1962).

32 John F. Kennedy Presidential Library, Luther Hodges, "Oral History Interview," Library Oral History Program, 9.

33 John F. Kennedy Presidential Library, Myer Rashish, "Oral History Interview," Library Oral History Program, 26.

34 Vinod K. Aggarwal refers to the LTA as "liberal protectionism"—for it allowed imports to keep rising (albeit at 5 percent a year). See Vinod K. Aggarwal, *Liberal Protectionism: The International Politics of Organized Textile Trade* (Berkeley: University of California Press, 1986).

35 *Business Week*, March 24, 1962, 32

36 Ibid.

37 Rashish, "Oral History Interview," 35.

38 Hodges, "Oral History Interview," 7.

39 Congressional Quarterly, *Special Report* (1962), 58–59.

40 Rashish, "Oral History Interview," 22.

41 John F. Manley, *The Politics of Finance: The House Committee on Ways and Means* (New York: Little Brown, 1970), 45.

42 Although there were members of the U.S. Chamber of Commerce, the AFL-CIO, the AFBF, the NFU, and the National Grange who were located in import-competing sectors, the position of these organizations reflected the interests of their members in export-oriented sectors.

43 John F. Kennedy Presidential Library, Master List of Association Positions, Davies File, Howard C. Petersen, Box 6, Folder "Company Positions on H.R. 11970."

44 Master List of Association Positions, Davies File.

45 Congressional Quarterly, *Special Report*, 20.

46 Ibid., 18–23.

47 Ibid., 30.

6

TRILATERALISM

The Trade Act of 1974

> The international trading system is now at a watershed from which it can either drift toward protectionism or continue its past hard-won progress toward a more open and prosperous world economy. [The United States] must face up to more intense long-term competition in the world's markets rather than shrink from it. Those who would have us turn inward, hiding behind a shield of import restrictions of indefinite duration, might achieve short-term gains and benefit certain groups, but they would exact a high cost from the economy as a whole.
>
> *Richard M. Nixon (1973)*

The Trade Act of 1974 marked the third major assertion of American world trade leadership in the postwar period and initiated a higher stage in the triumph of globalism in American trade politics. A response to the continued expansion of the European Community and the emergence of Japan as a major trading power, the Trade Act of 1974 was designed to encourage the European Community and Japan to assume responsibilities for the management of the GATT system commensurate with their economic power; specifically, by liberalizing their trade and economic policies within the framework of a new round of multilateral trade negotiations led by the United States. In order to entice the European Community and Japan into this new trilateral partnership, the Trade Act granted the president more power to reduce American trade barriers than any previous postwar trade statute. At the core of the Trade Act was congressional authorization for the president, for a period of five years, to reduce U.S. tariffs by 60 percent of their prevailing rates; to reduce tariffs of 5 percent or less to zero; and to take all "appropriate and feasible" steps within the president's power to "harmonize, reduce, or eliminate" nontariff trade barriers or other distortions of international trade (subject to a congressional fast-track procedure). It was under the auspices of the Trade Act that the United States launched the third watershed trade round of the postwar period, the Tokyo Round of Multilateral Trade Negotiations.

The origins of the Trade Act are to be found in a global trade policy planning alliance between internationally oriented corporate elites—many intimately involved with the CED and the CFR—and the Nixon White House. Not only were members of this alliance responsible for formulating the Nixon administration's trade bill, but they coordinated the campaign for the measure's enactment by Congress. That they were successful in this effort was the product of America's superpower position in world trade; for this position enabled the framers of the Trade Act to mobilize export-oriented domestic economic groups and their supporters in Congress around a major new assertion of U.S. world trade leadership. And while enactment of the Trade Act required more concessions to protectionist economic groups and their supporters in Congress than ever before, none of these concessions fundamentally challenged the chief negotiating authorities contained in the Act.

The Global Challenge: European Community Growth and the Rise of Japan

The period between the conclusion of the Kennedy Round in June 1967 and the enactment of the Trade Act in January 1975 was one of great challenges for the world economy and the international trading system. Some of these challenges grew out of the success of the Kennedy Round in reducing tariff barriers among the advanced industrial countries to their lowest levels in history (about 8 percent for dutiable imports), which, along with innovations in communications and transportation technologies, and the rise of multinational corporations, paved the way for an increase in the trade-related integration of national economies and a concomitant intensification of international competition. Other challenges grew out of a rapid rise in oil prices, spreading stagflation, and international monetary disorder. In response to these challenges the major trading nations, including the United States, increasingly turned to so-called nontariff trade barriers (NTBs) to help ameliorate the effects of the Kennedy Round tariff cuts, ease national economic adjustment to the rapid rise in oil prices, promote domestic employment at a time of spreading stagflation, and deal with competitive problems brought about by the turmoil in global financial markets. Perhaps the most pernicious of these NTBs were the use of state-sponsored export subsidies to gain global market share, the imposition of import quotas, and the negotiation of orderly marking agreements and Voluntary Export Restraints (VERs) to slow the pace of import penetration. In addition to these developments, the success of the Kennedy Round in reducing tariffs as a major barrier to trade revealed a vast network of NTBs—many tied to domestic economic and social programs—that had existed prior to the Kennedy Round and that posed major problems for the advancement of trade liberalization among developed countries going forward.

Yet the most important challenges for the GATT system were the continued growth of the European Community, the meteoric rise of Japan as a major world trader, and the policies and practices of these great economic powers. At the core of these challenges was an altered competitive environment, one in which the European Community and Japan were increasingly able to challenge the dominance of the United States in world markets. This new competitive environment posed a problem for the GATT system because many of the trade and domestic economic policies pursued by the European Community and Japan ran counter to the GATT's rules of multilateralism, non-discrimination, and trade liberalization. Many of these policies and practices were not new; moreover, at least through the early 1960s, the United States had tolerated them as part of its efforts to rebuild the war-torn world economy. However, as the European Community and Japan grew as great economic powers, the deleterious impact of these policies and practices on patterns of world trade grew apace.

Four aspects of European Community trade and domestic economic policies posed problems for the GATT regime. One was the Community's CAP. Initially contemplated in the Treaty of Rome (1958) and embodied in detailed proposals in 1960, the CAP came into full force in 1966. The foremost goal of the CAP was to make the Community as self-sufficient in agriculture as possible. At the heart of the CAP was a system of price supports, variable levies, and export subsidies. Price supports were used to keep farmers on the land by giving them direct cash payments to support production. Variable levies (usually in the form of quotas or high tariffs) were used to raise the selling price of targeted farm imports to levels above those of comparable Community products. Export subsidies were used to reduce the selling price of farm products on world markets (dumping), and were a necessary counterpart to the high domestic farm prices produced by the Community's system of price supports and variable levies (which otherwise would have priced European agricultural exports out of world markets).[1] Although many countries, including the United States, supported programs designed to support their agricultural sectors, the CAP was a particularly protectionist and discriminatory arrangement. Not only did it undermine the efforts of more efficient agricultural producers to sell in the Common Market, but it undermined their ability to sell in world markets (a direct consequence of dumping). While the CAP had emerged as a problem in the early 1960s, it was left largely untouched during the Kennedy Round of GATT trade negotiations.

The second challenge of the European Community to the GATT system was its program of Preferential Trade Agreements (PTAs). Beginning in the early 1960s, and gaining momentum thereafter, the Community began to enter into discriminatory trade agreements with non-Community countries and dependent territories. These PTAs gave non-Community members preferred access to the Common Market, usually through lower tariffs and larger quotas than extended to the outside world. Moreover, many of these PTAs contained a "reverse preference" provision, which was included in agreements with less-developed countries and dependent territories. These reverse-preference PTAs required non-Community signatories to give Community exports preferred access to their markets in exchange for preferred access to the Common Market. By the mid-1970s, PTAs extended to nearly eighty countries and dependent territories, most in southern Europe and Africa. While regular (non-reverse) PTAs discriminated against non-PTA exports to the Common Market, reverse-preference PTAs hindered non-Community exports to many less-developed countries and territories.[2]

A third challenge posed by European Community policy was its discriminatory treatment of Japanese exports. Between the early 1960s and the early 1970s, Japan's share of world exports doubled—from approximately 3 to 6 percent; and while many countries (including the United States) responded to this challenge with restrictive and discriminatory devices, Community practice was by far the worst. Indeed, as a partial result of these devices (usually high tariffs and quantitative restrictions), by 1970 the United States took 30 percent of Japanese exports, while the European Community took only 6 percent.[3] As one report put it, this created a "triangular problem" for the world trading system, one that placed unfair and unnecessary burdens on the United States.[4] Not only was Community practice inconsistent with GATT rules, but it made Japan less likely to liberalize its own economy. Moreover, by encouraging Japan to focus disproportionately on the American market, it threatened to undermine U.S. domestic support for the GATT system.

Finally, there was the problem of Community enlargement itself, and the chance that it would lead to new policies and practices which could threaten the future of the world trading system. By the late 1960s, the Community was engaged in negotiations with four countries to admit them as full members, three of which—England, Ireland, and Denmark—were admitted in 1973. As part of these negotiations the Community began to discuss a number of new policies which would discriminate against non-Community countries and disadvantage certain foreign producers in the Common Market. These policies included a "Buy European" policy linked to a pooling of member-government procurement of high-technology products; a common industrial policy which had the potential of incorporating restrictions on foreign trade and investment; and tougher technical standards for goods entering the Common Market—particularly in advanced manufactured products. Added to these measures was the Community's Value Added Tax scheme, which could be manipulated to raise the price of foreign products in the Common Market.[5] Perhaps most importantly, the enlargement of the Community held the potential (as did its creation in 1958) to generate an inward-looking orientation, one that could result in a turning away from the multilateral trading system in favor of a protectionist and discriminatory regional economic bloc.

As for Japan, the problems were twofold. One was the pace of Japanese trade liberalization. While Japanese exports grew at about 20 percent a year in the

1960s (more than twice as fast as world exports), the nation's imports increased at a slower rate. In part, this was due to Japanese tariffs, which were somewhat higher than those in the European Community and the United States through the 1960s. In larger measure, however, it resulted from a wide range of NTBs, which were designed to aid Japan's domestic economic development and protect its farmers from international competition. Among the most trade-distorting of these NTBs were import quotas, import-licensing schemes, and restrictive administrative rules and regulations governing imports.[6]

The second problem posed by Japan was the role of its state in the nation's economy. While controversy surrounds the actual economic effect of what one analyst has called Japan's "developmental state,"[7] there is general agreement that in the postwar era the Japanese state has taken a hands-on approach to national economic development.[8] More specifically, at least through the early 1970s, the Japanese state employed a wide range of measures designed to foster export-oriented development. These measures included an industrial policy through which the Japanese state sought to encourage high-growth industries with significant export potential; formation of tax and credit policies directed toward export-oriented industries; a system of "administrative guidance" to assure state–business cooperation in setting and achieving domestic industrial policy goals; state policies of preferential credit rates, tax incentives, and special depreciation allowances for export industries; a foreign aid program which tied the provision of aid to the purchase of Japanese products; and state support of export cartels which developed integrated and cooperative programs for the penetration of foreign markets.[9] The Japanese state was generally able to secure private sector cooperation in meeting industrial policy goals through its control over the major sources of investment funds, import licenses, technology imports, direct foreign investment, and other "leverage points." Japan's approach to its national economic development raised serious questions about the fairness of its competitive edge. This was particularly true for the United States, which by the mid-1960s was running a persistent and growing trade deficit with Japan in major industrial sectors; most importantly, textiles and apparel, iron and steel, automobiles, consumer electronics, and certain types of machinery.

The task of resolving the impact of the European Community and Japan on the world trading system fell to the United States, which by virtue of its super-power position within the GATT was the only nation with the capacity to steer these trading powers toward a more outward-looking and regime-consistent trade policy. The question was, how to do it? The answer was the Trade Act of 1974, which was designed to forge a trilateral partnership between the United States, the European Community, and a more muscular Japan within the framework of a new global trade round—a round designed to expand the scale and scope of the GATT and more fully integrate the European Community and Japan into the regime. In light of growing protectionist pressures in the United States in the late 1960s and early 1970s, this was no easy task. That it was accomplished reflected the efforts of internationally oriented corporate elites and the Nixon White House to define America's national trade interest in systemic terms; and to mobilize export-oriented domestic economic groups, and their supporters in Congress, around a major new assertion of U.S. world trade leadership.

The Formation of the Trade Act of 1974

The years immediately following the conclusion of the Kennedy Round were difficult times for the forces of world trade leadership. In the wake of the round, Congress and a wide range of domestic economic groups mounted a vigorous campaign to protect the American market from rising import competition and, in general, to move U.S. trade policy in a more nationalistic direction. In the fall of 1967 Congress failed to approve two agreements consummated in the Kennedy Round: one to repeal the so-called American Selling Price system, which established a system of customs valuation designed to shield the chemical industry from international competition; and another to implement a GATT anti-dumping code.[10] Moreover, in the two years following the conclusion of the Kennedy Round, nearly 300 quota bills were introduced into Congress covering major industrial and agricultural sectors facing or fearing growing competition in the American market. The most important of these sectors included textiles and apparel, iron and steel, chemicals, footwear, consumer electronics, and dairy and meat products. Moreover, in 1969, following months of pressure from the industry and Congress, the Department of State caved-in and negotiated a VER agreement with the European Community and Japan, limiting their steel exports to the United States. And between 1968 and 1972, three omnibus trade bills were introduced in Congress which, if enacted, would have ended nearly three decades of American world trade leadership.[11]

This is not to say that the president and his internationally oriented corporate allies were inactive during this period; although they *were* ineffective. In March 1967, as the Kennedy Round was drawing to a close, President Johnson directed his Special Trade Representative (STR), William M. Roth, to initiate a study of future U.S. trade policy and to make recommendations for a new trade bill designed to shift policy-making power from Congress to the chief executive. A member of the CFR, Roth was an international shipping executive from California who served on the CED's Research and Policy Subcommittee.[12] To assist Roth, President Johnson appointed a special Public Advisory Committee on Trade Policy. Chaired by Roth, the Advisory Committee was dominated by high-ranking officers from more than two dozen internationally oriented corporations and banks, including the Ford Motor Company; the General Motors Corporation; the General Electric Company; IBM; Texas Instruments; Mobil Oil Corporation; the Boeing Company; Bank of America; the Chase National Bank; and Goldman, Sachs & Company.[13]

Given the fact that the implementation of Kennedy Round tariff cuts would be phased in over a period of five years (and thus no new trade round was immediately needed), Roth and the Public Advisory Committee produced a minimalist trade bill, the Trade Expansion Act of 1968. The only significant provisions of the bill were a request for repeal of the American Selling Price system and authorization for the president—for a period of two years—to make minor adjustments in tariff rates on a housekeeping basis, but with no new negotiating authority.[14] Unlike the Roosevelt and Kennedy administrations, which launched major campaigns to secure congressional enactment of the RTAA of 1945 and the TEA of 1962, the Johnson administration, distracted with other problems, made little effort to push the TEA of 1968 through Congress. As a result, the bill died in the House Committee on Ways and Means.[15] It was the first time since the original RTAA of 1934 that Congress had rejected a presidential trade bill.

A second attempt to push a new trade bill through Congress was made during the first year of the Nixon administration. Shortly after taking office, President Nixon appointed a new STR, Carl J. Gilbert, to replace William M. Roth, who shortly after departing the Johnson Administration had replaced Howard C. Petersen as chairman of the CED's International Studies Committee.[16] Gilbert was Chairman of the Gillette Company and a longtime member of the CED and the CFR. He had been a participant in the Johnson administration's Public Advisory Committee on Trade Policy and was a past director of the Committee for a National Trade Policy—the corporate free trade lobbying group which George W. Ball had helped to found in the 1950s. Working closely with the ECAT, a free trade corporate lobbying group launched in 1967 by William M. Roth, investment banker and CFR leader, David Rockefeller, and vice chairman and president of IBM, Arthur K. Watson, Gilbert was given the task of drafting a new trade bill for the Nixon Administration.[17] However, like the trade bill drafted by Roth in the Johnson White House, the legislation produced by Gilbert—the Trade Act of 1970—was an attenuated measure. Indeed, the act only requested Congress—for a period of two years—to grant the president the power to cut U.S. tariffs by up to 20 percent of their prevailing rates.[18] As was the case in the closing days of the Johnson administration, in the early days of the Nixon administration, little effort was made to organize a vigorous campaign for congressional enactment of the Trade Act, which died quickly in Congress.

Following the demise of the Trade Act of 1970, the Nixon administration quickly began work on a new trade bill—this time putting behind it the full weight of the executive branch. This effort began in May 1970, when Nixon appointed a high-profile Commission on International Trade and Investment Policy to make an analysis of the principal problems faced by the United States as a result of changes in the world economy since 1945, and to produce a set of policy recommendations based on this analysis for the 1970s. The principal idea in founding the Commission was to meet the challenge of the new protectionism in Congress by beginning the process of building a new national consensus in favor of a renewed world trade (and monetary) leadership role for the United States. To serve as chairman of the Commission, Nixon tapped Albert L. Williams, head of IBM's Finance Committee and an Honorary Trustee of the CED.[19] Of the Commission's twenty-seven members, seventeen were high-ranking officials of major multinational corporations and banks, including Honeywell; the General Electric Company; Motorola; General Motors; Cargill; Monsanto; Standard Oil; Wells Fargo Bank; and the First National Bank of Chicago. The Commission also included Alfred C. Neal, President of the CED.[20] Rounding out the Commission were two representatives of organized labor drawn from the United Steel Workers of America and the International Association of Machinists and Aerospace Workers; one farm organization (the National Council of Farmer Cooperatives); and six academics.

Following a year of intensive work, in July 1971 the Commission on International Trade and Investment Policy (known informally as the "Williams' Commission") transmitted its final report to the president. Declaring that "the world has changed radically from the one we knew after World War II," the Commission argued that a "crisis of confidence" had developed in the United States with respect to the nation's continued participation in the multilateral trading system. According to the Commission, this crisis could be traced to a surge of imports into the American market since the mid-1960s (mostly from Japan), and a growing sense that the European Community and Japan were not assuming enough responsibility for the management of the international economic system.[21] The Commission concluded that the United States possessed a deep and ongoing national interest in maximizing international trade flows, and therefore needed to take immediate action to restore domestic confidence in the GATT system. Toward this end, the Commission recommended that the United States immediately launch a new round of GATT trade negotiations with the European Community and Japan (and other interested countries), designed to "prepare the way for the elimination of all barriers to international trade and capital movements within 25 years."[22] In addition to proposing that the president be granted major new trade-negotiating authority, including the power to negotiate on NTBs, the Commission argued that any new trade bill should strengthen provisions of U.S. trade law designed to safeguard domestic industries from both fair and unfair import competition.[23] The recommendations of the Williams' Commission were accepted by President Nixon in July 1971, and were used as a framework to guide the drafting of the administration's Trade Reform Act of 1973.[24]

The work of the Williams' Commission was only one facet of the Nixon administration's effort to lay the groundwork for a major new assertion of U.S. world trade leadership. Another was the creation of a White House Council on International Economic Policy (CIEP) in January 1971. A cabinet-level, interdepartmental committee, the CIEP was designed to oversee and coordinate all foreign economic policy—including trade—within the executive branch; and to provide a forum within which various bureaus and agencies could work out their differences. The CIEP served as the institutional nerve-center of the Administration's effort to formulate its Trade Reform Act.

The first chairman of the CIEP was Peter G. Peterson, who also served as Assistant to the President for International Economic Affairs. Peterson was Chairman of the Bell and Howell Company, a founding member of the ECAT, a member of the Board of Trustees of the CED, and a high-ranking official in the CFR (which he would lead as Chairman of the Board after leaving government service, replacing David Rockefeller).[25] As one White House staffer put it: Peterson was Nixon's "number one intellectual concubine" on matters of international economic policy.[26]

For his first task, Nixon directed Peterson to prepare an analysis of the changing world economy to serve "as background for the formulation of U.S. international economic policy in the seventies."[27] Completed in December 1971, Peterson's report closely paralleled the analysis and policy recommendations of the Williams' Commission. It argued that the growth of the European Community and the emergence of a more muscular Japan had created a "new era" in the development of the world economy—one marked by "basic structural and competitive changes."[28] As a result of these changes, "the forces of history [are] pointing toward a world of mutually receding and inward-looking blocs, precariously and even dangerously divided in asymmetrical mistrusts."[29] The best way for the United States to respond to this new environment, the report argued, was for the nation to take the lead in the creation of "a more open, outward-looking, multilateral, prosperous, and increasingly symmetrical and well balanced world—in which a commonly accepted system of rules and behavior patterns will assure the continuing prosperity of each and all."[30] With respect to trade, the report called on the president to launch a major, new GATT trade round—one marked by "shared leadership, shared responsibility, and shared burdens," especially between the United States, the European Community, and Japan.[31] Along with the report of the Williams' Commission, the Peterson report provided the basic policy framework within which the Nixon administration would develop its trade policy proposals.

The Nixon administration's effort to defuse the new protectionism in Congress and to seize the initiative on trade policy moved into high gear in August 1971. Under the political cover of the Williams' Commission report (which urged immediate and drastic action to respond to changes in the world economy), on August 15 the president shocked the nation and the world by announcing a New Economic Policy (NEP) for the United States. In addition to instituting domestic wage and price controls to fight inflation, the NEP suspended the convertibility of the U.S. dollar into gold, and imposed a temporary 10 percent surcharge on all imports into the United States. In addition to encouraging international monetary reform, the closing of the gold window and the import surcharge were designed to force an immediate devaluation of the dollar against the currencies of America's major trading partners so as to promote U.S. exports while curtailing the nation's imports. Although the suspension of the dollar's convertibility into gold and the import surcharge were condemned abroad (and by some at home) as bald economic nationalism, according to Peterson, their purpose was internationalist in nature—designed to head off the forces of economic nationalism at home and abroad and to provide a shock to the world economy which would open the way for the reform of the international economic system.[32]

Confirming Peterson's assessment, shortly after Nixon announced the NEP, the administration began behind-the-scenes negotiations with the European Community and Japan to persuade them to join with the United States in launching a major, new trade round under GATT auspices.[33] These negotiations led to joint declarations by the United States, the European Community, and Japan in support of a new trade round, which would include tariffs and NTBs on industrial and agricultural products. By the end of 1972, a new GATT Preparatory Committee was established to lay the groundwork for the round, and a consensus was reached between the United States, the European Community, and Japan to begin formal negotiations in September 1973.[34]

In preparation for the anticipated Nixon Round of Multilateral Trade Negotiations (which were renamed the Tokyo Round once the president resigned), and the drafting and submission of major, new trade legislation to Congress, in the fall of 1971, Nixon moved to strengthen the office of the STR. On the advice of Peter G. Peterson, the president appointed a new STR to replace Carl J. Gilbert. This individual was W. D. Eberle. In addition to being President of American Standard, a Fortune 500 company which produced industrial and farm equipment, and a member of the CFR and the CED, Eberle had just finished chairing a CED subcommittee charged with the tasks of examining the trade relationship between the United States and the European Community and making recommendations concerning U.S. trade policy toward the Common Market.[35] Eberle was allowed to hire two deputies (Gilbert had not been allowed even one): one to work with Congress and the private sector; the other to maintain ongoing consultations with foreign governments. To fill the first slot, Eberle hired W. R. Pearce, Vice President of the Cargill Corporation, and a member of the CFR and the Williams' Commission. For the second post, he hired Harald B. Malmgren, a Wall Street lawyer, CFR member, and advisor to the CED.

With the Williams' Commission report completed and the STR strengthened, and with agreement by the European Community and Japan to enter into a new round of multilateral trade negotiations, work to produce a new trade bill began in earnest in early 1972, following a change in the leadership of the CIEP. In January of that year, after appointing Peterson to be Secretary of Commerce, President Nixon tapped Peter M. Flanigan to be the new Assistant to the President for International Economic Affairs, as well as the new director of the CIEP. Flanigan was Vice President of the New York investment firm Dillon, Reed and Company; as well as member of the CFR. And it was under his direction that the administration's trade bill was drafted.

The work of drafting the administration's trade bill moved into high gear in June 1972, when Flanigan accepted a proposal from W. D. Eberle to use the recommendations of the Williams' Commission (which were echoed in the Peterson report) as the basis for interagency discussion on the new trade bill.[36] At the same time, Flanigan accepted a report from the CIEP's working-level Operations Group requesting a clear statement of the broad goals of administration trade policy, so as to guide the detailed work ahead. This statement was quickly drafted and drawn directly from the Williams' Commission report: to enter into multilateral trade negotiations in order "to prepare the way for the elimination of all barriers to international trade and capital movements within the next 25 years."[37] Over the next ten months the CIEP coordinated the work of eight executive branch bureaus and agencies in the formulation of a new trade bill: the Departments of State, Treasury, Commerce, Labor, and Agriculture; the office of Special Trade Representative; the Office of Management and Budget; and the Council of Economic Advisors. Although conflicts emerged among these participants, most involving the nature and scope of those parts of the trade bill designed to cushion domestic producers from rising imports, none of these conflicts spilled over into the CIEP's discussions on the bill's principal negotiating objectives, on which there was consensus. Indeed, after agreement on these negotiating objectives, all other issues were seen as "subsidiary."[38]

The most important drafting and strategy sessions on the administration's trade bill were held in December 1972 and January 1973. The overriding goals of these sessions were to build interagency agreement on the full bill (negotiating authority and domestic provisions), and to shape a proposal that could win in Congress. Agreement was reached early on that the bill would have to be comprehensive in scope. In addition to including a request for presidential authority to negotiate trade agreements on tariffs and NTBs covering industrial and agricultural products, participants in the CIEP's discussion agreed that it was strategically necessary for the bill to make some concessions to protectionist interests in Congress; specifically, by strengthening safeguards for domestic industries from both fair and unfair import competition. According to Flanigan, these concessions were necessary to build "a new coalition of forces . . . in the business community and Congress . . . [for] an outward-looking trade policy."[39] What conflicts emerged in the discussions over these concessions were worked out by Flanigan and Dean R. Hinton, Deputy Director of the CIEP, a career civil servant, and a member of the CFR. When Flanigan and Hinton were unable to resolve disputes, they turned to Treasury Secretary George P. Shultz, who chaired the newly created Council on Economic Policy and was President Nixon's chief economic advisor.[40] For his part, President Nixon stayed out of the drafting process until near the end, when final decisions needed to be made.

The administration's trade bill, the Trade Reform Act of 1973, was a complex document nearly 100 pages long. While the bill contained numerous provisions concerning relief for domestic producers facing foreign import competition, it requested more negotiating power for the president than ever before in the history of the trade agreements program: a five-year grant of authority to cut U.S. tariffs to zero; and a statutory mandate to negotiate on NTBs, subject to a congressional veto within ninety days of the submission of NTB agreements to Congress.

Prior to the introduction of the Trade Reform Act to Congress, the Nixon administration took a range of actions designed to enhance the chances for the bill's enactment. First, in May 1972, the administration negotiated a renewal of the steel VERs with the European Community and Japan, which were extended through 1974. These were paralleled by textile VERs with Japan and other East Asian countries; and by continuing administration efforts to negotiate a new and greatly expanded GATT textile agreement covering man-made fibers, and cotton textiles. The textile VERs were designed to replace the Long-Term Textile Agreement negotiated by the Kennedy administration in early 1960s and went into effect in January 1974. The negotiation of the steel and textile VERs were undertaken with a tacit agreement by the steel and textile industries that they would not oppose the administration's trade bill in Congress. Removing these industries from the legislative picture was crucial for the administration and its prospects for pushing its trade bill through the national legislature. Indeed, as one observer put it: "Steel and textiles, once you keep them out of a trade bill, you can resist the efforts of the other interests." According to another participant, "once it became apparent that we were getting agreement on these, everything else became easier."[41]

Furthermore, in the first few months of 1973, Peter M. Flanigan worked closely with a number of free trade oriented business groups to line them up for the coming congressional fight on the trade bill. In particular, the CIEP director maintained close contact with the ECAT, the United States Chamber of Commerce, and the NAM, which had moved into the free trade camp due to the rising export interests of its members during the 1960s. He also maintained a hectic schedule, meeting with representatives of major industries which were believed to oppose portions of the trade bill in an attempt to work out differences before the debate began in Congress. In addition, Flanigan, Eberle, and Pearce held numerous meetings with members of Congress to inform them about the administration's trade bill; to line them up to support the bill; and in general, "to defuse any potential resistance" that might emerge in Congress.[42] The most important of these meetings were held with the House and Senate leadership as well as with ranking members of the House Committee on Ways and Means and the Senate Committee on Finance.

Finally, the CIEP implemented a "marketing strategy" for the trade bill. This strategy centered on the CIEP's coordination of executive branch efforts to deal with Congress; the creation of a Public Advisory Board to permit constant, regular and direct interaction between the CIEP and industry, labor, and agricultural organizations; and the mobilization of "influential organizations and individuals who may be able to sway . . . Members of Congress."[43] Most importantly, the CIEP worked to mobilize the nation's multinational corporations. Indeed, between December 1972 and April 1973, when the Trade Reform Act was submitted to Congress, the CIEP maintained an active correspondence with more than seventy-five multinational corporations and their peak associations; while paying little attention to organized labor and the nation's leading farm groups.[44]

With a new round of GATT negotiations scheduled to begin in September 1973; the steel and textile industries placated with VERs; the proposed expansion of the nation's fair and unfair trade laws; leading members of Congress lined up to support the administration's trade policy proposals; and a public relations campaign focused on the mobilization of "influential organizations and individuals," on April 10, 1973, the Nixon administration introduced the Trade Reform Act to Congress. In submitting the act to the national legislature President Nixon cast the administration's trade proposals as vital to the national interest and American leadership in creating a more prosperous and peaceful world:

> The world today is embarked on a profound and historic movement away from confrontation and toward negotiation in resolving international differences. Increasingly in recent years, countries have come to see that the best way of advancing their own interests is by expanding peaceful contacts with other peoples. We have thus begun to erect a durable structure of peace in the world from which all nations can benefit and in which all nations have a stake . . . This structure of peace cannot be strong, however, unless it encompasses international economic affairs. . . . It is imperative, therefore, that we promptly turn our negotiating efforts to the task of resolving problems in the economic arena. . . . My trade reform proposals would equip us to meet this challenge.[45]

The Enactment of the Trade Act of 1974

Given the efforts of the Nixon administration to prepare Congress to enact the Trade Reform Act of 1973 (which was subsequently renamed the Trade Act of 1974), the skids for the movement of the legislation through the national legislature were well greased. Indeed, coterminous with opening public hearings on the bill in the House Committee on Ways and Means, in May 1973, Committee Chairman Wilbur D. Mills declared that he was in substantial agreement with the administration's trade proposals; and that he expected the Committee and the House to pass the legislation "changing the way the lady is dressed."[46] That said, Mills' endorsement of the Trade Reform Act was not shared by organized labor, which emerged as the chief opponent of the administration's proposals. After reviewing the bill in mid-April, the president of the AFL-CIO, George Meany, declared:

> The President's proposals do not meet the grave problems of trade which we have detailed time and again . . . . [They] provide no specific machinery to regulate the flood of imports and, indeed, some would increase the amount of damage to American employment and industrial production. The

proposals would open the door to further deterioration of America's position in the world economy and to the further export of American jobs.[47]

Moreover, at the request of the AFL-CIO, Massachusetts congressman James A. Burke and Indiana Senator Vance Hartke—both Democrats—reintroduced their Foreign Trade and Investment Act of 1971 into the House and the Senate to serve as a rallying point for opponents of the Trade Reform Act. However, as was the case two years earlier, the so-called Burke-Hartke Bill, which would have placed quotas on most American imports and limited the foreign direct investment activities of American multinational corporations, went nowhere.

On May 19, 1973, the House Committee on Ways and Means opened a month of public hearings on the Trade Reform Act. During these hearings the Committee took testimony from the administration and scores of economic groups. As per tradition, the administration presented it views first. The administration's case was made by the main bureaus and agencies which had participated in drafting the act: the CIEP, the STR, and the Departments of Treasury, State, Commerce, Agriculture, and Labor. The testimony of officials from these bureaus and agencies was worked out well in advance and coordinated through the CIEP and the STR. The representatives from the CIEP, the STR, and the Treasury and State Departments presented the overall rationale for the legislation. They argued that the bill was needed to allow the United States to respond to the continuing growth of the European Community and the emergence of Japan as major economic power, to persuade these traders to assume more responsibility for managing the GATT system, and to further the process of international trade liberalization—all of which were necessary to avoid "a return to the protectionist isolationism of the 1930s," which contributed to the Great Depression and World War II.[48]

The testimony of officials from the Departments of Commerce, Agriculture, and Labor was geared toward their domestic constituencies. Yet, in each case, these officials aligned their departments with that part of their constituency which was export oriented. Commerce Secretary F. B. Dent stressed the importance of the bill to the maintenance and expansion of U.S. manufacturing exports.[49] Agriculture Secretary Earl Butz argued that the bill would help to expand farm exports and thereby promote the growth and rationalization of the farm sector as a whole.[50] And in a complete break with the AFL-CIO, Labor Secretary Peter J. Brennen endorsed the bill as vital to export-led job creation.[51]

Business support for the administration's trade bill was anchored in organizations representing exporters, importers, and multinational corporations; and was led by the ECAT, the United States Chamber of Commerce, and the NAM. Agricultural support came from the AFBF, the National Grange, and the NFU. While the U.S. Chamber of Commerce, the NAM, the AFBF, the NFU, and the National Grange contained members who faced stiff import competition, these organizations aligned themselves with that part of their membership which benefited from exports. Outright opposition to the Trade Reform Act was led by the AFL-CIO. Although the AFL-CIO supported the TEA of 1962, by the late 1960s it had adopted a protectionist and nationalist position on U.S. trade policy, due to the rise of foreign imports in the American market and the growth of U.S. multinational corporations, both of which were seen as undermining production and jobs in the American economy. The AFL-CIO was joined by a number of affiliated and non-affiliated unions, as well as by agricultural producers and business firms who faced or feared rising import competition.[52]

After more than six weeks of meeting in closed session to mark up the trade bill, which included the participation of ten members of the administration, on October 10, 1973, the Ways and Means Committee voted 20–5 in favor of an amended version of the Trade Reform Act (H.R. 10710). While the administration endorsed the amended bill and declared it to be "a very substantial compromise of existing views," the AFL-CIO called it "worse than no bill at all."[53] During these sessions, James A. Burke made two spirited attempts to have the Committee adopt key sections of the Burke-Hartke Bill—the legislation endorsed by the AFL-CIO. One of these amendments would have imposed quotas on most imports into the United States to hold them at 1973 levels; the other would have automatically imposed quotas on imports once they captured 15 percent or more of the American market. Both of these proposals were voted down, 7–16. As for the amendments made by the Committee to the Administration's trade bill, none fundamentally threatened the objectives of the legislation as submitted to Congress. With respect to presidential negotiating authority, the Committee granted the chief executive the power, for five years, to reduce American tariffs by up to 60 percent, and to reduce to zero tariffs of 5 percent or less. This was the largest grant of tariff-cutting power ever delegated to the president; and while the administration's trade bill had requested unlimited tariff-cutting power, the Committee's amendment represented a minor change. At the same time, the Committee granted the president the power, for the first time in the history of the trade agreements program, to negotiate on NTBs—subject to a negative veto within ninety days of implementing legislation being submitted to Congress (as requested in the administration's bill). Finally, the Committee strengthened the provisions of the administration's bill which provided safeguards for domestic industry harmed by both fair and unfair import competition.

The Committee's amended trade bill was sent to the floor of the House on December 10, 1973, with a recommendation by the House Rules Committee that it be considered under a modified closed rule. As a result of congressional reforms designed to democratize the legislative process in the House, the modified closed rule required the support of a majority of that chamber. Thus, the Trade Reform Act, as amended by the Ways and Means Committee, faced two crucial votes on the House floor: one to adopt the modified closed rule, which was designed to preserve the work of the Ways and Means Committee by making it out of order to amend the bill on the floor except under specified conditions; the other on the bill itself.[54] After voting to accept the rule, the House passed the

Committee's amended version of the Trade Reform Act, 272–140. The core of the winning coalition was composed of Republicans and Southern Democrats— the so-called "conservative coalition"—who between them accounted for 220 votes.[55] In addition to voting with their party and the president, by the early 1970s most Republicans were ideologically committed to free trade and were able to justify their votes in terms of the major economic interests in their districts.[56] For their part, Southern Democrats voted for the bill largely as a *quid pro quo* for the efforts of the Nixon administration to protect the textile and apparel industries. Opposition to the bill was concentrated among Northern Democrats, who voted 2–1 against it (52–101). Generally speaking, in voting against the bill, Northern Democrats were supporting the position of the AFL-CIO; as well as making an effort to defeat a Republican president's policy initiative.

Following the vote in the House, which was seen as a great victory for the administration, the Trade Reform Act was sent to the Senate Finance Committee for consideration. In opening the Finance Committee's public hearings, committee Chairman Russell B. Long, a Democrat from Louisiana, declared that the Senate would take a tougher line on trade than the House Committee on Ways and Means:

> A great deal of international economic history has been written since Congress last delegated the Executive negotiating authority in the Trade Expansion Act of 1962. In my opinion, much of that history has been unfavorable to the United States. . . . I still desire an "open, non-discriminatory, and fair world economic system" [as the House bill's preamble stated], but I am tired of the United States being the "least favored nation" in a world which is full of discrimination. We can no longer expose our markets, while the rest of the world hides behind variable levies, export subsidies, import equalization fees, border taxes, cartels, and a host of other practices which effectively bar our imports.[57]

However, despite Long's rhetoric, the bill produced by the Senate Finance Committee made only minor changes to the House bill. Indeed, after holding public hearings that closely paralleled those in the House, and after its mark-up sessions, the Committee voted 17–0 to report a slightly amended trade bill to the full Senate. The most important changes made by the Committee to the House bill were to require that all NTB implementing agreements be submitted to Congress for an affirmative (rather than a negative) vote within sixty days of being submitted to Congress (the so-called "fast track" authority); and to further strengthen the nation's fair and unfair trade laws.[58] In explaining the Committee's change in the NTB authority, the Report of the Finance Committee stated: "Virtually all nontariff barriers in the U.S. are matters of [domestic] law. If the Congress were to delegate to the President the power to change domestic law, subject only to a Congressional veto, it would not only be a reversal of the constitutional roles of the legislative and executive branches, but also an abrogation of legislative responsibilities."[59] This change was acceptable to the administration. As W. D. Eberle put it, "As long as they can't hold us up on procedures, that's the key."[60]

The Trade Act of 1974 (as it was now called) reached the floor of the Senate in mid-December 1974, where it faced two critical votes: one on a rule to prevent popular but non-germane amendments; another on the bill itself. After approving the rule on non-germane amendments, 71–19, the Senate passed the Trade Act, 77–4. And after minor changes were made in the Trade Act in a House–Senate Conference Committee (none of which touched the act's negotiating authorities), the House passed the act, 323–26. The Senate passed the act, 72–4. And on January 3, 1975, the Trade Act of 1974 was signed into law by President Gerald R. Ford, who declared it to be

> the most significant trade legislation passed by the Congress since the beginning of the trade agreements program some four decades ago. [This act] demonstrates our deep commitment to an open world economic order and interdependence as essential conditions of mutual economic health. [It] will enable Americans to work with others to achieve expansion of the international flow of goods and services, thereby increasing economic well-being throughout the world . . . [and] . . . affords us a basis for cooperation with all trading nations.

The president concluded, "Alone, the problems of each can only multiply; together, no difficulties are insurmountable. We must succeed. I believe we will."[61]

Conclusion: The Triumph of Globalism in the Trade Act of 1974

With the signature of President Ford, the Trade Act of 1974 shifted trade policy-making power from Congress to the chief executive for the purpose of another major assertion of American world trade leadership. Indeed, it was under the authority of the Trade Act that American trade officials negotiated the Tokyo Round of Multilateral Trade Negotiations.

This chapter has argued that the Nixon Administration's trade policy was a reaction to external events: the continued expansion of the European Community, the rise of Japan as a great economic power, and the challenges of their trade and economic policies for the world trading system. In particular, America's response to these international challenges was the result of a collaborative effort between international corporate elites acting through the Williams' Commission, the CIEP, and the STR and the Nixon White House. This globally oriented, free trade alliance was unambiguously anchored in America's superpower position in world trade—for it fused the economic interests of multinational corporations with the foreign policy interests of the president.

Yet this superpower alliance was not able to implement its trade policy without convincing Congress to delegate its Article I, Section 8 power to "regulate commerce with foreign nations" to the president. As a result, the administration worked to build a legislative coalition in Congress that would support its Trade Reform Act. It did so by undermining protectionist interests in Congress by taking the textile and steel industries out of the legislative picture; strengthening the nation's import-relief laws; mobilizing internationally oriented businesses and their peak associations; and casting the Trade Act as a matter of vital national interest—specifically, the continued expansion of the GATT system and the exercise by the United States of a world trade leadership role. That they were successful in the face of rising import competition, stagflation, rising energy prices, and the Watergate scandal, is truly remarkable; and in the final analysis reflected America's superpower position in the world trading system as reflected in the capacity of the president and his international corporate allies to dominate the trade policy-making process. Viewed in this light, the triumph of globalism in the Trade Act of 1974 reflected a pattern of domestic trade politics anchored in the nation's superpower position in world trade—a pattern that expressed the power and interests of the nation's largest and most internationally oriented corporations and the executive branch of the American state.

Notes

1 Commission on International Trade and Investment Policy, *United States International Economic Policy in an Interdependent World* (Washington, D.C.: Government Printing Office, July 1971), 141–143.
2 *International Economic Report of the President* (Washington, D.C.: Government Printing Office, March 1973), 38.
3 Commission on International Trade and Investment Policy, *United States International Economic Policy*, 219.
4 Ibid.
5 Ibid., 199–211.
6 T. J. Pemple, "Japanese Foreign Economic Policy: Domestic Bases for International Behavior," in Peter J. Katzenstein, ed., *Between Power and Plenty: Foreign Economic Policies of Advanced Industrial States* (Madison: The University of Wisconsin Press, 1984).
7 Chalmers Johnson, *MITI and the Japanese Miracle* (Palo Alto, CA: Stanford University Press, 1982).
8 Commission on International Trade and Investment Policy, *United States International Economic Policy*, 215–217.
9 Ibid., 218–226.
10 Stephen D. Krasner, "US Commercial and Monetary Policy: Unraveling the Paradox of External Strength and Internal Weakness," in Peter J. Katzenstein, ed., *Between Power and Plenty: Foreign Economic Policies of Advanced Industrial States* (Madison: The University of Wisconsin Press, 1984), 79.
11 The first of these measures was the Fair International Trade Act (1968), which would have set quotas on most imports at mid-1960s levels. Another was the so-called Mills

Bill (1970), which imposed quotas on textiles and shoe imports, and made it easier for firms and workers to receive import relief. The third was the Burke-Hartke Bill (introduced in Congress in 1971 and 1972), whose principal backer was the AFL-CIO. The Burke-Hartke Bill increased taxes on multinational corporations and repealed pre-existing legislation which provided incentives for foreign investment. Further-more, the bill contemplated the creation of a Foreign Trade and Investment Com-mission—independent from the president—to coordinate the nation's trade policy; imposed quotas on nearly all imports based on the average annual quantity of goods imported between 1965 and 1969; strengthened the nation's anti-dumping law; and disallowed U.S. patent holders from producing with U.S. patents abroad. Perhaps most importantly, none of these bills contained provisions shifting trade policy-making power to the president. As it turned out, the Fair International Trade Act and the Burke-Hartke Bill died in the House Committee on Ways and Means. For its part, the Mills Bill passed the House and made it to the floor of the Senate before being scuttled in the face of an inevitable presidential veto.

12 Committee for Economic Development, *The United States and the European Commu-nity: Policies for a Changing World Economy* (New York: CED, November 1971), 5.

13 Report to the President submitted by the Special Representative for Trade Negotia-tions, *Future United States Foreign Trade Policy* (Washington, D.C.: Government Print-ing Office, January 1969), iv–v.

14 Alfred E. Eckes, Jr., *Opening America's Market: U.S. Foreign Trade Policy since 1776* (Chapel Hill: University of North Carolina Press, 1995), 210.

15 Cynthia Clark Northrup and Elaine C. Prang Turney, eds., *Encyclopedia of Tariffs and Trade in U.S. History*, Volume 1 (Westport, CT: Greenwood Publishing Group, 2003), 394; C. Fred Bergsten, "Crisis in U.S. Trade Policy," *Foreign Affairs,* 49 (July 1971): 619.

16 Committee for Economic Development, *The United States and the European Commu-nity*, 6.

17 Steve Dryden, *Trade Warriors: USTR and the American Crusade for Free Trade* (New York: Oxford University Press, 1995), 119.

18 U.S. Congress. Senate. *Staff Suggestions on Amendments to the Trade Act of 1970*, Com-mittee on Finance, United States Senate, 91st Congress, 2nd sess., 1.

19 Committee for Economic Development, *The United States and the European Community*.

20 Commission on International Trade and Investment Policy, v–vi.

21 In particular, and with respect to trade, the Commission singled out the European Community's CAP, Preferential Trade Agreements (PTAs), discrimination against Japanese exports, and enlargement as major areas of concern. In the case of Japan, the Commission singled out that nation's extensive use of nontariff trade barriers (NTBs) and its system of administrative guidance as the source of significant problems.

22 Commission on International Trade and Investment Policy, 1.

23 These safeguards were the adjustment assistance program, the escape clause (fair trade), as well as the anti-dumping and countervailing duty codes (unfair trade).

24 The recommendations of the Williams' Commission were rejected by its two labor representatives, who argued that they paid only "lip-service" to their central con-cern: the rise of multinational corporations and their shifting of production and jobs overseas. See Commission on International Trade and Investment Policy, Minority Report, 338–342.

25 Steve Dryden, *Trade Worriers*, 119.

26 Ibid., 147.

27 Peter G. Peterson, *The United States in the Changing World Economy: A Foreign Economic Perspective* (Washington, D.C.: Government Printing Office, December, 1971), front piece.

28 Ibid., i.

29 Ibid., 1.

30 Ibid.

31 Ibid., 50.

32 Ibid.

33 Also confirming Peterson's assessment, in December 1971, the 10 percent import surcharge was lifted following the negotiation of the Smithsonian Agreement, which began the process of a multilateral realignment of the world's major currencies.

34 Gilbert R. Winham, *International Trade and the Tokyo Round Negotiation* (Princeton: Princeton University Press, 1986), p. 15.

35 See Committee for Economic Development, *The United States and the European Community: Policies for a Changing World Economy* (New York: CED, November 1971), 5. In 1972, while still serving as STR, Eberle joined the CED's Program Committee, where he participated with William M. Roth and Howard C. Petersen in a study of U.S. foreign economic policy and the domestic economy. See Committee for Economic Development, *U.S. Foreign Economic Policy and the Domestic Economy* (New York: CED, July 1972), 4.

36 This suggestion was made by STR Deputy, W. R. Pearce, who had served on the Commission. See Robert A. Pastor, *Congress and the Politics of U.S. Foreign Economic Policy* (Berkeley: University of California Press, 1980), 139.

37 National Archives. Nixon Historical Materials Project. Dean R. Hinton Memo, June 20, 1972, "Follow-Up on Williams Commission Report," White House Central Files/(TA) Trade Subject Files, Box 4, Folder EXTA Trade (25 of 57, May–June, 1972).

38 Hinton Memo.

39 National Archives. Nixon Historical Materials Project. Peter M. Flanigan Memo, December 12, 1972, White House Central Files (TA) Trade, Box 5, Folder EXTA (Trade) (33 of 57, December 1–14, 1972).

40 Flanigan Memo.

41 Pastor, *Congress and the Politics of U.S. Foreign Economic Policy*, 158.

42 Ibid., 146.

43 National Archives. Nixon Historical Materials Project. Larry Brady Memo, "Marketing Plan for Administration Trade Bill," White House Central Files (TA) Trade, Box 5, Folder EXTA (Trade) (33 of 57, December 1–14, 1972.

44 National Archives. Nixon Historical Materials Project. Communications File, White House Central Files (TA) Trade.

45 Message of the President, Trade Reform Act, 1973.

46 Cited in, National Archives. Nixon Historical Materials Project. White House Central File (TA) Trade, Subject Files, Box 6, Folder EXTA (44–57, May 11–30, 1973).

47 *Congressional Quarterly Annual Report*, 29 (1974), 836.

48 U.S. Congress. House. *Hearings before the Committee on Ways and Means on H.R. 6767, the Trade Reform Act of 1973*, House of Representatives, 93rd Congress, 1st sess., Peter M. Flanigan testimony, 171.

49 Ibid., 162–163.

50 Ibid., 496.

51 Ibid., 492.

52 *Hearings before the Committee on Ways and Means*.

53 *National Journal*, "Administration's Reform Bill Threatened by Dispute over Relations with Russia," 5 (28) (November 24, 1973), 1742, 1752. The title of this article needs some elaboration. The dispute over relations with Russia concerned a section of the Trade Reform Act which granted that country continued most-favored-nation (MFN) status in its trade with the United States. With respect to this section a move was made in both the House and the Senate to tie continued MFN status to Russia's

relaxation of Jewish emigration—the so-called Jackson-Vanik Amendment. The fight over this Amendment in both the House and the Senate delayed the enactment of the Trade Reform Act for nearly a year, and was abandoned only after Secretary of State Henry Kissinger said he would recommend that President Nixon veto the whole trade bill if it included the Amendment. As a result, the Amendment was abandoned. See Pastor, *Congress and the Politics of U.S. Foreign Economic Policy*, 174–176.

54 The modified closed rule provided that only members of the Ways and Means Committee could offer amendments from the floor; and that other amendments could be offered only to deal with technical aspects of the legislation.

55 Congressional Quarterly, *Congressional Quarterly Almanac*, 29 (Washington, D.C.: Congressional Quarterly, Inc., 1974), 841–843.

56 Many Republicans came from districts which were home to export-oriented agricultural and industrial producers.

57 U.S. Congress. Senate. *Hearings on H.R. 10710, the Trade Reform Act of 1973*, Senate Finance Committee, 93rd Congress, 2nd sess., 1.

58 In the case of an implementing agreement that affected revenues, the Senate's bill stipulated that Congress would have 90 days to vote on the measure. In addition to strict time limits for congressional consideration of NTB implementing agreements, the fast-track procedure made congressional amendments—either from the floor, or committee—out of order.

59 Cited in Pastor, *Congress and the Politics of U.S. Foreign Economic Policy*, 163–164.

60 Cited in Ibid., 164.

61 Gerald R. Ford: "Remarks Upon Signing the Trade Act of 1974," January 3, 1975, *The American Presidency Project*, http://www.presidency.ucsb.edu/ws/?pid=4849 (accessed June 14, 2013).

7

THE NEW MULTILATERALISM

The Omnibus Trade and Competitiveness Act of 1988

Well, we're here to sign a piece of legislation that will help our economy continue to grow and compete. Our administration and Congress have come together in an effort to ensure open markets around the world. And yet this bill is just the latest step in that direction, in that effort, which began the first day that George Bush and I entered office and has already opened vast markets to American products all around the globe. It hasn't been easy, but I've never doubted our ultimate victory because we're riding a global wave. Country after country is recognizing that free trade is the key to a more prosperous future and that protectionism protects no one. . . . This bill will help us continue our efforts to open markets.

Ronald Reagan (1988)

The OTCA of 1988 is often considered the most protectionist and mercantilist trade act of the postwar period; and to some extent this is true: the act produced the most comprehensive overhaul of the nation's fair and unfair trade laws in the history of the trade agreements program. Yet this overhaul—spearheaded by Congress—was a movement within free trade; for the OTCA continued the nation's postwar drive to exercise world trade leadership, and led to a major expansion in the trade-negotiating authority of the president. Indeed, the OTCA was designed to allow the United States to participate in the fourth watershed trade round of the postwar period—the Uruguay Round of Multilateral Trade Negotiations, which was launched by the United States in 1986. Toward this end, the OTCA authorized the president, for a period of five years, to reduce U.S. tariffs by up to 50 percent of their prevailing rates; and to harmonize, reduce, or eliminate NTBs subject to a congressional fast-track procedure. While the fair and unfair trade provisions of the act were drafted in Congress, the act's liberalized negotiating authorities were formulated by the executive branch with the participation of globally oriented economic elites; and with the support of multinational corporations and their organizations. Therefore, while it cannot be said (as was the case with the RTAA of 1945, the TEA of 1962, and the Trade Act of 1974) that the OTCA originated in the executive branch, its freer trade provisions did. Furthermore, it was through active administration opposition to the congressionally initiated bill that became the OTCA that its most protectionist and mercantilist features were watered down so as to bring it into conformity with the president's free trade objectives. And while the Reagan administration took more protectionist and unilateral trade actions than any previous administration in the postwar period, these moves were designed to head off congressional adoption of a nationalist trade policy; and to plow the field for congressional adoption of new negotiating authorities for the president.

The Global Challenge: The European Community, Japan, and the Newly Industrialized Countries

From the point of view of new negotiating authorities for the president, the purpose of the OTCA was to allow the United States to respond to the trade and economic policies and practices of an expanding European Community, a more muscular Japan, and a handful of newly industrialized countries (NICs); and their deleterious impact on the GATT system. It also was designed to allow the United States to take the lead in expanding GATT disciplines to cover new sectors of the world economy (most importantly, agriculture, services, trade-related investment, and intellectual property rights); to better deal with the trade-distorting effects of NTBs (including domestic policies not directly related to trade, such as consumer health and safety laws and government procurement policies); and to strengthen the GATT's dispute settlement system. At the broadest level, the negotiating authorities contained in the OCTA were designed to forge a new multilateralism in the GATT system, one that would encourage the European Community, Japan, and the NICs to assume more responsibility for the system's management commensurate with their growing economic power.

For the European Community and Japan, assuming more responsibility meant adopting trade and economic policies that would better foster trade liberalization and multilateralism. For the NICs it meant reducing the degree of state involvement in the promotion of exports, and the use of various devices to limit competitive imports. Although none of these world traders had taken actions expressly designed to undermine the GATT system, various features of their trade and economic policies and practices posed significant problems for the system, as well as for specific sectors and industries in the United States. Many of these policies and practices were not new; yet the stronger the European Community, Japan, and the NICs became, the more their policies and practices grew problematic for the world trading system.

By the mid-1980s, four aspects of the European Community's trade and economic policies posed problems for the GATT regime, and for specific sectors and industries in the United States. One was the perennial problem of the Community's CAP. As will be recalled, at the heart of the CAP was a system of price supports, variable levies, and export subsidies. Not only did the CAP undermine the efforts of more efficient agricultural producers to sell in the Common Market, but, due to dumping, it undermined their efforts to sell in world markets as well. The CAP continued to pose a direct challenge to many nations (including the United States) which exported non-tropical agricultural products to the Community and throughout the world. Although agriculture received some attention in the Tokyo Round, the CAP was left virtually untouched.

Another ongoing problem was the Community's Preferential Trade Agreements (PTA) program. As will be recalled, PTAs were discriminatory trade agreements with non-Community countries and dependent territories. PTAs gave non-Community members preferred access to the Common Market—usually through lower tariffs and larger import quotas than were extended to the outside world. Moreover, many PTAs contained a "reverse preference" provision. Reverse-preference PTAs required signatories to give Community exports preferred access to their markets in exchange for preferred access to the Common Market. Although PTAs directly challenged the GATT's principles of multilateralism, the European Community continued to use them.

A third challenge was the Community's continued discriminatory treatment of Japanese exports. By the mid-1980s, the Community had negotiated an extensive array of quota agreements with the Japanese to limit their exports to the Common Market. The most significant of these quotas covered steel, automobiles and other transportation equipment, electronics products, and machine tools. Although many countries (including the United States) imposed restrictions on Japanese exports, Community practice was the most egregious.[1] As was the case in the early 1970s, Community protection against Japan created a triangular problem for the GATT system. Not only was Community practice inconsistent with the GATT's principles of multilateralism and trade liberalization, but it made Japan more reluctant to liberalize its own economy and to adopt a regime-consistent trade policy. Moreover, it forced Japan to concentrate its exports on the American market, which served to undermine U.S. domestic support for the GATT regime. Indeed, by the mid-1980s, fully one third of America's burgeoning trade deficit was accounted for by Japanese imports.

Finally, there was the relatively new problem of state-sponsored industrial targeting among Community members. While industrial targeting had been a feature of Community development since its creation in 1958, in the increasingly competitive world economy of the 1980s, it took on new significance. According to a study conducted by the United States International Trade Commission (USITC), by the mid-1980s the member states of the European Community actively supported a wide range of policies designed to enhance the international competiveness of targeted industries, including aircraft and aerospace; automobiles and transportation equipment; computers; electric machines; semiconductors; telecommunications equipment; steel; and textile and apparel products.[2] While some U.S. practices fell within the USITC's definition of industrial targeting (such as the protection of particular domestic markets through tariffs and quotas), the United States did not engage in the same level of coordinated targeting activities as did the European Community. The Community's industrial targeting posed two problems for the world trading system: it increased tensions within the GATT by raising the issue of what constituted fair trade; and to the extent that industrial targeting involved subsidies and discriminatory treatment of imports, it challenged the GATT's core principles of multilateralism and trade liberalization.

With respect to Japan, the problems remained what they had been in the early 1970s. One was the pace of Japanese import liberalization. Following a pattern set in the 1960s, during the 1970s and the 1980s, Japan's exports continued to grow at a much faster pace than imports. Indeed, by the late 1980s Japanese exports exceeded imports by almost 50 percent. Although Japanese tariffs were as low as those in the United States and the European Community, the nation continued to maintain a wide array of NTBs designed to aid Japanese industry and to protect its farmers. These NTBs included import quotas; import-licensing schemes; and a network of restrictive administrative rules and regulations governing imports. They also included a government-supported domestic distribution system which made it difficult for foreign companies to break into the Japanese market.[3]

The second problem posed by Japan was the unabated role of its developmental state in national economic activities, especially those designed to foster export-led domestic economic growth.[4] As Japan's power within the world economy grew, its approach to national economic development raised more and more questions about the nature and fairness of its competitive edge. This was particularly the case with respect to a number of large industries which were targeted for growth and which emerged in the 1970s and 1980s as major global competitors, most importantly automobiles, computers, iron and steel, machine tools and robotics, semiconductors, telecommunications equipment, and shipbuilding.

For their part, the NICs posed a challenge to the GATT system to the extent to which they utilized state-sponsored industrial targeting to promote the development of domestic industries, to expand exports, and to curtail competitive imports. While the nature of state intervention varied among the NICs, four countries epitomized the problem: Brazil, Mexico, South Korea, and Taiwan. Between the early 1970s and the late 1980s, these countries nearly doubled their share of total world exports and generally moved from large trade deficits to large trade surpluses.[5] Each of these countries supported trade and domestic economic policies that targeted major industrial sectors for development, most importantly, automobiles, computers, semi-conductors, electrical machinery, pharmaceuticals, textiles and apparel, shipbuilding, steel, telecommunications, machine tools and robotics, and chemicals.[6] These were industries within which intense competition already existed among the world's most developed nations; and the emergence of these (and other NICs) made global competition in these industries even more fierce. More than this, however, given the world export position of the NICs, their use of state intervention to promote industrial development generated problems for the GATT regime; specifically, it undermined confidence in the GATT's capacity to enforce discipline among its members, and raised questions about fair trade within the world trading system.

By virtue of its superpower position, the task of resolving these problems fell largely to the United States, whose response came in the form of the initiation of a major new GATT trade round: the Uruguay Round of Multilateral Trade Negotiations. United States participation in this round was made possible by the negotiating authorities contained in the OTCA of 1988.

The Formation of the Omnibus Trade and Competiveness Act of 1988: The Role of the Reagan Administration

The bulk of the OTCA of 1988 was formulated in Congress. Indeed, congressional involvement in the formation of the act was greater than at any time since the Smoot-Hawley Act of 1930. Yet most of the provisions in the OTCA that came from Congress were domestically oriented and dealt with strengthening the nation's fair and unfair trade laws, while the push for new negotiating authorities for the president, and the drive for a new GATT trade round, were executive in origin.

The Reagan administration's drive for a major new assertion of American world trade leadership began during the first few months of the president's second term. Early in 1985 United States Trade Representative (USTR) William E. Brock asked Edmund T. Pratt to conduct a major survey of private sector views on the initiation of a new GATT trade round.[7] The overriding purpose of this survey was to begin the process of building domestic support for the initiation of a new GATT trade round. Pratt was uniquely situated to initiate this process. Pratt was the Chairman and CEO of the Pfizer Corporation, a member of the CFR and CED, director of the ECAT, and Chairman of the President's Advisory Committee on Trade Negotiations (ACTN)—an official private sector committee established by Congress in the Trade Act of 1974 to advise the president and the USTR on trade policy. Pratt's involvement in the CFR and the CED was far from perfunctory. Indeed, as ACTN's chairman he played a leadership role in these organizations' trade policy work in the mid-1980s, when they undertook major studies designed to guide American policy with respect to the challenges confronting the world trading system.

The CFR's trade policy study began early in 1985 with the creation of a new international trade project: "The Future of the World Trading System and the Challenges for U.S. Trade Policy."[8] The steering committee of this international trade project was composed of over forty individuals, the bulk of whom were corporate business leaders, investment bankers, and corporate lawyers. Most importantly, the Chairman of the CFR's international trade project was Edmund T. Pratt, who worked alongside trade policy leaders W. D. Eberle, W. R. Pearce, and Harald B. Malmgren—all of whom were involved in the trade policy work of the Nixon administration.

The first publication of the CFR's project examined changes in the world economy which threatened the future of the GATT system, and called for a major new assertion of American leadership to respond to these changes: *Trade Talks: America Better Listen!*[9] The most important global challenge noted in this study was the "return of world-wide economic nationalism."[10] More specifically, the study noted that protectionism was on the rise, and that more and more countries were adopting "domestic industrial and economic policies . . . that give their . . . exports an unfair, favorable advantage in world markets."[11] These policies and practices threatened "to destroy the world trading system as we know it."[12] While the CFR's study was geared toward changes within the world economy as a whole, it was particularly concerned about the policies and practices of the European Community, Japan, and the NICs, which had embraced state intervention as the key to national economic development. The overriding issue with these and other countries was one of "rules and disciplines [within the GATT regime], of who obeys and who does not, and of what is fair and what is not." As Pratt put it:

> It is clear to those of us engaged in international business on a day-to-day basis that the rules governing the world marketplace must be improved if we are to maintain fair and equitable access to international markets by exporting and investing abroad. If the GATT is allowed to weaken further, the resulting contraction in world trade not only could trigger a world-wide recession, but could well lower the standard of living of all peoples—including the American people.[13]

The study argued that it was imperative that the United States initiate "a new round of multilateral trade negotiations" to respond to the deteriorating conditions within the GATT regime. Moreover, the study suggested an ambitious agenda for a new GATT trade round: "the unfinished business of previous trade rounds, such as emergency import protection, subsidies and non-tariff barrier codes; strengthening the trading system, by bringing sectors such as agriculture, textiles, and steel back under the auspices of GATT; and extending GATT disciplines to new areas such as services, high technology, investment, and intellectual property."[14] Finally, the study argued that the GATT itself was due for reform; in particular, its ability to enforce discipline among its members needed to be strengthened.[15]

For its part, the trade policy work of the CED was conducted within the context of a larger project examining the domestic and international consequences of global economic integration. Over seventy CED members participated in this project—the vast majority of whom were high-ranking officers in major internationally oriented corporations and investment banks.[16] Moreover, nearly a third of the participants in the CED's globalization project were also members of the CFR—including Edmund T. Pratt, Chairman of the CFR's international trade project. Like the CFR, the main concern of the CED was the deterioration of discipline within the world trading system. In particular, the first report of the globalization project, *New Dynamics in the Global Economy*, pointed to the "persistence of restrictive and distortive practices abroad" as a major cause of tension within the GATT. These practices included the use of NTBs, subsidies, and industrial targeting to enhance the competitiveness of domestic industries and agricultural sectors in world markets. The CED's report was particularly critical of the European Community and Japan; although its criticisms extend to the NICs and some underdeveloped countries as well. In addition to the deterioration of GATT disciplines, the report cited the lack of world trade rules covering intellectual property, services, and trade-related investment as contributing to this deterioration. The report concluded that the best way to deal with these problems was through the GATT; specifically, "through practical rules and remedies that encourage rather than discourage world trade." Toward this end, the participants in the CED's globalization project called for an American-led effort to initiate a new GATT trade round.

Pratt's participation as chairman of the CFR's international trade project and his participation in the CED's globalization project, coupled with his chairmanship of the President's Advisory Committee on Trade Negotiations, formed a bridge between the trade policy work of the CFR and the CED and the Reagan administration. In particular, in his capacity as Chairman of the ACTN, Pratt mobilized the organization's more than thirty private sector advisory committees to build support for a new global trade round and to produce a report on American trade policy for the president and the USTR. The report that emerged expressed an overall interest in a new round of multilateral trade negotiations, but only if new areas (including services, trade-related investment, intellectual property rights, and agriculture) were brought under GATT auspices.[17] Submitted to the USTR in the spring of 1985, Pratt's report helped to frame the administration's efforts to promote a major new assertion of American world trade leadership.[18]

Pratt's efforts were only one facet of the Reagan administration's drive to lay the groundwork for a new assertion of American world trade leadership. Another was the creation of the Economic Policy Council (EPC) in April 1985. The EPC was a high-level, interdepartmental committee established to oversee and coordinate economic policy-making within the executive branch. Between 1985 and 1988, all major decisions concerning the administration's trade policy were made by the EPC.[19] The EPC was formally chaired by the president, but operational power rested with the Secretary of the Treasury, James A. Baker, who served as the EPC's Chairman *pro tempore*. In addition to Baker, the EPC included the Secretaries of State, Commerce, Labor, Agriculture, and Transportation; the USTR; the Director of the Office of Management and Budget; and the Chairman of the Council of Economic Advisors. The EPC formed a bridge between the Reagan administration, the CFR, and the CED. Among the major players on trade policy, only James A. Baker was not associated with one of these private organizations. Secretary of State George P. Shultz, a former board member of the Bechtel Corporation, was an advisor to the CED and the CFR. Secretary of Commerce Malcolm Baldrige was a member of the CFR; and newly appointed USTR Clayton Yeutter, former director of the Chicago Board of Trade and ConAgra, was a member of the Chicago affiliate of the CFR.[20] Moreover, while not a formal member of the EPC, Edmund T. Pratt attended many of its meetings and continued to serve in the capacity of chief private sector advisor to the president and the USTR.

The trade policy work of the EPC began shortly after its creation. In the summer of 1985, Clayton Yeutter and USTR staff began negotiations with the European Community and Japan to persuade them to join with the United States in launching a new GATT trade round, which quickly produced agreement.[21] Over the next year preparatory negotiations were held under GATT auspices, and in September 1986 a new round was launched in Punte del Este, Uruguay. At the initial Uruguay meeting, the Reagan administration won a negotiating agenda which reflected the suggestions of the first report of the CFR's international trade project, as well as the ACTN report prepared by Pratt. Specifically, the administration succeeded in placing the following items on the Uruguay Round's agenda: agriculture, services, trade-related investment, intellectual property rights, high technology trade, NTBs, and GATT reform. In addition to a genuine desire to strengthen and expand the GATT system, the administration saw the inclusion of these agenda items as a vital ingredient in building domestic support for U.S. participation in the round. In particular, their inclusion reflected the administration's desire to knit together a new internationally oriented domestic coalition supportive of a major new assertion of American world trade leadership—a coalition comprised of services corporations, high technology industries, export-oriented agricultural organizations, and businesses with an interest in stronger foreign investment and intellectual property protection. Moreover, with a new trade round underway, the administration placed pressure on Congress to give the president new trade-negotiating authority; for if this authority was not granted, the United States could not meaningfully participate in the Round, and the nation clearly would be seen as turning its back on the GATT system.

In addition to preparing for a new GATT trade round, in the summer and fall of 1986 the EPC put together an administration trade bill. During these months the administration's legislative strategy and basic policy proposals were worked out. The overriding objective of the EPC during its bill-drafting process was to build interagency consensus on the legislation and to design a proposal which could win in Congress. Early on in these meetings agreement was reached that the foremost objective of a new trade bill was to secure a major grant of presidential negotiating authority from Congress. Although conflicts emerged in the bill-drafting process (mostly concerning the strengthening of the nation's fair and unfair laws), these conflicts were resolved by James A. Baker within the context of the EPC. For his part, President Reagan stayed out of the drafting process until near the end, when final decisions needed to be made.

The bill which emerged from the EPC, the Trade Competiveness Act of 1987, represented a substantial comprise of bureau and agency views. At the heart of the administration's trade bill was a presidential request for greatly expanded trade-negotiating authority. More specifically, the bill called for permanent standing authority for the president to negotiate NTB agreements (subject to a ninety-day congressional fast-track procedure); and a ten-year extension of unlimited tariff-cutting authority.[22] The act also explicitly called for negotiations on services, agriculture, trade-related investment, intellectual property rights, and high-technology products. At the same time, the bill expanded most of the provisions of U.S. trade law granting import relief; specifically, trade adjustment assistance; the escape clause; Section 301 (authorizing the president to retaliate against foreign unfair trade practices); and the nation's three traditional unfair trade laws: the Anti-dumping (AD) law, the Countervailing Duty (CVD) law, and Section 337 (relating to unfair trade laws not covered by the AD and CVD laws). The expansion of these domestically oriented provisions was calculated to secure a broad base of support for the administration's request for new negotiating authority, principally by taking the steam out of protectionist economic groups and their supporters in Congress.

Beyond these domestically oriented provisions within the text of its trade bill, the Reagan administration took a number of additional actions designed to increase the likelihood that Congress would grant the president new negotiating authority. One of these has already been mentioned: the efforts by Edmund T. Pratt to mobilize the private sector advisory committees of the ACTN to support the administration's trade bill. More than this, as chairman of the ECAT, Pratt worked closely with the presidents and CEOs of more than fifty multinational corporations to mobilize them for the legislative fight ahead.

In addition to Pratt's efforts, and the inclusion of expanded, domestically oriented provisions in U.S. trade law, the administration took a number of actions designed to head off the potential lobbying efforts of several major protectionist industries. These industries, which carried substantial weight in Congress, included machine tools, textiles and apparel, semi-conductors, and steel. The economic situation of the machine tool industry was of particular concern to members of Congress from industrial states in the North, Midwest, and Far West. The economic situation of the textile and apparel industries was of particular concern to members of Congress from the South; and that of the semi-conductor industry to members from New England and California. The economic situation of the steel industry was of particular concern to members of Congress from large industrial states, in particular Pennsylvania, Ohio, Indiana, and Michigan. If a majority of members of Congress from these regions and states joined together in opposing new negotiating authority for the president, the chances of a major new assertion of world trade leadership would be next to zero.

The Reagan administration's strategy for dealing with these industries and their supporters in Congress was to undermine their potential opposition by addressing their special problems outside the text of the president's trade bill. Toward this end, in May 1986, the administration negotiated VER agreements with Japan, West Germany, Taiwan, and Switzerland, to cut machine-tool exports to the United States.[23] This was followed in June 1986 with two international agreements. One expanded and strengthened the multilateral quota agreement on textiles and apparel (the so-called Multi-Fiber Agreement); the other committed Japan to expanding its purchases of American-made semi-conductors, while cutting its own semi-conductor exports to the United States.[24] Finally, in January 1987, the administration initiated negotiations with the European Community and Japan to renew their VERs on steel exports to the United States, which resulted in agreements to extend these agreements for three additional years.[25]

With the machine tool, textile and apparel, semi-conductor, and steel industries covered by special protectionist agreements; multinational corporations mobilized through the ACTN and the ECAT; and with the most extensive array of domestically oriented provisions ever included in a postwar trade act written into its bill, the Reagan administration submitted the Trade Competiveness Act to the House Committee on Ways and Means in February 1987.[26] However, unlike the RTAA of 1945, the TEA of 1962, and the Trade Act of 1974, the administration's bill never made it out of committee; indeed, it was never even considered. That said, the major new negotiating authorities called for by the bill found their way into the final act passed by Congress. Since these negotiating authorities were the most important provisions in the administration's trade bill, their inclusion in the OTCA of 1988—albeit in revised form—marked a major victory for the president and America's continued exercise of world trade leadership.[27] Indeed, as one trade insider put it: "while [a new] trade round was not its principal objective, it was ultimately the reason a bill was enacted into law."[28]

The Enactment of the Omnibus Trade and Competiveness Act of 1988

The legislative foundations of the OTCA of 1988 were worked out during the 99th Congress in 1985 and 1986. During the first session of the 99th Congress more than 600 trade bills were introduced in the House and the Senate.[29] While the vast majority of these measures were narrow in scope, three were designed to expand and strengthen the nation's fair and unfair trade laws. One of these measures was sponsored by the House Republican Party Caucus; another by a House Democratic Task Force on Trade; and a third by the Democratic and

Republican party leadership in the Senate. Although these measures differed as to particulars, each contemplated an overhaul of the domestically oriented provisions of U.S. trade law, and was designed to respond to the concerns of economic groups which faced or feared increasing foreign competition in American and world markets.[30]

Due to time constraints, the first session of the 99th Congress ended without any formal action on the three omnibus trade bills. Yet, early in the second session, the Subcommittee on Trade of the House Committee on Ways and Means began two months of public hearings on trade policy reform. The Subcommittee was particularly interested in hearing the views of economic groups on the omnibus trade bills produced by the House Republican Caucus and the Democratic Task Force on trade in 1985.[31] During the course of these hearings scores of economic groups testified in support of trade reform, including the United States Chamber of Commerce, the NAM, the AFL-CIO, and the National Grange. In addition to these broad-based groups, support for trade reform also came from businesses and unions in five major sectors: textile and apparel, iron and steel, chemicals, non-electrical machinery (including machine tools), and electrical machinery (including computers, telecommunications equipment, and semi-conductors).

For its part, the Reagan administration worked to defuse the drive for major trade policy reform. At the Subcommittee's hearings, USTR Clayton Yeutter testified that the administration was flatly opposed to a major revision in the nation's fair and unfair trade laws. He argued that "Congress is attempting to cure a myriad of problems that really should not be cured through the legislative process," and warned that many of the changes the Subcommittee was considering "will devastate the international trading environment."[32] In a refrain that would be repeated throughout the bill-drafting process, Yeutter told the Subcommittee that the president would not hesitate to veto a new trade bill containing a major revision of the nation's fair and unfair trade laws, and that while changes were needed in the world trading system, the best way to address them was through a new round of GATT negotiations.

Notwithstanding Yeutter's threat of a presidential veto, following the Subcommittee's hearings the full Ways and Means Committee moved into executive session to draft an omnibus trade bill. In the early phases of the Committee's mark-up, support for a major overhaul of the nation's fair and unfair trade laws enjoyed bi-partisan support. However, when the Committee's Democratic majority voted to include the so-called Gephardt Amendment in its omnibus trade measure, Committee Republicans turned against the bill.[33] Despite this opposition, however, Committee Democrats drafted the most domestically oriented trade bill since the Smoot-Hawley Act of 1930. In addition to including the Gephardt Amendment, the Committee's bill strengthened and expanded the nation's fair and unfair trade laws. Moreover, while the bill authorized the president to enter into tariff and NTB agreements, at this stage of the bill-drafting process, this authority was highly circumscribed.[34]

The Ways and Means Committee bill was sent to the floor of the House in May 1986 under a modified closed rule. Debate on the bill (H.R. 4800) lasted for two days, during which time Republican opponents of the measure offered three major amendments designed to weaken or eliminate key parts of the legislation. The most important amendment, however, was a Republican substitute for the Committee's bill, which, while similar to the Ways and Means proposal, was less far-reaching in its strengthening of the nation's fair and unfair trade laws. All of these amendments were voted down; and the Ways and Means Committee bill passed the House 295–115. Following the House vote, President Reagan announced that he would veto the measure, calling it "Kamikaze" legislation which would "plunge the world into a trade war, eroding our relations with our allies and free-world trading partners."[35]

The vote on H.R. 4800 was bi-partisan. Almost 40 percent of House Republicans voted with nearly all Democrats in favor of the measure. The defection of nearly 40 percent of the president's party from the administration's position clearly reflected the surge of imports into the American market as well as the rise of domestic opposition to further trade liberalization. As one member of Congress explained it, "Republicans are displaying the same kind of protectionist urges that Democrats are showing because their constituents are showing it. They are reflecting what their constituents feel."[36] Overall, support for H.R. 4800 was strongest among Representatives from regions and states with industries hard hit by foreign imports, or home to export industries (including agriculture) which faced foreign trade barriers. In particular, there was strong bi-partisan support for the bill among Representatives from New England, the South, and a number of large states with heavy industries, in particular Michigan, New Jersey, Ohio, and Pennsylvania.[37]

Following the House vote, H.R. 4800 moved to the Republican-controlled Senate. However, due to presidential opposition to the bill and a tight legislative calendar, the House-passed trade bill was allowed to die in the Senate Finance Committee. As a result, Congressional action on trade reform was postponed until the first session of the 100th Congress, in 1987.

At the start of the first session of the 100th Congress, Speaker of the House Jim Wright (D–Texas) introduced a new trade bill (H.R. 3). With only minor changes, H.R. 3 was identical to the bill passed by the House the previous year. At the same time, the Reagan administration sent its own trade bill (the Competitiveness Trade Act of 1987) to the Ways and Means Committee for consideration. As previously noted, the core provisions of the administration's bill concerned its request for major new negotiating authority for the president. More specifically, the Competitiveness Trade Act called for permanent standing authority for the president to negotiate NTB agreements (subject to a ninety-day congressional fast-track procedure); and a ten-year extension of unlimited tariff-cutting authority.[38] The act also explicitly called for negotiations on services, agriculture, trade-related investment, intellectual property rights, and high-technology products.

The administration did not offer its trade bill as a substitute for H.R. 3 but, rather, as a counterpoint, one that stressed the need for new negotiating authorities. Yet, because Congress was so far along in drafting its own trade bill, the administration's bill received little attention. That said, because the administration had launched the Uruguay Round negotiations in September 1986, it forced the Ways and Means Committee to consider this presidential request; for without major new presidential negotiating authorities, Congress would be put in the position of torpedoing the new GATT round. With the question of presidential negotiating authority squarely on the table, H.R. 3 became the vehicle for a major new assertion of American world trade leadership as well as for an expansion in the nation's fair and unfair trade laws. Indeed, in opening hearings on H.R. 3, Chairman of the Ways and Means Committee Dan Rostinkowski (D–Illinois) made it clear that he would attempt to strike a balance between the administration's request for new negotiating authority and those pressing for an expansion in the nation's fair and unfair trade laws. "I'm not trying to write legislation to please Lane Kirkland [President of the AFL-CIO]; I'm trying to write legislation that will be signed by the President."[39] For his part, Lane Kirkland signaled that if the Ways and Means Committee swung too far in the direction of the administration, the AFL-CIO would be forced to come out against H.R. 3.

> This is where Congress must exercise its responsibility to defend the national interest. Although sorely needed, tinkering with changes in trade law is not enough. The country needs more than a process bill. It needs legislation that recognizes the magnitude of our problem . . . Anything less is just smoke and mirrors.[40]

Beginning on February 3, the House Committee on Ways and Means opened a month of hearings on H.R. 3. These hearings were similar to those held in 1986—only with more emphasis on the new GATT trade round, which the administration declared would lead to results "in the very near future."[41] While similar to the Committee's hearings in 1986, with presidential negotiating authority at stake, a coalition of organizations representing multilateral corporations came out in support of H.R. 3 (although with lukewarm support or outright opposition to the bill's domestically oriented provisions). The most important of these groups were the CED, the ECAT, the U.S. Council for International Business, the Business Roundtable, and the Coalition of Service Industries, including representatives from the banking, insurance, telecommunications, data processing, entertainment, engineering, construction, food, and medical industries. The coalition also included Consumers for World Trade, an organization of multinational corporations and export-oriented businesses and farm groups, including, the Caterpillar Tractor Company, Chevron Corporation, IBM, Mobile Oil Company, Phillips Petroleum, RCA Corporation, the American Soybean Association, Continental Grain Company, and the National Corn Growers

Association.[42] Support for H.R. 3 also came from important constituency organizations, which approved of both major new negotiating authorities for the president as well as a major expansion in the nation's fair and unfair trade laws: the United States Chamber of Commerce; the NAM; the AFBF; the Labor–Industry Coalition for International Trade; and the Trade Reform Action Coalition—the last two bringing together companies and unions. Finally, the AFL–CIO threw its support to H.R. 3, but with an important *quid pro quo*: that the legislation contain the Gephardt Amendment.[43]

The administration's position on H.R. 3 was presented by the Chairman of the President's EPC, James A. Baker, and the USTR, Clayton Yeutter. Baker argued that the central principle behind U.S. trade policy was to unleash market forces at home and abroad, and that any action contrary to this would undermine the American and world economies. Furthermore, he stated that in its present form H.R. 3 was unacceptable to the administration and that the president would be forced to veto it—whether or not it contained new negotiating authorities.[44] Yeutter echoed Baker's position. In addition, he argued that any concerns about "equity and fairness" in the world trading system should be addressed within the context of the Uruguay Round and not through domestically oriented trade legislation. Like Baker, Yeutter stressed that the inclusion of the Gephardt Amendment in a new trade act would prompt a swift presidential veto.

Following its hearings, the Ways and Means Committee moved into executive session to draft a new bill. Going into the mark-up, Committee Chairman Dan Rostenkowski again reiterated that he would attempt to strike a balance between a major expansion in the nation's fair and unfair trade laws and the administration's request for new negotiating authorities. Thus, under Rostenkowski's direction, the Committee modified or eliminated a number of provisions of H.R. 3 that the administration found most objectionable. Most importantly, he persuaded Richard A. Gephardt to withdraw his amendment and offer it instead on the House floor.[45] Despite these changes, however, the amended version of H.R. 3 expanded and strengthened the bill's domestically oriented provisions. Yet unlike H.R. 4800, passed in the 99th Congress, the amended version of H.R. 3 granted the president major new power to negotiate on tariffs and NTBs. While these new authorities were somewhat less than the administration wanted, they represented an important presidential victory. With respect to negotiating authority, H.R. 3 granted the president, for a period of six years, unlimited tariff-cutting authority; and at the same time extended the president's NTB negotiating authority on a fast-track basis for four years, subject to a two-year renewal if the president could show that progress was being made in the Uruguay Round.[46] In light of Rostinkowski's changes, the new H.R. 3 was approved by the Ways and Means Committee in a lopsided, bi-partisan vote, 32–2.

H.R. 3 was sent to the full House in April 1987. It arrived under a modified closed rule which allowed more than a dozen amendments, the most important of which was the Gephardt Amendment. The Gephardt Amendment caused deep fissures in the Democratic Party—particularly among the leadership. Despite this split, however, the amendment narrowly passed, 218–214.[47] Following the vote on the Gephardt Amendment, Republicans offered a substitute for H.R. 3, which included all of the bill's provisions as originally reported by the Ways and Means Committee (i.e., absent the Gephardt Amendment). However, the Republican substitute was defeated in a party-line vote, 268–156. After this, the House voted to pass H.R. 3 as amended on the floor by a veto-proof majority, 312–107. Not surprisingly, President Reagan declared the bill to be protectionist, and stated that "Any protectionist legislation that comes across my desk is going to have a big fat V-E-T-O written right across it."[48]

Following the House vote, the action moved to the Senate, where the Finance Committee had been holding hearings on its own omnibus trade bill (S. 490). S. 490 was co-sponsored by a bi-partisan coalition of fifty-six Senators, and in broad outline was similar to the House bill. As was the case with Rostenkowski in the House, Finance Committee Chairman Lloyd Bentsen (D–Texas) signaled early on that he would direct the Committee's mark-up process with an eye toward producing a bill the president could sign. Yet, as it emerged from the Committee, the administration again signaled that the president would veto the measure. As one trade official put it within hours of the Finance Committee's vote, the Senate bill "contains provisions that could create trade conflicts without opening overseas markets and would make it easier for uncompetitive industries to get import relief at the expense of consumers and exporting industries. Unless substantial improvements are made, the president's advisors cannot recommend that he approve the legislation."[49] As passed by the Finance Committee, S. 490 strengthened the nation's fair and unfair trade laws, although it did not contain the equivalent of the Gephardt Amendment. At the same time, S. 490 granted the president major new negotiating authorities, although more circumscribed than in the House bill. More specifically, while S. 490 granted the president the authority to enter into NTB agreements on a fast-track basis for six years, it required the chief executive to submit all tariff agreements to Congress as well. Moreover, the Committee added a new procedure which allowed Congress to withdraw the president's fast-track authority at any time (the so-called "reverse fast track"). That said, the bill stipulated that the reverse fast track could be implemented only via a fast-track procedure of its own, which would make it very difficult for Congress to act under this provision.

The Senate Finance Committee introduced S. 490 into the full Senate in June 1987, under the threat of a presidential veto. Indeed, in a rare appearance at the Capitol, ten days before Senate floor debate commenced, the president held a luncheon with Senate Republicans where he urged them to wage a floor fight to eliminate the worst sections of S. 490, which he termed "dangerous."[50] From this point on, the administration began what one Senator called "a full court press" to prevent a veto-proof majority in the Senate. Republicans who were considered fence-sitters were visited by Treasury Secretary and EPC Chairman, James A.

Baker, and White House Chief of Staff, Howard H. Baker. White House lobbying, plus a last-minute blow-up over a provision of the bill concerning the rules governing the export of Alaskan oil, eroded Republican support for the measure. When the final vote was taken, the bill passed overwhelmingly (63–36), but three votes shy of the two-thirds majority needed for a veto override. Perhaps most importantly, just prior to the vote, the Senate adopted a strong but less dramatic alternative to the Gephardt Amendment by a lopsided margin of 87–7. This amendment, which became known as "Super 301," significantly strengthened and expanded Section 301 of U.S. trade law; and put pressure on the president to retaliate against countries which discriminated against U.S. exports.[51]

The Senate and House bills were reconciled in a conference committee which softened many of the most objectionable features of both measures. Most importantly, the committee dropped the Gephardt Amendment from the House bill; although it accepted the Super Section 301 amendment passed in the Senate. At the same time, it granted the president more negotiating power than at any time since the enactment of the Trade Act of 1974. More specifically, the conference bill authorized the president to enter into tariff agreements for a period of five years; to cut U.S. tariffs by up to 50 percent of their prevailing rates without returning to Congress; and to enter into NTB agreements subject to an initial three-year grant of fast-track authority followed by an additional two years of authority if the president could certify that more time was needed to complete negotiations.[52] The conference committee bill passed the House by a veto-proof majority, 312–107. The Senate, on the other hand, voted to uphold the president's anticipated veto, 61–37.

Once passed by the Senate, the conference committee's bill, the Omnibus Trade and Competitiveness Act of 1988, was sent to President Reagan, who promptly vetoed it. Yet the president's veto was not directed at the changes made in the nation's fair and unfair trade laws. Although the administration had repeatedly threatened a veto over changes in these provisions, the president's veto was directed against other provisions in the bill, especially a section dealing with plant closings. With respect to the bill's fair and unfair trade provisions, the administration decided that it would have to live with them if it wanted a major new grant of presidential negotiating authority.

In the wake of the president's veto, House and Senate leaders removed the sections of the bill which the administration did not like and brought the measure to the floors for another vote. In the House, the OTCA passed, 376–45. In the Senate, it passed, 85–11. The lopsided nature of these votes was facilitated by President Reagan's announcement—prior to the voting—that he intended to sign the legislation, which he did on August 23, 1988. In reflecting on the final measure, and the president's willingness to sign it, one trade official declared, "Few of the statutory changes [in the act] . . . involved activities that could not already be undertaken under existing law." And that despite the most congressional involvement on trade since the Smoot-Hawley Act in 1930, when it came to the fundamentals, "the 1988 act was fully consistent with the other trade laws of the [postwar] era."[53]

Conclusion: The Triumph of Globalism in the Omnibus Trade and Competitiveness Act of 1988

Unlike the other trade acts examined in this study, the lion's share of the Omnibus Trade and Competitiveness Act of 1988 was drafted in Congress, with little participation by the executive branch. Yet the constant threat of a presidential veto over early versions of the legislation—and particularly the failure of the Senate to pass S. 490 with a veto-proof majority—meant that the administration played an important role in softening the major domestically oriented provisions of the act dealing with fair and unfair trade laws. That said, from the point of view of America's world trade leadership role, the most significant provisions in the OTCA involved a major new grant of presidential negotiating authority; and this portion of the act originated in the executive branch, and was designed to respond to the challenges posed to the GATT system by the European Community, Japan, and the NICs.

Moreover, the negotiating authorities contained in the president's trade bill were formulated in the EPC, which included USTR Clayton Yeutter, former director of the Chicago Board of Trade and ConAgra, and a member of the Chicago affiliate of the CFR. Furthermore, the president's special private sector advisor on trade, Edmund T. Pratt (who worked closely with Yeutter), was Chairman of the Pfizer Corporation, the Chairman of the USTR's ACTN, the Chairman of the ECAT, the Chairman of the CFR's international trade project, and a member of the CED's project on the international and domestic consequences of internationalization. The participation of Yeutter and Pratt in the EPC, as well as Yeutter's creation of an ad hoc "insiders' group," served as a bridge between the nation's largest and most internationally oriented corporations and the executive branch; and it continued the domination of the superpower alliance in the trade policy-making process. The link between the nation's largest and most internationally oriented corporations and the executive branch was further solidified by the congressional lobbying efforts of multinational corporations, which were the strongest supporters of new negotiating authority. As will be recalled, the interests of these companies were represented in congressional hearings by the CED, the ECAT, the U.S. Council for International Business, Consumers for World Trade, the Business Roundtable, and the Coalition of Service Industries. The coming together of these corporations and the executive branch's lobbying efforts speaks to the confluence of interests between these globally oriented sectors of American society and state—a confluence structurally anchored in America's superpower position in world trade. And while the president was forced to respond to the concerns of protectionist and mercantilist economic groups and their supporters in Congress, these efforts were designed to clear the way for the president's trade policy proposals in the national legislature as well as to counter more assertive action by Congress. In the final analysis, then, and despite its strengthening of the nation's fair and unfair trade laws, the OTCA of 1988 continued America's postwar drive for a more open world trading system; and it led to a new and higher stage in the triumph of globalism. Indeed, not only did the negotiating authorities in the act significantly strengthen the hand of the president vis-à-vis Congress in the trade policy-making process, but they allowed U.S. trade negotiators to deploy these authorities in the fourth watershed trade round of the postwar era: the Uruguay Round of Multilateral Trade Negotiations, which led to the creation of the WTO.

Notes

1 Enzo Grill and Enrico Sassoon, *The New Protectionist Wave* (New York: New York University Press, 1990), 151.
2 This study is summarized in U.S. Congress, House, *Trade Reform Legislation, Hearings before the Subcommittee on Trade of the Committee on Ways and Means*, 99th Congress, 2nd sess., Part I, 458–475. These policies included research and development grants; preferential loans; state encouragement of mergers and the formation of cartels; state-led research projects designed for commercial applications; direct production subsidies; discriminatory government procurement policies for targeted industries; special tax measures; rationalization of industries according to state plan; nationalization of industries; state-led development of new industries; discriminatory licensing policies; local content laws; and various tariff and quota schemes designed to limit or eliminate foreign competition in the Common Market.
3 Office of the United States Trade Representative, *1990 National Trade Estimate Report on Foreign Trade Barriers* (Washington, D.C.: Government Printing Office, 1990), 107–125.
4 These policies and practices included an industrial policy through which the Japanese state sought to encourage high-growth industries with significant export potential; tax and credit policies directed toward high-growth industrial exporters; a system of administrative guidance to assure state–business cooperation in setting and achieving industrial policy goals; a foreign aid program which tied the granting of aid to the purchase of Japanese exports; and state support of export cartels, which developed integrated and cooperative programs for the penetration of world markets.
5 United Nations, *Yearbook of International Trade Statistics* (New York: United Nations, 1988), 994. The pace of the combined world export shares of these countries was about double the world average over the same period.
6 Committee on Ways and Means, *Trade Reform Legislation*, 458.
7 C. Michael Aho and Jonathan David Aronson, *Trade Talks: America Better Listen!* (New York: Council on Foreign Relations, 1985), 62.
8 Ibid., x.
9 Ibid.
10 Ibid., ix.
11 Ibid.
12 Ibid.
13 Ibid., ix.
14 Ibid., 7.
15 Ibid.
16 See membership list in William J. Beeman and Isaiah Frank, *New Dynamics in the Global Economy* (New York: CED, 1988).

17 Aho and Aronson, *Trade Talks*, 61–62.
18 In addition to the work of Pratt and the ACTN, in mid-June 1987, USTR Clayton Yeutter formed an ad hoc, private sector advisory committee comprised of "a select group of [more than 30] lobbyists for U.S. companies and business associations" who met regularly and on an off-the-record basis with Yeutter. This group was nicknamed the "insiders' group," and "help[ed] the Reagan administration shape the final version of the trade bill, in exchange for the opportunity to press their own views on Yeutter." Among the companies and business associations represented in this group were Pfizer, Caterpillar, International Paper, Philip Morris, Xerox, the NAM, and the ECAT. See Steve Dryden, *Trade Warriors: USTR and the American Crusade for Free Trade* (New York: Oxford University Press, 1995), 338; fn. 19.
19 United States Trade Representative, *1990 Trade Policy Agenda and 1989 Annual Report of the President of the United States on the Trade Agreements Program* (Washington, D.C.: Government Printing Office, 1990), 88, fn. 2.
20 The CFR's membership list is found in Council on Foreign Relations, *Annual Report, 1987* (New York: CFR, 1987). For Shultz's advisory role to the CED, see *National Journal*, 4 (25) (June 17, 1972), 1019.
21 Aho and Aronson, *Trade Talks*, 59.
22 United States Congress, *The Trade, Employment, and Productivity Act of 1987: Message from the President of the United States Transmitting a Draft of Proposed Legislation, 100th Congress, 1st Session* (Washington, D.C.: Government Printing Office, 1987), Title V, Subtitle A, Trade and Competiveness Act of 1987, 433.
23 Congressional Quarterly, *Congressional Quarterly Almanac, 1986*, 42 (Washington, D.C.: CQ Press, 1986): 343.
24 Gary C. Hufbauer, et al., *The Free Trade Debate* (New York: Priority Press Publications, 1989), 113–120.
25 *National Journal*, 19 (3) (January 17, 1987): 124. The VERs on steel were last negotiated with the EEC and Japan in 1982. In addition to these trade policy moves, in the fall of 1985, U.S. Secretary of the Treasury, James Baker, successfully negotiated an international agreement designed to push down the value of the dollar against other major currencies (the so-called Plaza Accord). From the administration's point of view, the chief aim of the Plaza Accord was to respond "to heightened support in Congress . . . for restrictive trade policies." See Congressional Quarterly, *Congressional Quarterly Weekly Report*, 43 (39) (Washington, D.C.: CQ Press, September 28, 1985): 1911.
26 The Trade Competitiveness Act was part of a larger bill submitted to Congress, The Trade, Employment, and Productivity Act of 1987, which had five titles containing 20 different bills.
27 As USTR, Clayton Yeutter told a group of reporters in February 1986, while the CEP was beginning the process of putting together its trade bill, the only item considered essential by the administration was its negotiating authority for a new GATT trade round. See Congressional Quarterly, *Congressional Quarterly Weekly Report*, 44 (10) (Washington, D.C.: CQ Press, March 8, 1986): 558.
28 Susan C. Schwab, *Trade-offs: Negotiating the Omnibus Trade and Competitiveness Act* (Boston: Harvard Business School Press, 1994), 4.
29 *National Journal* (January 17, 1987), 124.
30 Congressional Quarterly, *Congressional Quarterly Almanac, 1985* (Washington, D.C.: CQ Press, 1986), 254. Between 1980 and 1988, America's trade deficit jumped more than 400 percent, from 25 billion to 114 billion dollars.
31 Congressional Quarterly, *Congressional Quarterly Almanac, 1986* (Washington, D.C.: CQ Press, 1986).
32 *National Journal*, 18 (2) (March 22, 1986): 709.
33 The Gephardt Amendment was sponsored by Missouri Democrat Richard A. Gephardt and championed by the AFL-CIO and the Motorola Company. The amendment

stipulated that if a country maintained a large trade surplus with the United States, the president was *required* to negotiate a trade agreement with the country aiming for annual 10 percent reductions in their trade surpluses. Furthermore, if the country failed to meet these "surplus reduction goals" the president was required to take whatever retaliatory action was necessary to achieve them, although the president could avoid the automatic retaliation provision if it was determined that taking such action would cause "substantial harm" to the American economy as a whole. In 1986, Japan, West Germany, and Taiwan would have been affected by the Gephardt Amendment.

34 The Committee's bill limited the president's negotiating authority to one year and for the first time required that all tariff agreements be submitted to Congress on a fast-track basis. (In all previous postwar trade acts the president was allowed to proclaim tariff cuts without returning to Congress.) As in the past, all NTB agreements were subject to the fast-track procedure.

35 Congressional Quarterly, *Congressional Quarterly Almanac, 1986* (Washington, D.C.: CQ Press, 1986), 343.

36 Ibid., 344.

37 Ibid., 40-H, 41-H. Broadly speaking, the major industries in New England affected by rising imports or the trade policies and practices of foreign countries included, electrical machinery, non-electrical machinery, computers, paper and paper products, and leather and leather products. The major industries in the South included textiles and apparel, chemicals, electrical machinery, and timber and wood products. The industries in the major industrial states included iron and steel, automobiles, and non-electrical machinery.

38 United States Congress, *The Trade, Employment, and Productivity Act of 1987*, 100th Congress, 1st sess., 433.

39 Congressional Quarterly, *Congressional Quarterly Weekly Report*, 45 (10) (Washington, D.C.: CQ Press, March 7, 1987): 433.

40 U.S. Congress. House. *Comprehensive Trade Legislation: Hearings before the Committee on Ways and Means of the House of Representatives and its Subcommittee on Trade, on H.R. 3*, 100th Congress, 1st sess., 1987, 55.

41 Congressional Quarterly, *Congressional Quarterly Weekly Report*, 45 (10) (Washington, D.C.: CQ Press, March 7, 1987): 433. As it turned out, the Uruguay Round of Multilateral Trade Negotiations would last eight years (1986–1994).

42 *Comprehensive Trade Legislation*, 1451.

43 Since the fight over the Trade Act of 1974, when the AFL-CIO came out strongly against new negotiating authorities for the president, the union had come to the conclusion that it could not stop the free trade orientation of American trade policy. As Howard D. Samuel, President of the Industrial Union Department of the AFL-CIO explained it: "We have learned that our economy is no longer an island. We have become thoroughly internationalized. We know it is enviable. I do not think anyone is trying to put their finger in the dike to stop that process." Committee on Ways and Means, *Trade Reform Legislation*, 10.

44 *Comprehensive Trade Legislation*, 99.

45 Congressional Quarterly, *Weekly Report*, 43 (Washington, D.C.: CQ Press, 1988): 640–641.

46 Although this "reverse fast track" provision required the president to request an extension of fast-track authority after four years, the Committee's bill established rules that made it difficult for Congress to deny the request. Under these rules, the vote on fast track extension was a vote to *disapprove* new authority; in other words, the president would be allowed to retain fast-track authority unless Congress voted to take it away. Furthermore, congressional consideration of a "disapproval resolution" was itself subject to fast-track rules, which streamlined congressional procedures, limited floor debate, prohibited amendments, and generally made disapproval difficult.

47 Of the 55 Democrats who joined with 159 Republicans in opposing the Gephardt Amendment, the bulk were from coastal states heavily involved in foreign trade; in particular, California, Oregon, Washington, Florida, and New York. Of the 17 Republicans who voted with 201 Democrats in support of the amendment, the majority were from Northeastern states with heavy industries; most importantly, New Jersey, Pennsylvania, and Michigan. See Congressional Quarterly, *Congressional Quarterly Almanac, 1987* (Washington, D.C.: CQ Press), 24-H, 25-H.

48 Congressional Quarterly, *Weekly Report*, 45 (21) (Washington, D.C.: CQ Press, May 23, 1987).

49 Congressional Quarterly, *Congressional Quarterly Almanac*, 650.

50 Ibid., 651.

51 The Administration came out strongly against this provision, but to no avail. As USTR Clayton Yeutter put it in his testimony to the Finance Committee, "Section 301 is the H-Bomb of trade policy; and in my judgment, H-Bombs ought to be dropped by the President of the United States and not by anyone else." "In the long term," he continued, "we cannot repeatedly bludgeon other nations into opening their markets with threats of U.S. [retaliation]. Rather we must be able to negotiate credibly for global trade liberalization." U.S. Congress. Senate. *Improving Enforcement of Trade Agreements, Hearing Before the Committee on Finance on S. 490, S.539, and H.R. 3.* United States Senate, 100th Congress, 1st sess., 19.

52 This additional two-year authority was subject to a disapproval resolution (i.e., a "reverse fast track" vote).

53 Schwab, *Trade-Offs*, 222.

PART IV
Conclusions

8

TRIUMPH OF GLOBALISM
Politics, Theory, Policy

> What counts in any attempt at social prognosis is not the Yes or No that sums up the facts and arguments which lead up to it but those facts and arguments themselves. They contain all that is scientific in the final result. Everything else is not science but prophecy. Analysis, whether economic or other, never yields more than a statement about the tendencies present in an observable pattern. And these never tell us what will happen to the pattern but only what would happen if they continued to act as they have been acting in the time interval covered by our observation and if no other factors intruded. "Inevitability" or "necessity" can never mean more than this.
>
> *Joseph A. Schumpeter (1942)*

Schumpeter's epigraph sounds an important warning. I have argued that the triumph of globalism has been a constituent feature of American trade politics since World War II; and that this phenomenon has had a definite historical trajectory from less to more. Therefore, it might be tempting to conclude that this trajectory will continue into the future. Yet, as noted by Schumpeter, assertions of future developments based upon past developments are fraught with danger. Past patterns are not always predictors of future patterns. Therefore, in concluding this book, I eschew any predictions about the future course of America's exercise of world trade leadership or the triumph of globalism. Instead, this chapter reviews the book's main findings concerning the triumph of globalism and the political pattern that produced it. It then moves to a consideration of theory; specifically, the contributions which the book's external–internal approach may make to the study of American politics and public policy more generally. Finally, the chapter ends on a normative note by briefly exploring some actions that might be taken to ameliorate the impact of America's exercise of world trade leadership on the nation's democratic domestic political regime.

Politics

The central descriptive problem asserted in this book is that America's exercise of world trade leadership has rested on the transfer of trade policy-making authority from Congress to the president, and from the American state to the GATT/WTO regime: what I have called the triumph of globalism. If Congress and the president were similar institutions, or if the representation of citizen interests were the same at the domestic and global levels, this shift of trade policy-making power would have little effect on the organization of America's democratic domestic political regime. However, Congress and the president are radically different institutions and the representation of citizen interests is profoundly different in the domestic and international realms. The most significant differences between the president and Congress that affect citizen–state relationships are the institutions' orientation to the domestic and international levels as well as their internal political structures. On the one hand, the executive branch is a centralized institution (with the president at its apex) with a global orientation. On the other hand, compared to the president, Congress is a profoundly decentralized institution with a domestic orientation. The outward orientation and centralized political structure of the presidency makes the chief executive comparatively more attuned to the needs of American citizens with global economic and political interests and more insulated from domestic politics than is Congress; while the inward orientation of Congress and its decentralized political structure make it comparatively more responsive to American citizens with domestic economic and political concerns and considerably more removed from global politics than is the president. Furthermore, this transfer of trade policy-making power from Congress to the president has made possible a related shift of power from the American state to the GATT/WTO regime, which severs the citizen–state relationship almost completely. It does so by moving the trade policy-making process from the national level, where citizen–state relationships are constituted, to the realm of global politics, where the operative political relationships are state-to-state. As a result, the triumph of globalism has important consequences for the representation of citizen interests in trade politics and policy-making. It alters who gets what, when, and how.

Yet, the argument that America's exercise of world trade leadership has led to the triumph of globalism in postwar American trade politics begs a fundamental question: what accounts for the policy of world trade leadership? And here this book has argued that the answer is found in a pattern of domestic trade politics anchored in America's superpower position in world trade, what I have termed "superpower trade politics." More specifically, America's superpower position in world trade has generated a confluence of interests at the domestic level between the largest and most internationally oriented corporations, their organizations, and high-ranking corporate leaders and the executive branch of the American state; the first rooted in globally oriented economic power and interests, the second rooted in the power and interests of the president as the nation's foreign policy leader. The confluence of this deep structure of globally oriented power and interests has led to an enduring alliance between the nation's largest and most internationally oriented corporations, their organizations, and high-ranking corporate leaders and the President of the United States. At least with respect to the four crucial trade acts examined in this study, since the end of World War II this superpower alliance has dominated American trade politics; principally by formulating the nation's postwar policy of world trade leadership and fighting for the expansion of the president's international trade-negotiating authority. Moreover, the formulation of this policy has been in response to external events: the vacuum generated by World War II in the world trading system (RTAA of 1945); the rise of the EEC in the late 1950s (TEA of 1962); the trade and economic policies of a growing European Community and Japan (TA of 1974); and the trade and economic policies of an enlarged European Community, a more muscular Japan, and a handful of NICs, as well as the need to reform the GATT to cover more sectors and policy areas and strengthen its dispute settlement system in the face of a rapidly internationalizing world economy (OTCA of 1988).

However, the global policy objectives of the superpower alliance (i.e. the creation, maintenance, and expansion of an international trade regime through the initiation of GATT trade rounds) could not be realized without the president gaining negotiating authorities from Congress. For while Article 2 of the Constitution grants the president the power to enter into negotiations with foreign governments, Article I, Section 8 of the Constitution grants Congress the power to "regulate commerce with foreign nations." As a result, in order to exercise world trade leadership the president has been forced to approach Congress for the power to implement international trade agreements; and this fact of constitutional design has made Congress a player in the trade policy-making process. However, due to its decentralized and inward-looking political organization, and its concomitant sensitivity to the pleas of domestic economic groups opposed to the policy of world trade leadership, the national legislature has been a reluctant partner in the quest of the superpower alliance to promote the construction of an open world trading system. Moreover, as the result of an increasingly competitive world market (and especially the rise of foreign competition in the American market) over the course of the postwar period, Congress has become more and more reticent about granting the president the power needed to launch GATT trade rounds. Indeed, nearly every aspect of postwar American trade policy that has been protectionist or mercantilist in orientation can be traced to Congress, either directly or by its putting pressure on the president.

Yet, while Congress has won many battles, the president has won the war. The chief executive has done so in three ways. First, the president and his trade policy lieutenants have cast administration trade bills as matters of global policy vital to the national interest. Given the president's plenary powers in foreign affairs and his position as head of state, this has played to the advantage of the chief executive in his dealings with Congress. Most importantly, it has helped to skew the trade policy-making process in Congress toward the president. Second, the president and his trade policy lieutenants have worked to mobilize globally oriented economic groups to lobby Congress in support of a delegation of trade policy-making power to the president. In this way, the chief executive and his trade-policy lieutenants were able to create a free-trade coalition that straddled society and state; and that served as a counterpoint to the lobbying efforts of protectionist and mercantilist economic groups and their supporters in Congress. Third, over the course of the postwar period, the president has made special strategic concessions to major protectionist and mercantilist groups and their congressional supporters. These concessions, however, were movements within free trade, for they were the price to be paid for Congress's acquiesces to administration requests for trade-negotiating authority. Thus, by casting administration trade bills in terms of a global policy vital to the national interest, mobilizing free trade-oriented groups to lobby Congress, and making strategic concessions to protectionist and mercantilist groups and their supporters in Congress, the president (and the superpower alliance more generally) has been able to dominate postwar American trade politics. As a result, the exercise of world trade leadership has been the foremost feature of postwar American trade policy—a feature that has produced the triumph of globalism.

Theory

It has long been recognized that international structures and processes affect the internal politics of states. Among the giants of Western political thought, Thucydides demonstrated how the concerns of members of the Athenian Assembly about the city-state's external reputation (and therefore its capacity to manage its empire) played a central role in the debates over how to deal with the turn-tail Mytilenians. Machiavelli's *The Prince* explored the construction of state power within the strategic and military fields following the Medici restoration in Renaissance Italy. Tocqueville's analysis of the institutional organization of the American national state traced its relatively decentralized structure to the back-water position of the United States in the international state system in the early antibellum period. Marx pointed out how the expansion of the world market was essential to the growth of British industry and commerce and a force that would eventually draw all corners of the planet into its ambit. And Weber demonstrated how the emergence of the modern-rational state in Northwestern Europe drew heavily upon the Roman law tradition; and he explored how the position of great powers in the modern state system affects the formation of their states.[1]

Among pioneering twentieth-century social scientists, Otto Hintz argued that apart from class struggle it is the position of a nation in the international economic and state system that shapes its internal economic and political development. Karl Polanyi examined how the international political crisis that laid the foundations for World War II was anchored in the ways in which national states responded to the breakdown of the utopian attempt to reestablish the nineteenth-century gold standard in the wake of World War I. Alexander Gerschenkron contended that the power of Bismarck rested upon a marriage of iron and rye that was anchored in the external economic positions of German heavy industry and landlord–peasant agriculture. Harold Lasswell traced the development of what he called the "garrison state" to the strategic imperatives of World War II and its aftermath. Charles Tilly demonstrated how the emergence of the modern European national state was historically contingent, based on waging and winning wars, which itself was the product of differential combinations of coercion and capital within its territorial ambit. Immanuel Wallerstein argued that the international power of national states, as well as their domestic politics, can be understood only by locating their economies within an expanding capitalist world system composed of core, semiperipheral, and peripheral regions. Theda Skocpol traced the French, Russian, and Chinese revolutions to the weakening of their respective states as the result of strategic competition and war, which generated political opportunity structures at the domestic level conducive to revolutionary collective action. Peter J. Katzenstein traced the postwar economic success of small Western European states to the emergence of democratic-corporatist arrangements and flexible industrial policies at the domestic level which resulted, in part, from the competitive pressures of an increasingly open world economy. And Peter A. Gourevitch showed how different cross-class coalitions and state structures at the domestic level produced different policy responses by North American and European nations when confronted with a series of international economic crises.[2]

Given its long and rich ancestry, it might be thought that this "external-internal" approach has been broadly applied to the study of American politics. Yet this is not the case; for, despite its pedigree, this approach has not been systematically applied to the United States, where the study of American politics is largely divorced from explorations into how the international environment affects the domestic regime. As Ira Katznelson put it in the agenda-setting *Shaped by War and Trade: International Influences on American Political Development*, "[c]onspicuously absent are investigations by Americanists either of the international sources of domestic politics or the mutual constitution of international relations and domestic affairs."[3] The source of this analytical chasm is not hard to find. It is located in the remarkable disjunction, at both the theoretical as well as the institutional levels, between scholars concerned with American national politics and specialists in international relations. I believe it is also the result of the lingering perspective that somehow the United States is an "exceptional" nation—a point of view that lends itself to ignoring how American society and state are influenced by international forces that affect all nations (differentially, to be sure). This perspective wrenches the United States out of what Charles Tilly has termed the twin master processes of the modern era: a worldwide capitalist economy and an international system of states.[4] That American society and state are embedded in these twin master processes of the modern era is a point that should require little elaboration; for these

processes existed prior to the formation of the American state and the development of its economy. This point cannot be stressed enough: American society
and state are the products of a unique world historic development—the emergence during the long sixteenth century of an inextricably interlinked worldwide
capitalist economy and international state system. Lifting the United States out
of this economic and political field and, in effect, treating the nation as an island
has profound explanatory consequences; for it builds a deep-seated domestic bias
into analyses of American politics. This is not to say that the worldwide capitalist
economy and international state system determine American politics, or that, due
to its superpower status, the United States does not shape the international system
of which it is a constituent part. It is to say that students of American politics
should at least consider the domestic consequences of the nation's participation in
an international economic and political system, the dynamics of which affect all
countries. By way of analogy, divorcing the study of American politics from considerations of the impact of the international system on the domestic regime is the
macro-historical equivalent of attempting to explain the growth of a tree without
taking into account its root structure and the soil within which it grows.

  This book has endeavored to overcome this disjunction between external and
internal processes in the case of one public policy. It has argued that the triumph
of globalism in postwar American trade politics has been the result of the nation's
exercise of world trade leadership, which itself has been the product of a pattern
of domestic politics anchored in the nation's superpower position in world trade.
Of course one might argue that, due to its morphology, trade politics is uniquely
suited to the application of an external–internal approach. After all, a nation's
trade policy sets the rules that regulate the insertion of its domestic economy into
the world economy with respect to the cross-border exchange of goods, services,
trade-related investment, and intellectual property. As such, it naturally straddles
the external–internal divide and does so with respect to both society and state.
Yet it is precisely trade's morphological structure that makes it a potent advocate
for a more general application of an external–internal approach to the study of
American politics. This is the case because trade directly addresses some of the
enduring issues that have animated the study of American domestic politics for
generations; specifically, the pattern of class and group involvement in politics
and policy-making, the institutional organization of the American state, and the
relationships between them. In this sense, the study of trade politics takes on the
form of what Harry Eckstein has called a "plausibility probe," a case study that
"involve[s] attempts to determine whether [the] potential validity [of a theory]
may reasonably be considered great enough to warrant the pains and costs of test-
ing" in other times, places, and issue areas.[5] If this book has done its job, it suggests
a plausible research agenda for students of American politics that focuses on the
ways in which the evolving matrix of world capitalist economy and international
state system have affected domestic politics and policy-making from the earliest days of the Republic forward; especially with respect to patterns of class and

group mobilization into politics, the development of the institutional organization of the American national state, and the historically contingent relationships between the two.

On a more prosaic level, I believe it can be categorically stated that an external–internal approach is necessary for the analysis of the wide variety of public policies that are directly subject to the rules of the GATT/WTO. The reason is simple: there is no getting around the fact that these rules have an impact on the pattern of domestic politics and policy-making. As the Congressional Budget Office put it more than twenty years ago:

> Foreign trade can no longer be dealt with apart from other domestic economic policies and concerns. Governments often employ trade policies less for commercial ends than to achieve other goals—economic, political, and social. Significant trade liberalization thus means changing these national programs, and for this reason domestic policies will increasingly be the focus of trade negotiations.[6]

Many of these policies were outlined in Chapter 1; but they bear repeating. They include: environment, banking, and tax policy; foreign investment, financial services, and agricultural policy; telecommunications, technology, and intellectual property policy; small-business policy; government procurement policy, including affirmative action for minority-owned firms; and consumer health and safety policy. What is more, because the scope and jurisdiction of the WTO extend to all domestic policies and practices that may interfere with the regime's principles of multilateralism, non-discrimination, and trade liberalization (whether or not these policies were designed to interfere with freer trade), the number of policies potentially subject to WTO rules is as vast and varied as there are regulatory regimes at the local, state, and national levels.

Beyond those policies that are (or might become) subject to international trade laws, there are a number whose morphology suggests their analysis could benefit from an external–internal approach, such as national security policy; alliance formation; foreign aid policy; monetary policy; energy policy; and immigration policy. An external–internal approach also suggests itself with respect to the study of social movements, especially the labor movement; the environmental movement; and the anti-globalization movement. Finally, particularly in light of America's superpower position in the postwar international system, an evaluation of the impact of this status on the American state might lead to new insights in the fields of presidential studies, congressional studies, and studies of the changing nature of American federalism. This is not to say that these phenomena cannot be understood apart from the use of an external–internal approach, or even that the deployment of such an approach will yield new insights. It is to say that students of American politics would do well to at least consider the impact of the external environment on politics and policies that have traditionally been considered domestic.[7]

Policy

This book would be remiss if it concluded without some thoughts on how American trade policy might be reformed to lessen the sting of the triumph of globalism on the nation's democratic domestic political regime. Unfortunately, reform proposals are a dime a dozen; and reform is impossible without powerful political forces behind it. However, with this caveat in mind, it is possible to imagine reforms that would heighten considerations of democracy and domestic political autonomy without undermining America's exercise of world trade leadership. First, from the point of view of democracy and domestic political autonomy, the rules of the GATT/WTO regarding multilateralism and non-discrimination pose few issues; and indeed are worth keeping. One of the great successes of America's exercise of world trade leadership has been its drive to construct a world trading system based on cooperation among nations. This approach stands in stark contrast to the virulent forms of economic nationalism and trade warfare that marked the 1930s and that are generally seen as contributing to the global depression of that era and the outbreak of World War II. There is no inherent conflict between maintaining a cooperative international trading system and America's democratic domestic political regime. Where the problem emerges is with respect to the elevation of free trade over other social values. Indeed, when coupled with a commitment to ongoing trade liberalization, the increasing scope of the WTO's regulatory ambit necessarily means that its rules will push deeper and deeper into America's domestic regulatory regimes at the national, state, and local levels, thereby undermining domestic political autonomy. Yet this does not have to be the case. An international trade regime based on the principles of multilateralism and non-discrimination does not have to be one that sacrifices social values and the laws that implement them on the altar of freer trade. Indeed, it is possible to imagine a multilateral and non-discriminatory international trade regime that embodies values other than free trade; one that allows member states to pursue domestic social objectives without fear that they might be undermined by the rules of world trade.

With respect to the triumph of globalism itself, one can imagine a number of reforms that would lessen the sting of the GATT/WTO on America's domestic democratic regime. Although many may find these suggestions radical, I believe they are no more radical than the creation, maintenance, and expansion of an international regime for freer trade whose rules trump those of national governments. The first reform would be the easiest to attain, since it does not involve the creation of new institutions: the negotiation of a stand-still agreement. A stand-still agreement would simply allow the current rules of the WTO (including its dispute settlement system) to continue in their present form, but it would prevent the extension of international trade rules to new issue areas or moves to further liberalize the organization's myriad trade agreements. So as to be clear, this reform would not aim at rolling back existing rules, processes, or procedures.

It would simply acknowledge that the international rules governing trade have gone far enough. The main criticism that might be advanced with respect to this suggestion is what trade *cognizati* refer to as the "bicycle theory," which holds that if trade liberalization is not constantly moving forward the process itself will fall down, thus opening the window for a rise in protectionism. This might have been true prior to the creation of the WTO, when the GATT was a temporary agreement among nations with a weak dispute settlement system. The WTO is not the GATT. It is a permanent organization along the lines of the United Nations, the International Monetary Fund, the World Bank, and the International Court of Justice; and its rules are enforced by arguably the most effective dispute settlement system among international organizations. Furthermore, the Final Act of the Uruguay Round of Multilateral Trade Negotiations, which created the WTO, contains a "built-in" agenda for the (further) liberalization of trade in agriculture, basic telecommunication services, maritime transport services, movement of natural persons, financial services, subsidies, government procurement, safeguard measures, and professional services. A stand-still agreement would not affect this built-in agenda, nor would it undermine extant agreements, nor the operation of the WTO's dispute settlement system. Nor would the negotiation of a stand-still agreement undermine America's exercise of world trade leadership, for the United States could be the sponsor of such an arrangement.

If a stand-still agreement could be reached, further actions designed to enhance democratic accountability in American trade politics and the world trade regime might not be needed, for the triumph of globalism largely would be stopped in its tracks. However, if such an agreement could not be reached there are two reforms that would go a long way toward enhancing democratic accountability in American trade politics as well as in the international trade regime. With respect to American trade politics one can imagine the creation of a nationwide network of locally elected trade policy-making districts designed to incorporate citizen interests into the trade policy-making process at the national level. These local districts could feed into similar state-wide and regional districts, which would culminate in a standing national Citizens' Trade Congress. The Citizens' Trade Congress could be empowered to formulate policy which would be accorded special status within Congress and the executive branch. It could also be empowered to amend or veto international trade agreements negotiated by the president. Since the trade-related internationalization of the American economy and the rules of the WTO are having a growing impact on U.S. citizens, the virtue of this scheme is that it would allow for direct grassroots participation in the nation's trade policy-making process on a substantive rather than a consultative basis.[8] One also can imagine the creation of new institutions within the WTO itself, designed to build citizen participation into the process of global trade policy-making. This could be accomplished by creating a representative body within the WTO to which the citizens of member states elect representatives along the lines of the European Parliament. Although in recent years the WTO has moved to allow citizen-initiated *amicus curiae* briefs in its dispute settlement process (especially in cases involving the environment), and has opened some dispute settlement hearings to the public, these reforms have had little impact on the organization's policy-making process. As in the case of a stand-still agreement, the United States could exercise leadership in the construction of such a representative body.

In the end, however, absent the backing of powerful political forces, which are nowhere in sight, the prospect for these and other like-minded reforms are bleak. Moreover, even if these forces were to emerge, the triumph of globalism already has resulted in an institutional reorganization of the trade policy-making process within the United States which makes it difficult for American citizens to harness national state power to deal with the domestic consequences of trade-based globalization. As we look ahead, if the politics described in this book continue unabated, we should expect that the extant rules of the WTO will continue to push deeper and deeper into the domestic realm; and that the trade-related integration of the American and world economies on a freer trade basis will continue apace.

Notes

1   Thucydides, *History of the Peloponnesian War*, rev. ed., M. I. Finley, ed. (New York: Penguin Classics, 1954), "The Mytilenian Debate," Book III, 212–222; Niccolo Machiavelli, *The Prince* (New York: Bantam Classics, 1984); Alex de Tocqueville, *Democracy in America*, J. P. Mayer, ed. (New York: Harper Perennial, 1969), "History of the Federal Constitution," Volume One, 113; and "Accidental Causes That May Increase the Influence of the Executive Power," Volume One, 125–126; Karl Marx and Friedrich Engels, *Manifesto of the Communist Party* (London: Merlin Press, 1998), 14–15; Max Weber, *General Economic History* (Mineola, NY: Dover Publications, 2003), "The Rational State," 338–351; Max Weber, *Economy and Society: An Outline of Interpretative Sociology*, Guenther Roth and Claus Wittich, eds. (Berkeley: University of California Press, 1978), Volume 2, Chapter IX, "Political Communities," 910–920.
2   Otto Hintze, *The Historical Essays of Otto Hintze*, Felix Gilbert and Robert M. Berdahl, eds. (New York: Oxford University Press, 1975), "The Formation of States and Constitutional Developments," and "Economics and Politics in the Age of Modern Capitalism"; Karl Polanyi, *The Great Transformation: The Political and Economic Origins of Our Time* (Boston: Beacon Press, 2001); Alexander Gerschenkron, *Bread and Democracy in Germany* (Berkeley: University of California Press, 1943); Harold D. Lasswell, "The Garrison State," *The American Journal of Sociology* 46 (4) (January, 1941): 455–468; Charles Tilly, *Coercion, Capital and European States: AD 990–1992* (Malden, MA: Blackwell, 2000); Immanuel Wallerstein, *The Modern World System I: Capitalist Agriculture and the Origins of the European World Economy in the Sixteenth Century* (New York: Academic Press, 1974); Theda Skocpol, *States and Social Revolutions: A Comparative Analysis of France, Russia, and China* (New York: Cambridge University Press, 1979); Peter J. Katzenstein, *Small States in World Markets: Industrial Policy in Europe* (Ithaca, NY: Cornell University Press, 1985); Peter A. Gourevitch, *Politics in Hard Times: Comparative Responses to International Economic Crises* (Ithaca, NY: Cornell University Press, 1986).
3   Ira Katznelson, "Rewriting the Epic of America," in Ira Katznelson and Martin Shefter, eds., *Shaped by War and Trade: International Influences on American Political Development* (Princeton: Princeton University Press, 2003), 4.

4   Charles Tilly, *Big Structures, Large Processes, Huge Comparisons* (New York: Russell Sage Foundation, 2006).

5   Harry Eckstein, "Case Study and Theory in Political Science," in Fred I. Greenstein and Nelson W. Polsby, eds., *Handbook of Political Science*, vol. 7 (Reading, MA: Addison-Wesley Publishing Company, 1975), p. 108.

6   Congress of the United States, Congressional Budget Office, *The GATT Negotiations and U.S. Trade Policy* (Washington, D.C.: Congressional Budget Office, 1987), xii.

7   A more fully elaborated agenda for such an approach may be found in, Katznelson and Shefter, eds., *Shaped by War and Trade*. Some of this work is already being done. See, for example, Richard Rose, *The Postmodern President*, 2nd ed. (Chatham, N.J.: Chatham House, 1991); Aaron L. Friedberg, *In the Shadow of the Garrison State: America's Anti-Statism and Its Cold War Grand Strategy* (Princeton: Princeton University Press, 2000); Andrew D. Grossman, *Neither Dead Nor Red: Civil Defense and American Political Development during the Cold War* (New York: Routledge, 2001); Daniel Kryder, *Divided Arsenal: Race and the American State during World War II* (Cambridge: Cambridge University Press, 2001); and Aristide R. Zolberg, *A Nation by Design: Immigration Policy in the Fashioning of America* (Cambridge, MA: Harvard University Press, 2008).

8   Although the Trade Act of 1974 created an official Advisory Committee on Trade Negotiations to provide input into the USTR's international trade negotiating priorities, the Committee is appointed by the president, it possesses no substantive policy-making power, and the USTR is not required by law to heed its advice. Moreover, although the ACTN includes sub-committees on labor, agriculture, and the environment, as well as a sub-committee representing state and local governments, nearly 75 percent of its more than 500 members hail from corporations or business associations.

BIBLIOGRAPHY

Aggarwal, Vinod. *Liberal Protectionism: The International Politics of Organized Textile Trade.* Berkeley: University of California Press, 1986.

Aho, Michael C. and Jonathan David Aronson. *Trade Talks: America Better Listen!* New York: Council on Foreign Relations, 1985.

Allison, Graham. *Essence of Decision: Explaining the Cuban Missile Crisis.* New York: Little, Brown and Co., 1971.

Arndt, Heinz W. *The Economic Lessons of the Nineteen-Thirties.* London: Oxford University Press, 1944.

Bauer, Raymond A., Ithiel de Sola Pool, and Lewis A. Dexter. *American Business & Public Policy: The Politics of Foreign Trade.* 2nd ed. Chicago: Aldine, Atherton, Inc., 1972.

Beasley, William G. *Japanese Imperialism, 1984–1945.* London: Oxford University Press, 1987.

Bentley, Arthur K. *The Process of Government: A Study of Social Pressures.* Chicago: University of Chicago Press, 1908.

Bergsten, C. Fred. "Crisis in U.S. Trade Policy." *Foreign Affairs* (49) (July, 1971).

Bhagwati, Jagdish. *Protectionism.* Boston: MIT Press, 1988.

Biskupic, Joan and Elder Witt. *The Supreme Court and the Powers of the American Government.* Washington, D.C.: Congressional Quarterly, Inc., 1997.

Bloch, Marc. *The Historian's Craft: Reflections on the Nature and Uses of History and the Techniques and Methods of Those Who Write It.* New York: Vintage, 1964.

Buchanan, Norman S. and Friedrich A. Lutz. *Rebuilding the World Economy.* New York: Twentieth Century Fund, 1947.

Bull, Hedly. "International Theory: the Case for a Classical Approach." In *An Overview of International Studies,* ed., John R. Howard. New York: MSS Informational Corporation, 1972.

Business Week, March 1962.

Carr, E. H. *The Twenty Years' Crisis.* New York: Harper Collins, 1946.

Camps, Miriam and William Diebold, Jr. *The New Multilateralism: Can the World Trading System Be Saved?* New York: Council on Foreign Relations, 1986.

Chase National Bank. "The New European Market: A Guide for American Business-men." New York: The Chase National Bank, 1962.

Clark, Cynthia Northrup and Elaine C. Prang Turney, eds. *Encyclopedia of Tariffs and Trade in U.S. History*, vol. 1. Westport, CT: Greenwood Publishing Group, 2003.

Columbia University Rare Book and Manuscript Collection. Frank Altschul Papers, Organizations (CFR), General Correspondence, "Dinner in Honor of George W. Ball," 1961.

Commission on International Trade and Investment Policy. *United States International Economic Policy in an Interdependent World*. Washington, D.C.: Government Printing Office, 1973.

Committee for Economic Development. *United States Tariff Policy*. New York: Committee for Economic Development, 1954.

——. *Common Market: Economic Foundations for a U.S. of Europe?* New York: Committee for Economic Development, 1959.

——. *The European Common Market and Its Meaning to the United States*. New York: Committee for Economic Development, 1959.

——. *Taxes and Trade: 20 Years of CED Policy*. New York: Committee for Economic Development, 1963.

——. *The United States and the European Community: Policies for a Changing World Economy*. New York: Committee for Economic Development, 1971.

——. *U.S. Foreign Economic Policy and the Domestic Economy*. New York: Committee for Economic Development, 1972.

——. *New Dynamics in the Global Economy*. New York: Committee for Economic Development, 1988.

Congress of the United States. Congressional Budget Office. *The GATT Negotiations and U.S. Trade Policy*. Washington, D.C.: Congressional Budget Office, 1987.

Congressional Quarterly. "Extension of Reciprocal Trade Agreements." *Congressional Quarterly Annual Report*. Washington, D.C.: Congressional Quarterly Press, 1945.

——. *Special Report: The Trade Expansion Act of 1962*. Washington, D.C.: Congressional Quarterly Press, 1962.

——. *Congressional Quarterly Almanac*. Various issues.

——. *Congressional Quarterly Almanac*. Various issues.

Corwin, Edward S. *The President: Office and Powers*. 5th rev. ed. New York: New York University Press, 1984.

Council on Foreign Relations. *Studies of American Interests in the War and the Peace*. Memorandum E-B 32, "Economic War Aims: General Considerations." New York: Council on Foreign Relations, 1941.

——. Memorandum E-B 36, "Economic War Aims: Main Line of Approach." New York: Council on Foreign Relations, 1941.

——. Memorandum E-B 57, "Possible Revisions of the Trade Agreements Act." New York: Council on Foreign Relations, 1942.

——. E-B 76, "Coupling Economic Adaptation with Trade Policy." New York: Council on Foreign Relations, 1945.

——. *By-Laws with a List of Officers and Members*. New York: Council on Foreign Relations, 1945.

——. *The War and Peace Studies of the Council on Foreign Relations*. New York: Council on Foreign Relations, 1946.

——. *Annual Report of the Council on Foreign Relations, with List of Members and By-Laws*. New York: Council on Foreign Relations, 1961.

———. *Annual Report, 1987.* New York: Council on Foreign Relations, 1987.

Cronin, Thomas E. *The State of the Presidency.* Boston: Little, Brown, and Co., 1980.

Croome, John. *Reshaping the World Trading System: A History of the Uruguay Round.* Geneva: World Trade Organization, 1995.

Davidson, Roger H. and Walter J. Olezek. *Congress and Its Members,* 3rd ed. Washington, D.C.: Congressional Quarterly, Inc., 1990.

Destler, I. M. *American Trade Politics,* 2nd ed. Washington, D.C.: Institute for International Economics, 1992.

Destler, I. M., John Odell, and Kimberly Ann Elliot. *Anti-Protection: Changing Forces in United States Trade Politics.* Washington, D.C.: Institute for International Economics, 1987.

Diebold, William Jr. "A Watershed with Some Dry Sides: the Trade Expansion Act of 1962." Revised text, n.d.

Dryden, Steve. *Trade Warriors: USTR and the American Crusade for Free Trade.* London: Oxford University Press, 1995.

Easton, David. "The Political System Besieged by the State." *Political Theory* 9 (3) (August 1981): 303–325.

Eckes, Alfred E. *Opening America's Market: U.S. Foreign Trade Policy since 1776.* Chapel Hill: University of North Carolina Press, 1995.

———. "Interview with W. Michael Blumenthal. In *Revisiting U.S. Trade Policy.* Athens: Ohio University Press, 2000.

Eckstein, Harry. "Case Study and Theory in Political Science." In *Handbook of Political Science,* Vol. 7, Fred L. Greenstein and Nelson Polsby, eds. Reading, MA: Addison-Wesley Publishing Company, 1975.

Eichengreen, Barry and Douglas A. Irwin. "Trade Blocs, Currency Blocs and the Reorientation of World Trade in the 1930s." *Journal of International Economics* 38 (February 1995): 1–24.

Elliot, William Y. *The Political Economy of American Foreign Policy.* New York: Henry Holt and Company, 1955.

European Commission. *Market Access Sectoral and Trade Barriers Database,* "United States: General Features of Trade Policy, 2003."

Eustat. http://www.eustat.es/elementos/ele0002500/tbl0002544_i.html#axzz2cYSsHhA3

Fenno, Richard E. *Home Style: House Members in Their Districts.* Boston: Little, Brown, and Co., 1978.

Finlayson, Jock A. and Mark W. Zacher, "The GATT and the Regulation of Trade Barriers: Regime Dynamics and Functions." In *International Regimes,* ed., Stephen D. Krasner. Ithaca, NY: Cornell University Press, 1983.

Ford, Gerald R. "Remarks Upon Signing the Trade Act of 1974," January 3, 1975, *The American History Presidency Project,* http://www.Presidency.ucsb.edu/ws/?pid=4898.

Fortune Magazine. http://money.cnn.com/magazines/fortune/global500/2005/index.html.

———. "The Fortune Directory of the Largest U.S. Corporations." July 1961.

———. "The Fortune Directory of the 100 Largest Industrial Corporations Outside the United States." August 1961.

———. "The Fortune Directory of the 500 Largest Industrial Corporations." May 1971.

———. "The 200 Largest Industrial Companies Outside the United States." August 1971.

———. "The 500 Largest Industrials." May 1981.

———. "The Foreign 500." August 1981.

———. "The World's Biggest Industrial Corporations." July 1991.

——. "The World's Largest Corporations." July 2001.

Friedberg, Aaron L. *In the Shadow of the Garrison State: America's Anti-Statism and Its Cold War Grand Strategy*. Princeton: Princeton University Press, 2000.

Froman, Lewis A. *Congressmen and Their Constituencies*. Chicago: Rand McNally and Co., 1963.

Gabaccia, Donna R. *Foreign Relations: American Immigration Policy in Global Perspective*. Princeton: Princeton University Press, 2012.

Gerschenkron, Alexander. *Bread and Democracy in Germany*. Berkeley: University of California Press, 1943.

Gourevitch, Peter. *Politics in Hard Times: Comparative Responses to International Economic Crises*. Ithaca, NY: Cornell University Press, 1986.

Government Accounting Office. *World Trade Organization: Standard of Review and Impact of Trade Remedy Rulings*. Report to the Ranking Minority Member, Committee on Finance, U.S. Senate, GAO-03-824, July 2003.

Grill, Enzo and Enrico Sassoon. *The New Protectionist Wave*. New York: New York University Press, 1990.

Grossman, Andrew D. *Neither Dead nor Red: Civil Defense and American Political Development during the Cold War*. New York: Routledge, 2001.

Hawkins, Harry C. and Janet L. Norwood. "The Legislative Basis of U.S. Commercial Policy." In *Studies in United States Commercial Policy*, ed., William B. Kelly, Jr. Chapel Hill: University of North Carolina Press, 1963.

Herring, E. Pendleton. Book Review. "Politics, Pressures and the Tariff." *American Political Science Review* 30 (2) (April 1936): 374–375.

Hinshaw, Randall. *The European Community and American Trade*. New York: Praeger Publishers, 1964.

Hintze, Otto. "Economics and Politics in the Age of Modern Capitalism." In *The Historical Essays of Otto Hintze*, Felix Gilbert and Robert M. Berdahl, eds. London: Oxford University Press, 1975.

Hirschman, Albert O. *National Power and the Structure of Foreign Trade*. Berkeley: University of California Press, 1945.

Hiscox, Michael J. *International Trade and Political Conflict: Commerce, Coalitions, and Mobility*. Princeton: Princeton University Press, 2001.

Hoffman, Stanley, ed. *Gulliver's Troubles; or, the Setting of American Foreign Policy*. New York: McGraw Hill, 1968.

Hufbauer, Gary C. et al. *The Free Trade Debate*. New York: Priority Press Publications, 1989.

Hull, Cordell. "National Foreign Trade Week." *Department of State Bulletin* 10 (256) (1944): 480.

——. *The Memoirs of Cordell Hull*, vol. II. New York: The Macmillan Company, 1948.

Internal Revenue Service. *Tax Statistics 2000*. www.irs.gove/uac/SOI-Tax-Stats-Table-3-Corporation Returns-With-Net-Income.

International Economic Report of the President (Washington, D.C.: Government Printing Office, March, 1973).

Irwin, Douglass A. "Multilateral and Bilateral Trade Policies in the World Trading System: An Historical Perspective." In *New Dimensions in Regional Integration*, eds., Jamie de Melo and Arvind Panagariya. New York: Cambridge University Press, 1993.

Jackson, John H. "The General Agreement on Tariffs and Trade in United States Domestic Law." *Michigan Law Review* 66 (1967): 249–322.

Jackson, John H., William J. Davey, and Alan Ol Sykes. *Legal Problems of International Economic Relations*, 3rd ed. Minneapolis: West Publishing Company, 1995.

John F. Kennedy Presidential Library. Committee for a National Trade Policy, Board of Directors. Petersen Box 14, Finney File, CNTP Information Kit.

John F. Kennedy Presidential Library. Howard C. Petersen, Chronological File, Box 1, August 1961–September 1962.

John F. Kennedy Presidential Library. Library Oral History Program. Luther Hodges, "Oral History Interview."

John F. Kennedy Presidential Library. Library Oral History Program. Myer Rashish, "Oral History Interview."

John F. Kennedy Presidential Library. Master List of Association Petitions. Davies File, Howard C. Petersen, Box 6, Folder "Company Positions on H.R. 11970."

Johnson, Chalmers. *MITI and the Japanese Miracle*. Palo Alto: Stanford University Press, 1982.

Kaiser, Robert G. and John Burgess. 1999. "A Seattle Primer: How Not to Hold WTO Talks." *Washington Post*, December 12.

Katzenstein, Peter J. *Small States in World Markets: Industrial Policy in Europe*. Ithaca, NY: Cornell University Press, 1985.

Katznelson, Ira and Martin Shefter, eds. *Shaped by War and Trade: International Influences on American Political Development*. Princeton: Princeton University Press, 2003.

Kennedy, John F. State of the Union Address, January 11, 1962. www.infoplease.com/t/his/state-of-theunion/175.html.

Kennedy, John F. "Trade Expansion Act of 1962 Signed." *Department of State Bulletin*, October 29, 1962.

Keohane, Robert O. *After Hegemony: Cooperation and Discord in the World Political Economy*. Princeton: Princeton University Press, 1984.

——. "Problematic Lucidity: Stephen Krasner's 'State Power and International Trade'." *World Politics* 50 (1) (October 1997): 150–170.

Keohane, Robert O. and Joseph S. Nye. *Power and Interdependence*, 2nd ed. Boston: Scott, Forseman and Company, 1989.

Kindleberger, Charles P. *The World in Depress, 1929–1930*. Berkeley: University of California Press, 1986.

Koenig, Louis W. *The Chief Executive*. New York: Harcourt Brace Javanovich, Inc., 1975.

Koh, Harold H. "The Fast Track and United States Trade Policy." *Brooklyn Journal of International Law* XVII (1992): 143–180.

Kraft, Joseph. *The Grand Design: From Common Market to Atlantic Partnership*. New York: Harper and Brothers Publishers, 1964.

Krasner, Stephen D. "State Power and the Structure of International Trade." *World Politics* 28 (3) (April 1976): 317–347.

——. "United States Commercial and Monetary Policy: Unraveling the Paradox of External Strength and Internal Weakness." In *Between Power and Plenty: Foreign Economic Policies of Advanced Industrial States*, ed., Peter J. Katzenstein, Madison: University of Wisconsin Press, 1978.

——, ed. *International Regimes*. Ithaca, NY: Cornell University Press, 1981.

Kryder, Daniel. *Divided Arsenal: Race and the American State during World War II*. New York: Cambridge University Press, 2001.

Lake, David A. *Power, Protection, and Free Trade: International Sources of U.S. Commercial Strategy, 1887–1939*. Ithaca, NY: Cornell University Press, 1988.

Lasswell, Harold D. "The Garrison State." *American Journal of Sociology* 46 (4) (January, 1941): 455–468.

List, Friedrich. *The National System of Political Economy, Volume II, the Theory.* New York: Augustus M. Kelley, 1996.

Low, Patrick *Trading Free: The GATT and U.S. Trade Policy.* Washington, D.C.: Twentieth Century Fund, 1993.

Lowi, Theodore J. Book Review. "American Business, Public Policy, Case-Studies, and Political Theory." *World Politics* 16 (4) (July 1964): 677–715.

MacArthur, John R. *The Selling of "Free Trade."* New York: Hill and Wang, 2000.

Machiavelli, Niccolo. *The Prince.* New York: Harper Perennial, 1969.

Maddison, Angus. "Historical Statistics of the World Economy. www.ggc.net/maddison/Historical.../horizontal-file_02–2010.xls.

Manley, John F. *The Politics of Finance: The House Committee on Ways and Means.* New York: Little Brown, 1970.

Marx, Karl. "On the Question of Free Trade." In *Collected Works*, Vol. 6. Karl Marx and Fredrick Engels. New York: International Publisher, 1976.

Marx, Karl and Friedrich Engels. *The Manifesto of the Communist Party.* London: Merlin Press, 1998.

Mastanduno, Michael. "The United States Political System and International Leadership: A 'Decidedly Inferior' Form of Government." In *American Foreign Policy: Theoretical Essays*, 2nd ed., ed., G. John Ikenberry. New York: Harper Collins, 1996.

Mayhew, David R. *Congress: The Electoral Connection.* New Haven: Yale University Press, 1974.

McKeown, Timothy J. "Hegemonic Stability Theory and Nineteenth Century Tariff Levels in Europe." *International Organization* 37 (1) (December 1983): 73–91.

——. "The Limitations of 'Structural' Theories of Commercial Policy." *International Organization* 40 (1) (Winter 1986): 43–64.

Milner, Helen V. *Resisting Protectionism: Global Industries and the Politics of International Trade.* Princeton: Princeton University Press, 1988.

National Archives. Committee on Trade Agreements and Committee on Trade Barriers. International Trade Files. Trade Barrier Minutes. Box 101, "Legislative Program for Renewal and Expansion of Trade Agreements Authority for Multilateral Negotiations," February 6, 1945.

National Archives. Executive Committee on Economic Foreign Policy. Interdepartmental and Intradepartmental Committees. Box 47, ECEFP Docs., "Legislative Program on Trade Barriers, February 8, 1945.

National Archives. Interdepartmental and Intradepartmental Committees. Box 47, ECEFP Docs., "Objectives of a Legislative Program on Trade Barriers," March 2, 1945.

National Archives. Interdepartmental and Intradepartmental Committees. "Minutes of the Meeting of the Executive Committee on Economic Foreign Policy," Box 57, ECEFP Minutes Docs., March 9, 1945.

National Archives. Interdepartmental and Intradepartmental Committees. "Minutes of the Meeting of the Executive Committee on Economic Foreign Policy," Box 57, ECEFP Docs., March 16, 1945.

National Archives. Nixon Historical Materials Project. Dean R. Hinton Memo, June 20, 1972, "Follow Up on Williams' Commission Report," White House Central Files/ (TA), Trade Subject Files, Box 4, Folder EXTA Trade (25 of 57, May–June, 1972).

National Archives. Nixon Historical Materials Project. Peter M. Flanigan Memo, December 12, 1972, White House Central Files (TA) Trade, Box 5, Folder EXTA (Trade) (33 of 57, December 1–14, 1972).

National Archives. Nixon Historical Materials Project. Larry Brady Memo, "Marketing Plan for Administration Trade Bill," White House Central Files (TA) Trade, Box 5, Folder EXTA (Trade) (33 of 57, December 1–14, 1972).

National Archives. Nixon Historical Materials Project. Communications File, White House Central Files (TA) Trade.

National Archives. Nixon Historical Materials Project. White House Central File (TA) Trade, Subject Files, Box 6, Folder EXTA (44–57, May 11–30, 1973).

National Journal. Various issues.

National Lawyers Guild, Seattle Chapter. *Bringing in an Undemocratic Institution Brings an Undemocratic Response.* Seattle: National Lawyers Guild, Seattle Chapter, 2000.

Nettl, J. P. "The State as a Conceptual Variable." *World Politics,* 20 (4) (1968): 559–592.

New York Times. January 8, 1962.

Notter, Harley A. *Postwar Foreign Policy Preparation, 1939–1945.* Washington, D.C.: Government Printing Office, 1949.

Nye, Joseph S. and Robert Keohane. "Transnational Relations and World Politics: An Introduction." *International Organization* 25 (3) (Summer 1971): 329–349.

Odell, John S. *U.S. International Monetary Policy: Markets, Power, and Ideas as Sources of Change.* Princeton: Princeton University Press, 1982.

Office of the United States Trade Representative. *1990 National Trade Estimate Report on Foreign Trade Barriers.* Washington, D.C.: Government Printing Office, 1990.

——. *1990 Trade Policy Agenda and 1989 Annual Report of the President of the United States on the Trade Agreements Program.* Washington, D.C.: Government Printing Office, 1990.

O'Halloran, Sharyn. *Politics, Process, and American Trade Policy.* Ann Arbor: University of Michigan Press, 1994.

Olezek, Walter J., *Congressional Procedures and the Policy Process,* Washington, D.C.: Congressional Quarterly, Inc., 1989.

Paarlberg, Robert L. *Leadership Abroad Begins at Home: U.S. Foreign Economic Policy After the Cold War.* Washington, D.C.: The Brookings Institution, 1995.

Pastor, Robert A. *Congress and the Politics of U.S. Foreign Economic Policy.* Berkeley: University of California Press, 1980.

Pemple, T. J. "Japanese Foreign Economic Policy." In *Between Power and Plenty: Foreign Economic Policies of Advanced Industrial States,* Peter J. Katzenstein, ed. Madison: The University of Wisconsin Press, 1984.

Penrose, E. F. *Economic Planning for the Peace.* Princeton: Princeton University Press, 1953.

Peterson, Peter G. *The United States in the Changing World Economy: A Foreign Economic Perspective.* Washington, D.C.: Government Printing Office, 1971.

Pious, Richard M. *The American Presidency.* New York: Basic Books, 1979.

Polanyi, Karl. *The Great Transformation: The Political and Economic Origins of Our Time.* Boston: Beacon Press, 1975.

Preeg, Ernest H. *Traders and Diplomats: An Analysis of the Kennedy Round of Negotiations under the General Agreement on Tariffs and Trade.* Washington, D.C.: The Brookings Institution, 1970.

——. *Traders in a Brave New World: The Uruguay Round and the Future of the International Trading System.* Chicago: University of Chicago Press, 1995.

Program on International Policy Attitudes (PIPA). www.Americansword.org/digest/global_issues/intertrade/summary.

Public Law No. 79–130, 59 Stat. 410. *The Reciprocal Trade Agreements Act,* 1945.

Public Law No. 87–794, 76 Stat. 1962. *The Trade Expansion Act,* 1962.

Public Law No. 93–618, 88 Stat. 1978. *The Trade Act*, 1974.

Public Law No. 100–418, 102 Stat. 1107. *The Omnibus Trade and Competitiveness Act*, 1988.

Public Law No. 103–465, 108 Stat. 4809. *The Uruguay Round Agreements Act*, 1994.

Reagan, Ronald. "Remarks on Signing the Omnibus Trade and Competitiveness Act of 1988 in Long Beach, California." The American Presidency Project. http://www.presidency.ucsb.edu/ws/?pid=36289.

Ricardo, David. *The Principles of Political Economy and Taxation*. Amherst, New York: Prometheus Books, 1996.

Ripley, Randall. *Congress: Process and Policy*, 3rd ed. New York: W. W. Norton and Company, 1983.

Rogowski, Ronald. *Commerce and Coalitions: How Trade Affects Domestic Political Alignments*. Princeton: Princeton University Press, 1990.

Rose, Richard. *The Postmodern President*, 2nd ed. Chatham, N.J.: Chatham House, 1991.

Rosenau, James N., ed. *Domestic Sources of American Foreign Policy*. New York: The Free Press, 1967.

Rossiter, Clinton. *The American Presidency*. Baltimore: The Johns Hopkins University Press, 1960.

——, ed. *The Federalist Papers*. New York: Mentor, 1961.

Ruggiero, Renato. "Beyond Borders: Managing a World of Free Trade and Deep Interdependence." Speech delivered before the Argentina Council on Foreign Relations. World Trade Organization PRESS/55, September 10, 1996.

Schattschnieder, E. E. *Politics, Pressures and the Tariff: A Study of Free Private Enterprise in Pressure Politics, as Shown in the 1929–1930 Revision of the Tariff*. New York: Prentice-Hall, 1935.

——. Book Review. "American Business & Public Policy." *Public Opinion Quarterly* 29 (2) (Summer 1965): 343–344.

Schulzinger, Robert D. *The Wise Men of Foreign Affairs: The History of the Council on Foreign Relations*. New York: Columbia University Press, 1984.

Schumpeter, Joseph A. *Capitalism, Socialism, and Democracy*, 3rd ed. (New York: Harper & Row, 1950).

Schwab, Susan C. *Trade-offs: Negotiating the Omnibus Trade and Competitiveness Act*. Boston: Harvard Business School Press, 1994.

Shonfield, Andrew. "International Economic Relations of the Western World: An Overall View." In *International Economic Relations of the Western World, 1959–1971*, vol. 1, ed., Andrew Shonfield. London: Oxford University Press, 1976.

Shoup, Laurence H. and William Minter. *Imperial Brain Trust: The Council on Foreign Relations and United States Foreign Policy*. New York: Monthly Review Press, 1977.

Singer, J. David. "The Level of Analysis Problem in International Relations." *World Politics* 14 (1) (October 1961): 77–92.

Smith, J. Allen. *The Spirit of American Government*. New York: The Macmillan Company, 1907.

Snidal, Duncan. "The Limits of Hegemonic Stability Theory." *International Organization* 39 (4) (Autumn 1985): 579–614.

Special Representative for Trade Negotiations. Report to the President. *Future United States Foreign Trade Policy*. Washington, D.C.: Government Printing Office, 1969.

Stoneman, William E. and Frank Freidel, eds. *A History of Economic Analysis of the Great Depression in America*. New York: Taylor & Francis, 1979.

Strange, Susan. "Still an Extraordinary Power: America's Role in a Global Monetary System." In *The Political Economy of Domestic and International Monetary Issues*, eds., R. Lombra and W. Witte. Ames: Iowa State University Press, 1982.

———. "The Persistent Myth of Lost Hegemony." *International Organization* 41 (4) (Autumn 1987): 551–574.

Thucydides. *History of the Peloponnesian War*. M. I. Finley, ed. New York: Penguin Classics, 1954, rev. ed.

Tilly, Charles. *Coercion, Capital, and European States, AD 990–1992*. Cambridge, MA: Blackwell, 1994.

———. *Big Structures, Large Processes, Huge Comparisons*. New York: Russell Sage Foundation, 2006.

United Nations. "National Accounts Main Database. http://unstats.un.org/unsd/snaama/selbasicFact.asp.

———. *Yearbook of International Trade Statistics*. New York: United Nations, 1988.

———. *Economic Statistics*. http://unstats.un.org/unsd/snaama/dnllist.asp

United States v. Curtiss-Wright Corporation, 299 U.S. 304 (1936).

U.S. Census Bureau. *Statistical Abstract of the United States, 2003*. Washington: D.C.: Government Printing Office, 2004.

U.S. Congress. House Committee on Ways and Means. *1945 Extension of Reciprocal Trade Agreements Act: Hearings before the Committee on Ways and Means*, 79th Congress, 1st sess. on H.R. 2652, superseded by H.R. 3240, 1945.

———. House. *Foreign Trade Agreements: Report from the Committee on Ways and Means to Accompany H.R. 3240*, 79th Congress, 1st sess., 1945.

———. House. *Message from the President of the United States urging Extension of the Reciprocal Trade Agreements Program*, 79th Congress, 1st sess., March 26, 1945, Doc. 124.

———. Senate. *Staff Suggestions on Amendments to the Trade Act of 1970*. 91st Congress, 2nd sess. Washington, D.C.: Government Printing Office, 1970.

———. House. *Hearings before the Committee on Ways and Means on H.R. 6767, the Trade Reform Act of 1973*, 93rd Congress, 1st sess., 1973.

———. Senate. *Hearings before the Committee on Finance on H.R. 10710*, 93rd Congress, 2nd sess., 1974.

———. House. *Trade Reform Legislation: Hearings before the Subcommittee on Trade of the Committee on Ways and Means*, 99th Congress, 2nd sess., 1986.

———. House. *Comprehensive Trade Legislation: Hearings before the Committee on Ways and Means and Its Subcommittee on Trade* 100th Congress, 1st sess., 1987.

———. House. *The Trade, Employment, and Productivity Act of 1987: Message from the President of the United States Transmitting A Draft of Proposed Legislation*, 100th Congress, 1st sess., 1987.

———. Senate. *Improving Enforcement of Trade Agreements, Hearings before the Committee on Finance on S. 490, S. 539, and H.R. 3*, 100th Congress, 1st sess., 1987.

U.S. Department of Commerce. "U.S. Foreign Trade Associated with U.S. Multinational Corporations." *Survey of Current Business*, December 1972.

———. "U.S. Merchandise Trade Associated with U.S. Multinational Corporations." *Survey of Current Business*, May 1986.

———. "Operations of U.S. Multinational Corporations." *Survey of Current Business*, March 2002.

———. *A Profile of U.S. Exporting Companies, 2000–2001*. Washington, D.C.: Government Printing Office, 2002.

U.S. Department of State. "Threshold of a New Trading World." *Department of State Bulletin*, November 20, 1961.

——. "The Hour of Decision: A New Approach in American Trade Policy." *Department of State Bulletin*, December 25, 1961.

U.S. General Accounting Office. *World Trade Organization: Standard of Review and Impact of Trade Remedy Rulings*, GAO-03-824. Washington, D.C.: 2003.

Wala, Michael. *The Council on Foreign Relations and American Foreign Policy in the Early Cold War*. Providence: Berghahn, 1994.

Wallerstein, Immanuel. *The Modern World System I: Capitalist Agriculture and the Origins of the European World Economy in the Sixteenth Century*. New York: Academic Press, 1974.

Weber, Max. *Economy and Society*. Guenther Roth and Claus Wittich, eds. Berkeley: University of California Press, 1968.

——. *General Economic History*. Mineola, NY: Dover Publications, 2003.

Whinham, Gilbert R. *International Trade and the Tokyo Round Negotiation*. Princeton: Princeton University Press, 1986.

Wilcox, Clair. *A Charter for World Trade*. New York: Macmillan Company, 1949.

Wilson, Woodrow. *Congressional Government: A Study in American Politics*. New York: Houghton Mifflin Company, 1885.

World Trade Organization. *Final Act of the Uruguay Round of Multilateral Trade Negotiations*. www.wto.org/english/docs_e/legal_e.htm.

——. "Dispute Settlement—Index of Dispute Issues." www.wto.org/english/tratop_e/dispu_e/dispu_subjects_index-e.htm.

——. Trade Policy Review Body, "Trade Policy Review: United States, Doc. Number WT/TPR/S/88."

——. Statistics Database. "Time Series on International Trade." http://stat.wto.org/Home/WSDBHome.aspx?Language=E.

——. *Trading into the Future*, 2nd ed. Geneva: WTO, 1999.

Zolberg, Aristide R. *A Nation by Design: Immigration Policy in the Fashioning of America*. Cambridge, MA: Harvard University Press, 2008.

——. *How Many Exceptionalisms?: Explorations in Comparative Macroanalysis*. Philadelphia: Temple University Press, 2008.

INDEX